AF478904

The Eurogroup

Manchester University Press

European Policy Research Unit Series

Series Editors: *Simon Bulmer, Peter Humphreys* and *Mick Moran*

The European Policy Research Unit Series aims to provide advanced textbooks and thematic studies of key public policy issues in Europe. They concentrate, in particular, on comparing patterns of national policy content, but pay due attention to the European Union dimension. The thematic studies are guided by the character of the policy issue under examination.

The European Policy Research Unit (EPRU) was set up in 1989 within the University of Manchester's Department of Government to promote research on European politics and public policy. The series is part of EPRU's effort to facilitate intellectual exchange and substantive debate on the key policy issues confronting the European states and the European Union.

Titles in the series also include:

The Eurogroup

How a secretive circle of finance ministers
shape European economic governance

Uwe Puetter

Manchester University Press
Manchester and New York

distributed exclusively in the USA by Palgrave

Published by Manchester University Press
Oxford Road, Manchester M13 9NR, UK
and Room 400, 175 Fifth Avenue, New York, NY 10010, USA
www.manchesteruniversitypress.co.uk

Distributed exclusively in the USA by
Palgrave, 175 Fifth Avenue, New York,
NY 10010, USA

Distributed exclusively in Canada by
UBC Press, University of British Columbia, 2029 West Mall,
Vancouver, BC, Canada V6T 1Z2

British Library Cataloguing-in-Publication Data
A catalogue record for this book is available from the British Library

Library of Congress Cataloging-in-Publication Data applied for

ISBN 0 7190 7403 7 *hardback*
EAN 978 0 7190 7403 5

First published 2006

15 14 13 12 11 10 09 08 07 06   10 9 8 7 6 5 4 3 2 1

Typeset in Sabon
by Action Publishing Technology Ltd, Gloucester
Printed in Great Britain
by CPI, Bath

Contents

List of figures

List of tables

Abbreviations

BEPGs	Broad economic policy guidelines (the technical term used in EU language to refer to the 'broad guidelines of the economic policies of the Member States and of the Community' mentioned in Article 99.2, TEC)
COREPER	Committee of Permanent Representatives
DG ECFIN	Directorate General for Economic and Financial Affairs, European Commission
ECB	European Central Bank
ESCB	European System of Central Banks
ECOFIN	Economic and Financial Affairs Council
EFC	Economic and Financial Committee
EMU	Economic and Monetary Union
EP	European Parliament
EPC	Economic Policy Committee
EU	European Union
Euro 11	Eurogroup's name between June 1998 and June 2000
GDP	Gross domestic product
G7	Group of Seven (group of the world's major economic powers)
IGC	Intergovernmental Conference
IMF	International Monetary Fund
OMC	Open method of coordination
SGP	Stability and Growth Pact
Stage 3	Final phase of EMU. All legal provisions apply. Irrevocable fixing of the exchange-rates of those EU member states fulfilling the convergence criteria marks the creation of the single currency.
TEC	Treaty Establishing the European Community

Acknowledgements

The completion of a research project like the one presented in this book is not possible without the academic and personal support of numerous colleagues and friends, as well as the logistical and financial help of institutions. First of all, I would like to thank Antje Wiener and Paul Teague at Queen's University Belfast. Both have lent enormous support to the project. They have encouraged me to further follow up the traces of informal governance in the area of European Economic and Monetary Union at all stages of the project. Our intensive discussions played a pivotal role in the development of the theoretical framework of the research. Their cooperation and personal sympathy made the project a unique experience for me. In financial terms the research benefited from a three-year doctoral research grant sponsored by the Institute of European Studies and the School of Politics and International Studies at Queen's University. I also gratefully acknowledge the support through the European Union Social Science Information Research Facility (EUSSIRF) visiting scholarship programme at the library of the European University Institute in Florence. In addition, the project benefited from a two-year project scholarship of the European Political-economy Infrastructure Consortium (EPIC). I would like to thank Simon Bulmer, David Howarth and the participants of the EPIC workshops, as well as the members of the University Association of Contemporary European Studies' (UACES) study group on constitutionalism beyond the state for their comments on earlier versions of the manuscript or individual chapters. Moreover, writing this book would not have been possible without the practical experience I gained with European economic governance during my stay at the Secretariat of the Economic and Financial Committee and Economic Policy Committee in Brussels in 2002. I am particularly indebted to the former director of the secretariat Günter Grosche and would like to thank all my former colleagues in the secretariat and the Commission's DG ECFIN for sharing their views and experiences on the Eurogroup's work with me.

Finally, my parents and numerous friends provided vital help in managing the logistics of the 'pan-European' fieldwork behind this project.

Introduction

The informal Eurogroup, comprising the finance ministers of the euro area, plays a central role in the economic governance set-up of Economic and Monetary Union (EMU). This might seem surprising given that the group is deprived of any formal decision-making competences and keeps a low official profile. The group is the smallest coordination forum known in Brussels. Only the ministers themselves attend the meetings and they find no administrative infrastructure at their disposal. In fact, the Eurogroup pre-agrees all critical Council decisions with relevance for the euro area member states. It is within this group that ministers decide on the overall orientation of economic governance in the euro area and establish common interpretations of EMU's core policy instruments and their applicability. For example, the debates over the Stability and Growth Pact (SGP) and its interpretation with regard to the situation of individual euro area countries are conducted within this secretive forum. The intensive debates of euro area ministers within the Eurogroup have emptied out the agenda of the Economic and Financial Affairs Council (ECOFIN). In addition, the Commission consults the Eurogroup on all important decisions which fall under the responsibility of the supranational administration in the area of EMU. Most importantly, the discussions within the group also influence decision-making at the European and national level in a much more subtle way. Informal debates within the Eurogroup often stabilise delicate political situations and inter-institutional conflicts. Moreover, it is mainly through the group's ongoing debates about appropriate policy options that the rules and procedures of economic governance evolve over time. The explorative element of Eurogroup discussions is of particular importance within a decision-making environment, which implies genuinely new challenges to all involved parties. Finally, the outcome of the discussions within the group is reflected in the way individual ministers communicate with the media on EMU affairs. In addition, there is clear evidence that ministers act as advocates of common Eurogroup positions in the domestic process of decision-making and political debate.

The Eurogroup is not a formal Community institution. In legal terms the group is a mere discussion club of the euro area's top decision-makers involving the Commission and the European Central Bank (ECB). The 'Treaty establishing a Constitution for Europe' signed in Rome in October 2004 is the first legal document mentioning the Eurogroup. Nevertheless, even if ratified the Treaty would not change the informal character of the Eurogroup. This low official profile is not least the result of considerable political opposition against the creation of a supplementary body for the coordination of economic policy during 'Stage 3' – the final phase of the EMU project. Ever since the idea of such a coordination forum was floated concerns have been raised that the envisaged participation of the ECB might compromise the political independence of the central bank. Informality was made a precondition for the dialogue between monetary and economic policy authorities in EMU. Another reason why the group has been denied a greater official role in the canon of European Union (EU) institutions is the delicate relationship between the euro area countries and those EU member states outside the single currency zone. As the *de facto* decision-making forum for the euro area countries the Eurogroup's work is perceived as a threat to the integrity of the ECOFIN Council, which involves all twenty-five member states and is the only official decision-making body in this policy area. In the past, fears of non-euro member states – particularly the United Kingdom – have often forced the Eurogroup to navigate carefully through the institutional jungle of Brussels.

Despite the important role of the Eurogroup for the coordination of economic policies in the euro area the literature on EMU has widely ignored the group as an independent source of decision-making authority. Similarly, the conceptual challenge for political scientists implicit in the opaque and secretive structure of informal governance has not been well understood so far. This deficiency also applies to the wider literature in the sub-discipline of European studies. Although all Council formations see sporadically so-called informal meetings there are no systematic studies of informal deliberations among ministers.

The puzzle

Starting back in 1998 and continuing until today the Eurogroup has assembled the finance ministers of the euro area countries, the Commission and the ECB on an average of ten to twelve occasions a year. This synchronisation of the group's meeting cycle with the one of the most important EU Council formations – the General Affairs Council and the ECOFIN Council – suggests that the Eurogroup is of some relevance to decision-making within EMU or – in a wider sense – the EU. However, both the media coverage of the meetings and the academic literature on

European integration and EMU have so far failed to fully come to terms with this strange entity of an informal circle of ministers. So what are all those meetings behind closed doors really about? The *Financial Times* once published one of the rare background newspaper articles about the Eurogroup under the title 'Quiet men taking charge'.[1] Secrecy and the exercise of considerable political influence from behind-the-scenes seem to be the attributes of the Eurogroup.

It is another characteristic feature of the rare public statements of participants on the proceedings of Eurogroup meetings that the particular atmosphere in which discussions take place is praised. It is disclosed that, unlike at regular Council meetings, ministers share excellent and frank discussions within the Eurogroup. The content of these discussions, however, remains opaque. For this reason some members of the European Parliament (EP) have voiced their concerns about the elitist style of governance pursued within the group and the lack of transparency and democratic accountability. The concern is that the Eurogroup has effectively taken over decision-making on economic governance without being embedded in the official framework of Community institutions allowing at least a minimum degree of democratic control.[2] Consequently, the informal character of the group seems to be of a paradoxical nature. On the one hand, the Eurogroup is nothing more than a mere discussion club, which convenes outside the regular Community structure. Compared to the formal decision-making competences of the Council, the Commission and the ECB, the group is weak and without influence. On the other hand, however, what seems to be the Eurogroup's weakest link – the group's informal profile – is praised for providing a particular environment for discussions among ministers. Debates are seen to be more productive than the discussions within the ECOFIN Council.

The role of the Eurogroup within EMU's economic governance set-up provokes a series of questions: How can the paradoxical nature of the Eurogroup's informal status be explained? What is actually discussed within the meetings? How far are these discussions different from those in other contexts of EU decision-making – notably within the Council of Ministers? Does informality make a difference with regard to the conduct and the outcome of discussions? Moreover, how is it possible for a group which is deprived of any formal decision-making competences, to influence economic governance in EMU? How does the role of the Eurogroup affect the institutional balances between EMU's official decision-making bodies?

Finally, this book seeks to explore two hypotheses with regard to the foundation of an informal group for euro area discussions. Firstly, is the low profile of the group the result of a political compromise between the euro area countries and the rest of the EU member states? Or, secondly, does the loose framework for discussions on economic policy coordination simply represent the lowest common denominator of autonomously acting national governments, which try to escape close coordination?

In answering these interrelated questions the book aims to increase knowledge of an under-researched aspect of EU governance. Through presenting an in-depth study of the operation of the Eurogroup and its intervention in the decision-making processes this study contributes to a more complete picture of EMU's institutions. Such a contribution is of particular relevance to debates on the further evolution of the institutional framework of economic governance in the single currency zone. EMU is a relatively new area of EU activities. European monetary union poses genuinely new challenges to decision-makers in the area of economic policy. In this situation a better understanding of the applied forms of governance and their potential for further evolution is crucial. Moreover, there is great uncertainty with regard to the effects of the recent enlargement on the existing institutional set-up. A more precise knowledge of the functioning of the Eurogroup helps one to better understand the current institutional dynamics and clarifies the institutional options in the context of future modifications to the architecture. Since the Eurogroup is a relatively young institution there is also considerable room for a further refinement of its working methods. As the recent decision to create a two-year presidency and the introduction of new agenda items (such as the discussions on structural policy) have demonstrated, the work of the group is subject to continuing change. With regard to the wider EU context the analysis of the Eurogroup's informal working method has important implications for the debates on innovative modes of governance, such as on the principle of flexible integration and the so-called 'open method of coordination' (OMC).

The argument

This book is built around the assumption that the most plausible explanation as to why merely informal discussions can have such an impact on actual decision-making within EMU is that the group members voluntarily advocate the results of these discussions when they shape policies in other formal decision-making contexts. The latter may include the formal Community institutions such as the ECOFIN Council, the Commission and the ECB. A finance minister may also promote particular policy options, which were considered by the Eurogroup, when facing pressure from cabinet colleagues, parliament, interest groups or media representatives within the domestic arena. However, such behaviour is only likely to occur if participants identify themselves with the group's position. They must share the group's verdict that a particular policy option is appropriate and reasonable in a given situation. Only under this condition would individual ministers refrain from re-opening issues or watering down

Eurogroup positions. As an informal body the Eurogroup cannot sanction non-compliance with commonly agreed policy objectives. The 'exit'-option always remains open to participants. Consequently, the group's influence over economic governance depends on its ability to generate voluntary commitment to common positions. In other words, the outcome of Eurogroup discussions must be truly consensual.

Now the most characteristic feature of the Eurogroup, its informal character, appears in a different light. At first glance informality seemed to be the group's central weakness. Once considered as a working method the informal context of the discussions among ministers emerges as the group's most vital asset. What distinguishes the Eurogroup from other contexts in which ministers negotiate within the EU, i.e. the formations of the Council of Ministers, is its restricted format and the confidentiality of discussions. In other words, the Eurogroup brings the euro area's top decision-makers closer together than ever before and engages them in face-to-face dialogue, thus making it easier to explore diverging views and foster consensual outcomes. The Eurogroup institutionalises a process of continuing policy dialogue including the critical review of national policies and the collective definition of the common interest of the euro area. The outcome of these discussions functions in turn as a key reference point in situations in which national policies are inconsistent with the overall 'policy-mix' of the single currency zone and substantiates what is widely known as peer pressure (Figure 0.1).

This book, therefore, suggests an analytical framework, which is anchored in the constructivist concept of social interaction. On the one hand, social interaction is considered as a creative process constituting social reality. On the other hand, the results of this creative process constitute conditions of social interaction. The latter determine behaviour in the form of exogenously given factors such as power relations, interest maximisation and culture. In other words, interaction involves constraint as well as creativity – it is structuring and structured at the same time. This conceptual dualism opens access to a range of approaches within the area of international relations theory, public policy analysis and political economy, which have conceptualised and specified the conditions of consensual processes of policy formation, the construction of policy ideas and the nature of informal resources. The key theoretical challenge addressed by this book is to synthesise the findings of this literature and to specify the conditions under which they are applicable to the particular context of informal deliberations among ministers. This will allow a presentation of a conclusive set of hypotheses on how and under what conditions informal deliberations among ministers in the area of EMU generate powerful informal resources, which intervene at the various stages of European and domestic processes of policy formation. Finally, the differentiation between the *setting* and the *content* of negotiations lays

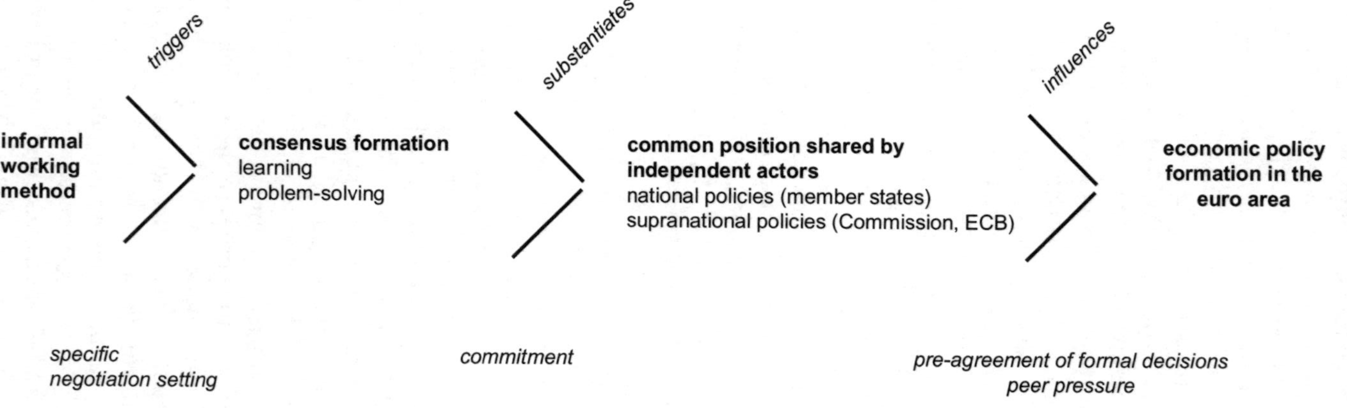

Figure 0.1   The Eurogroup's informal working method – chain of influence

the basis for the applicability of the results of the analysis of the Eurogroup to other policy areas.

Book outline

The book is split into seven chapters. Chapter 1 discusses the analytical framework of the analysis of informal governance within the Eurogroup. It reviews the current state of the literature on EMU, the Council of Ministers and on innovative modes of European governance. This literature focuses on the empirically most closely related institutions and styles of governance. By building on the findings of this literature and responding to its theoretical deficiencies the discussion then follows up the relevant theoretical pathways in more detail. The core argument of the book is substantiated through three central working hypotheses. The discussion concludes with the introduction of the methodology organising the analysis of the empirical information. Presenting first hand information from personal interviews with Eurogroup participants, Chapters 2–5 form the empirical core of the book. Chapter 2 puts the Eurogroup's work into the historical and institutional context of EMU. It explains how the creation of the Eurogroup responded to particular institutional deficiencies inherent to EMU's economic governance set-up. Moreover, the effects of the multi-speed nature of European monetary integration on the efforts to strengthen economic policy coordination in Stage 3 are considered. Chapter 4 then introduces the key features of the group's informal working method. Chapters 4 and 5 portray the Eurogroup's informal working method in action. The overview of the recurrent items on the Eurogroup's agenda in Chapter 4 demonstrates how informal governance responds to quite different political and economic-technical challenges. Building on this broader and contextual picture Chapter 5 then turns to the in-depth analysis of a particular discourse over policy within the group. The discussion refers to the Eurogroup's role in the operation of the SGP. It is explained how Eurogroup discussion has shaped the interpretation of the pact since it came into force, a process which also found its expression in the revisions made to the pact in March 2005. In addition, reference to four similar instances of non-compliance with common policy rules brings in a comparative dimension and seeks to account for the role of possible obstacles to informal policy deliberation such as political and economic pressure. Chapter 6 evaluates the empirical findings in the context of the analytical framework of this book. Finally, Chapter 7 concludes with highlighting the institutional implications of this study for economic governance in EMU and the wider EU.

Notes

1   *Financial Times* (8 February 2000).
2   This position is advocated by Christa Randzio-Plath, president of the
    Economic and Monetary Committee of the European Parliament, round
    table discussion, CEUS, University of Bremen, 28 January 2002.

1

Theorising informality

There is no ready-to-use approach for studying informal governance within the Eurogroup. Neither has the context of informal deliberations among ministers been subject to detailed empirical investigation, nor is there a conclusive theoretical concept explaining the particularities and dynamics of such an institutional context. This chapter, therefore, looks at the theoretical implications of a study of informal governance within the Eurogroup in more detail. It critically reviews existing approaches dealing with closely related phenomena in the area of EU governance. In addition, approaches on inter-subjective interaction in negotiation settings in the wider field of international relations, public policy analysis and political economy will be discussed. The chapter identifies the most promising theoretical pathways upon which an analytical framework and a conclusive set of working hypotheses can be based.

Studying EMU

The transition towards a single European currency and the negotiation of the Treaty provisions on EMU received a great deal of attention among scholars of European integration working in the discipline of political science (see notably Busch 1996; Cameron 1998; Campanella 1995; Dyson 1994; Dyson and Featherstone 1999; Hosli 2000; Howarth 2001; Kaelberer 2003; Liebert 2001, Marcussen 2000; McNamara 1998; Minkkinen and Patomäki 1997; Moravcsik 1998; Polster 2002; Risse et al. 1998; Sandholtz 1993; Schönfelder and Thiel 1996; Verdun 2000b, 1999; Wolf 1999). This literature helps one to better understand the institutional environment in which the Eurogroup was set up years later. However, it lacks analytical potential with regard to the task of explaining the actual functioning of EMU and its individual institutions and processes. Moreover, there is a general shortage of more recent political science studies covering the EMU process in operation. EMU is at the heart of EU governance and represents a policy area governed by a

Council formation, which convenes as many times as the General Affairs Council itself. Nonetheless, the area of policy coordination particularly has received relatively little attention compared to other areas of EU activity.

The reference to the Europeanisation frame has done a great deal to widen the knowledge about the impact of EMU on domestic policies and cultures and to raise awareness of the key challenges to EMU's institutional set-up (Dyson 2002). However, these studies are not sufficient to account for the inner-institutional dynamics within EMU's governance framework. Here, scholars have mainly focused on monetary policy and financial market issues (Heisenberg 2003; Howarth and Loedel 2002; Traxler 2003; Verdun 2000a). This leaves out the field of economic policy coordination in which the Eurogroup operates (exceptions are Hancké 2003; Heipertz and Verdun 2004).

One of the main insights of the literature on European political economy is that economic and social policies in the different EU member states are characterised and influenced by different policy traditions. These traditions often go back to different understandings of the state's fundamental role vis-à-vis the market (see e.g. Berger and Dore 1996; Crouch and Streeck 1997; Hall and Soskice 2001; Hollingswood and Boyer 1997; Kitschelt et al. 1999; Schmidt 2001; Somers 1998). Thus, one should expect policy-makers to approach particular economic situations in different ways. Continuing dialogue is important in order to take these different backgrounds into account and to review them collectively. Moreover, it is reasonable to assume that the discussion of different policy preferences among euro area finance ministers is facilitated by the fact that elite identity in this policy area is most pronounced compared to other fields of EU governance (Dyson and Featherstone 1999; Marcussen 2000; Ungerer 1997; Verdun 1999; Westlake 1999).

What can also be extracted from the more recent literature on EMU is the concern about the relative weight of the different EMU institutions in the wider economic governance set-up. The orientation of EMU towards price stability and the powerful role of the ECB as a sanctioning factor in the decision-making process (Howarth and Loedel 2002) figure uppermost in the research agenda of scholars working in the field. The provisions of the SGP are widely seen as a straightjacket, which ties the hands of economic policy-makers. The pact is associated with an essentially technocratic style of governance (Dyson 2000). Given the task of analysing the role of the Eurogroup in economic policy coordination the central questions would be: What difference do the informal governance structures make in this respect? How do these structures influence the diagnosed asymmetry between a powerful monetary pillar and a weak economic pillar of EMU and what scope for discretionary policy coordination remains for governments within this context?

It is in this area that a study on informal governance within the Eurogroup can make an important contribution to the political science literature on EMU. There is little disagreement in the literature about the key attributes of EMU's institutional architecture. However, not much is known about how these institutional coordinates became subject to contestation and readjustment since the single currency came effectively into being. The current understanding is largely informed by the blueprint of the economic governance set-up laid down in the provisions on EMU introduced with the Maastricht Treaty. Consequently, the views about the economic pillar have been heavily biased by the *formal role* assigned to the different Community institutions such as the ECB, the ECOFIN Council and the Commission. The impact of the *informal governance process* within the Eurogroup was – not surprisingly – widely overlooked. As a result the literature on EMU has largely ignored the Eurogroup both as an independent source of political authority and as a conceptual challenge to political scientists. Here, this book seeks to make an essential contribution.

Analysing the Council of Ministers

The institutional structure most closely related to the operation of the Eurogroup is that of the Council of Ministers (Hayes-Renshaw and Wallace 1997; Sherrington 2000; Westlake 1999). The idea of creating an informal forum for discussion among euro area ministers clearly emanates from the practice of the influential ECOFIN Council formation. The Eurogroup seems to be a kind of limited version of this formation – a 'euro area ECOFIN'. This analogy is not unproblematic because the Eurogroup is deprived of the ability to conclude formal decisions and is not considered to be an official Community institution. Chapter 6 will develop the comparison between the informal Eurogroup and the formal Council setting in greater detail.

The Council is the place for the articulation and formation of competing national interests as well as of the common interest of the member states. The organisational structure of the Council is intergovernmental. Nevertheless, actor behaviour is likely to be influenced by intergovernmental and supranational considerations simultaneously. Therefore, Alberta Sbragia has described the work of the Council as a 'balancing act' (quoted in Bulmer 1996: 18). Adopting a comparativist-federalist perspective he has pointed to the fact that the EU is characterised through the concentration of power and identity within the lower tier of its confederalist system. The legitimacy of EU governance depends on a collective system of decision-making in which this lower tier, i.e. the member states, is represented. The Council plays this pivotal role through mediating between 'the conflicting dynamics of cooperative federalism and entrenched territorialism' (Bulmer 1996: 32). Consequently, the value-added aspect of the Council with regard to the functioning of EU governance lies in its ability to provide a forum for consensus-building among territorially defined interests.

Consequently, a close-up picture of the negotiation process within the intergovernmental environment of the Council or similar structures does not necessarily imply a classical intergovernmentalist research agenda (Hoffmann 1995; Milward 1992; Moravcsik 1998; Taylor 1983). As a derivative of neo-realist international relations theory such a research programme would imply the explanation of negotiation behaviour and the choice of particular decision-making institutions through the exogenously given preferences of the involved actors. The collective decision-making in the Council would be mainly understood as the attempt by member states to remain in control of integration. Studies of the negotiation process would tend to be focused on the manifestation of the bargaining power of the respective countries in the Council. An example would be the study of the impact of voting rights on negotiation behaviour (Hosli 2002, 1996).

In contrast, the critics of pure intergovernmentalist approaches – coming from either the rational choice or the historical institutionalist camp (see for example Garrett and Tsebelis 1996; Pierson 1998) – have highlighted the relevance of lock-in-effects and unintended consequences for processes of EU decision-making. In other words, the institutional framework is treated as an independent source of actor behaviour. Bulmer (1998) has pointed to the analytical potential of this 'new institutionalism' with regard to the close-up or micro-level analysis of decision-making procedures. Such a micro-organisational perspective is adopted by this book. It assumes that EU decision-making is built on intergovernmental and supranational structures alike and engages in a close-up analysis of the dynamics of one particular mode or style of governance. What is of particular interest for the analysis of the Eurogroup is that this wider interpretation highlights the role of 'less formal arenas of politics' (Bulmer 1998: 369). Moreover, the functioning of formal institutions is not separable from underlying norms and codes of conduct which guide actor behaviour. Such an understanding of institutions allows, for example, the conceptualisation of a specific culture of decision-making as a characteristic feature of the work of the Council. As Jeffrey Lewis (2003: 151) has pointed out,

> The Council, as an institution, equals more than the sum of its parts (the member states). National actors in the Council also act collectively, and many develop a shared sense of responsibility that the work of the Council should move forward and the legislative output of the Council (even if in only one specialized policy area) should be a success.

Lewis has further pursued this sociological institutionalist perspective in connection with an in-depth analysis of the Council's diplomatic infrastructure (Lewis 2000, 1998a, 1998b; but see also Egeberg 1999). The culture of consensual and cooperative decision-making is particularly strong within the Committee of Permanent Representatives (COREPER) – the pre-negotiating body comprising the ambassadors of the EU member states. According to Lewis the intimate atmosphere provided by the negotiation setting is the main factor behind the evolution and strength of this cultural element. Such a negotiation setting provides for confidential negotiations among very senior civil servants who share a great deal of expertise and procedural knowledge on EU affairs. Lewis's findings are also confirmed by the wider literature on EU negotiations which is informed by other theoretical perspectives (Elgström and Jönsson 2000; Elgström and Smith 2000; Lodge and Pfetsch 1998). The emphasis on cultural and deliberative elements seems to be most pronounced within the *in camera* settings of COREPER. More generally, the literature on the Council draws attention to the multi-faceted picture of intergovernmental decision-making processes in the EU.

New modes of European governance

More recently, two modes of governance have received particular attention in the literature because they are considered to be innovative solutions to institutional dilemmas arising from the sometimes considerable degree of diversity among EU member states. Both the concept of flexible or differentiated integration and the 'open method of coordination' (OMC)[1] address the problem that member states differ in their commitment to core aspects of the integration process. Although the idea of the provision of policy instruments and transitional arrangements dealing with the effects of a non-simultaneous integration process is as old as the European integration project itself (Wallace 1985), the debate has resurfaced under the keywords 'flexibility' or 'closer cooperation' ever since the run-up to the Treaty of Amsterdam (see for example Edwards and Philippart 1999; Ehlermann 1998; Stubb 1997, 2000; Wallace 2000). These debates are motivated by the prevailing uncertainty with regard to the effects of the recent enlargement process on EU governance. It is not yet clear how the enlarged EU will cope with the fact that some of the old members already diverge in their commitment to common EU activities in highly sensitive areas such as monetary or foreign and defence policy. The debate about the use of flexibility centres mainly on the institutionalisation of decision-making procedures in the absence of full participation by all member states in a given policy area. At the same time the different proposals aim at preserving the overall institutional integrity of the EU. In contrast, contributions focussing on the OMC discuss the possibility of creating incentives for greater policy convergence through common policy guidelines, benchmarking and peer pressure in areas which fall under the exclusive or primary competence of the member states. Not surprisingly both strands of the literature are mainly influenced by normative considerations and have only just started to develop more analytical perspectives. Moreover, the literature on flexibility still seeks to establish a standardised terminology facilitating the navigation through the conglomerate of real world phenomena and normative concepts (see Tuytschaever 1999; Warleigh 2002).

In particular, legal approaches on flexibility (or differentiation) can provide valuable access-points to the study of informal governance in EMU. These approaches most plainly grasp the full scope of the idea of institutionalising a multi-speed integration process (Tuytschaever 2000). The concept of the legal integrity of the EU and the principle of non-discrimination to which EU law has to adhere in its application vis-à-vis the individual member states, goes to the heart of the integration project. Inevitably, the introduction of legal differentiation leads to tensions between member states and threatens the integrity of Community institutions. One could even say that flexibility is the expression of an insurmountable institutional dilemma rather than the definite solution to it. Consequently, scholars are largely divided on the issue of flexibility. It is not clear whether flexible integration is a suitable instrument for maintaining the overall coherence of the EU even in situations of fundamental disagreement over core EU policies.[2] As Chapter 2 will demonstrate, these considerations can help one to better understand the background of the events leading to the creation of the Eurogroup and the institutional constraints within which the group operates. Moreover, it will become clear why EMU's own flexibility regime has not been subsumed under the general flexibility provisions negotiated during the Intergovernmental Conferences in Amsterdam and Nice (see Stubb 2000). This puzzle has never been solved satisfactorily by the flexibility literature. In total, however, this literature is of less help when it comes to conceptualising the process of informal governance as such.

Here, contributions on the use of the OMC in the area of economic policy (De Búrca and Zeitlin 2003; Hodson and Maher 2001) can provide further guidance. The focus is on the creation, framing and application of what these contributions call soft law or soft policy. Despite the creation of a single currency economic policies remain essentially within the jurisdiction of the member states. However, as a consequence of monetary union, economic and institutional interdependencies increase irrespective of the continuing existence of far-reaching national competences in this policy area. The literature on the OMC acknowledges this particular context of coordination. It explores the scope for the application of a middle way between full integration on the one hand and completely unconnected policy-making by independent national decision-makers on the other. The OMC, as Dermot Hodson and Imelda Maher (2001: 739) have noted, 'seeks to make a virtue out of the inevitable and continuing diversity institutionally and ideationally in the way that Member States define and conduct their economic policy'.

The OMC emphasises particular modes of interaction which can be summarised as information exchange (Culpepper 2002) and policy learning in the widest sense. The latter comprises consensus formation around non-binding common policy guidelines and what the network analysis literature has called policy-transfer, i.e. instances in which successful policies are transferred from one country or sector to another (Hodson and Maher 2001: 727). The mere existence of a coordination mechanism such as the OMC is an indicator of the reluctance of member states to transfer sovereignty to the Community level indefinitely. At the same time, however, this coordination mechanism keeps all options open and triggers a continuing deliberative dialogue on newly arising policy problems. Gráinne De Búrca and Jonathan Zeitlin (2003: 2) have highlighted this consensual nature of the OMC by stressing that

> By committing the member states to share information, compare themselves to one another and reassess current policies against their relative performance, the OMC is also proving to be a valuable tool for promoting deliberative problem-solving and cross-national learning across the EU.

The soft policy nature of the OMC makes it an attractive case to study in connection with the analysis of informal governance. There are essentially two important parallels. The first parallel concerns the mode of governance. Similar to the OMC framework, decisions of the Eurogroup are not binding in the strict sense of Community law. Moreover, a continuing consensus-oriented policy dialogue is at the heart of the OMC. The second parallel concerns the agenda. The OMC emerged in the area of economic policy coordination in EMU in connection with the Lisbon European Council conclusions (European Council 2000). The method highlighted the importance of peer pressure, benchmarking and policy learning in the area of economic reform. In this respect, the OMC corresponds to the particular attributes of the Eurogroup's informal working method. However, as will be demonstrated, the OMC and the Eurogroup's informal working method are two distinct coordination mechanisms which coexist in the area of EMU. Nonetheless, the literature on the OMC provides further indications of which theoretical concepts might be particularly relevant to the analysis of soft policy approaches.

Constructing the analytical framework

The review of the literature on EU policies and institutions most closely related to the Eurogroup setting, presented many indications as to what to examine in more detail. Studies on the Council can provide a basis for a comparison between the Eurogroup's informal working method and formal decision-making within the Council. Most importantly, the review of the literature on the Council has pointed to the wide implications of a close-up study of Eurogroup negotiations. In political terms, EU governance is based on the constant mediation between a common policy framework and deeply rooted national interests. Intergovernmental negotiations should be understood as the main form of consensus-building as regards the formulation of common policy objectives in the EU polity rather than as an obstacle to political integration. Moreover, the literature on the Council has pointed to the particular relevance of cultural and normative elements in the analysis of intergovernmental negotiations within the context of the EU. In this context, one particular empirical finding of a number of EMU-related studies is noteworthy. European monetary and economic policy-makers obviously share a strong identity based on mutual ideational affinity with regard to assumptions on causal relations within the economy and between state action and market performance.

However, as indicated earlier there is no ready-to-use approach which could help in conceptualising the process of informal deliberations among euro area ministers more specifically. In order to construct such an analytical framework the following looks into approaches focusing on inter-subjective interaction in the wider field of international relations, public policy analysis and political economy. The main aim is to generate hypotheses on the conditions of such processes. In turn, this will then allow the determination of the impact the Eurogroup's informal working method has on negotiation behaviour and outcome.

As has been suggested above, this discussion is conducted within a constructivist frame which allows the conceptualisation of social interaction as a dual process. Actor behaviour is not seen as merely determined by structural conditions or exogenously given preferences but rather understood as creative behaviour leading in fact to the constitution of (changed) social structures and (altered) preferences (Christiansen, Jørgensen and Wiener 2001). The emphasis on the conceptualisation of social interaction as a constitutive process facilitates the identification of essential factors in processes of policy formation, which are easily overlooked by an analysis basing the assessment of intergovernmental decision-making on rational choice assumptions. The latter perspective is of great relevance to economic and political economy studies on EMU (see for example Artis and Buti 2000; Collignon 2001) but also implicit in the intergovernmentalist or strategic interactionist research agendas of political scientists (see for example Campanella 2000; Hosli 2002, 1996; Moravcsik 1998). As Emanuel Adler and Peter Haas (1992: 369) have noted with regard to theory formation in the area of international relations theory:

> We relate institutions to the dynamic interaction between domestic and international political games, and we describe these games not only in terms of material interests but also as part of the bargaining and negotiation that take place among different epistemic understandings and practices 'carried' by epistemic communities and later by policymakers as well.

This should not, however, imply that rational choice assumptions cannot provide valuable access points for the study of EMU. The argument here is rather that this book focuses on a question different from those approached within rational choice frameworks. This study does not seek to explain economic policy coordination within EMU as such. It does not ask why euro area member states choose to cooperate or opt for certain policies in a given situation but rather focuses on the process of informal coordination. Nevertheless, such a research agenda is likely to be of great interest also to rationalist scholarship in the area of EMU. Treating the context of informal deliberations as an independent source of actor behaviour is not without consequences for the formation of game theoretical models of economic policy coordination in EMU. In fact a perspective which treats preference formation as an endogenous process, can be seen as complementary to rationalist research programmes in international relations theory and political economy aimed at explaining coordination on the basis of non-cooperative game theory (Martin and Simmons 1998).

The relevance of deliberation

The initial assumption has been that the consensual nature of Eurogroup discussions is the main explanatory factor with regard to the group's ability to influence economic governance within the euro area. The argument was that only consensus-oriented negotiations would generate commitment to the results of group discussions on the part of individual decision-makers. In the absence of legal constraint personal conviction is the only motive for ministers to enact common policy objectives. Two main theoretical questions arise from this assumption. Firstly, what does deliberation actually imply and what is its political relevance? Secondly, why and how does this matter in the specific context of EU decision-making?

Throughout the book, deliberation is used in a very restrictive sense. It refers back to the philosophical idea that persuasion is an interactive process based on reason and rationality – be it in a scientific or practical political sense (Kant 1990, 1983). This implies that causal beliefs or political norms are not advocated or pursued by individuals because of external constraint but rather because of conviction. The normative aspect of this general theme has been followed up by democratic theory and contemporary political philosophy because of its wide implications for social interaction (Elster 1998; Habermas 1998, 1995). More specifically, the consequences for policy formation at the domestic level, as well as within structures of governance beyond the state, can be circumscribed as follows. In general, any decision, which affects others, should refer to 'arguments committed to values of rationality and impartiality' (Zürn 2000: 186). This implies the dictum that efficient policy formation directed at increasing general welfare is inconceivable without reference to the public interest as it is determined by policy deliberation in a particular situation (Majone 1993). Harald Müller and Thomas Risse have applied this notion of deliberation and arguing to the context of international negotiations. In their contributions they have repeatedly stressed that, in principle, negotiators have to be prepared to retreat from whatever their initial strategic motivation was if the discourse forces them to do so (Müller 2001, 1995, 1994; Risse 2000).

Although the deliberative principle can be seen as indeed 'the most ambitious conception of democracy' (Zürn 2000: 186) it is not considered here as some ideal world principle without relevance to empirical analysis. On the contrary, it is argued here that the existence or absence of a style of policy formation based on deliberation can have very practical consequences for the system of EU governance. The anarchic nature of the international system implies that there is no neutral third party to enforce agreements between states (Martin and Simmons 1998). This even applies to the EU which is bound together by a far reaching common policy framework. The common system of governance fully depends on the consent of the individual member states as regards the implementation and enforcement of common rules and policy objectives. Even supranational institutions such as the Commission and the ECB are toothless if a member state should eventually deny compliance with Community legislation or common policy guidelines. This is not to say that supranational institutions cannot bring a lot of pressure to bear on a non-complying member state through uniting the other member states within the Council. However, to avoid friction and to preserve the unity of the Community the system of EU governance relies on consensual decision-making. As Fritz Scharpf (2001: 6) has noted, this situation is unlikely to change and will not change as long as there is a lack of a 'strong European collective identity', which would legitimise the creation of more powerful supranational institutions. As it will be demonstrated in Chapter 2, this observation is all the more important with regard to the area of economic policy coordination in EMU.

The studies by Christian Joerges and Jürgen Neyer on the role of the EU committee system in the drafting of European law within the regulatory field (Joerges 2002; Joerges and Neyer 1997a, 1997b; Neyer 2000) provide the rare example of an analytical framework organised around the idea of the political – and in this case legal – relevance of the deliberative principle in EU governance. Departing from Joseph Weiler's famous 'inter-supra-infra trichotomy' (Weiler 1999: 274) EU governance can be characterised as follows. Within the EU system intergovernmental structures coexist alongside supranational ones and finally with the EU's committee system. The committees shape European law by bringing together officials from the national governments and the supranational institutions as well as experts and representatives of corporate interests – the system of 'infranationalism' in Weiler's terms. The committee system operates at the interface of intergovernmental control and supranational authority. Its role in the formation of European law explains the relevance of deliberation as an essential mode of interaction within the committees. As Joerges and Neyer argue, European law emerges by nature as a product of a conflict of laws. Its supremacy is only recognised as legitimate because it 'has repeatedly managed to civilise national idiosyncrasies on normatively good grounds' (Joerges 2002: 138). The committee system therefore implies the creation and protection of a space for deliberative interaction. In other words, the provisions governing the committee system are in fact 'legal principles and rules civilising the decision-making process and providing an institutional context for practical reasoning' (Joerges and Neyer 1997b: 299). The form of governance exercised through and within the committee system has been therefore called 'deliberative supranationalism' (ibid.).

To rephrase the problem in terms of cooperation theory, the main task of the Eurogroup is to solve a particular common action problem. As regards decision-making in the area of economic policy, the euro area countries are independent and competing political entities. Nevertheless, these countries share a common interest in policy coordination as members of a single currency zone. The solution to cooperation dilemmas depends on an institution's ability to influence the behaviour of actors in such a way that the orientation towards the common interest prevails over the narrow concentration on the individual interest (Gehring, 1994: 215). Consequently, one should expect that processes of common interest formation based on deliberation are the most effective. Policy deliberation is most likely to generate a high degree of commitment to policies which are compatible with the common interest. This is especially important in 'weak' or less institutionalised contexts of coordination which lack the mechanisms to sanction inappropriate behaviour. Herein lies the main reason for the expected central role of the Eurogroup's informal working method. It is only the analysis of the conditions under which the policy dialogue takes place, which will enable the assessment of the group's ability to foster processes of policy deliberation. In analogy to the EU committee system the Eurogroup would create a space for policy deliberation. However, it is noteworthy that the committee system has *formally* institutionalised the deliberative principle in the way that procedural rules require expert hearings and demand the review of different technical and legal options by senior civil servants. As is demonstrated in Chapter 3 literally no *formal* provisions conducting the work of the Eurogroup exist. The conditions of the policy dialogue itself, the factors influencing discussion behaviour and routinised informal procedural rules are therefore likely to play a central role. In other words, what is true for policy deliberation networks in general, is likely to be all the more important for the Eurogroup. Deliberation presupposes 'the existence of goodwill on the side of the participating actors' (Zürn 2000: 193).

However, the above does not imply that discussions among ministers within the Eurogroup are exclusively conducted in the manner of policy deliberation. As is known from the negotiation literature, one should always expect that negotiators have to deal with unbridgeable ideological cleavages, distributional conflicts or merely technical exchanges of information, which do not imply a commitment to any particular kind of action on the part of one of the involved parties. In this context, a particularly fruitful debate in the German journal of international relations – the *Zeitschrift für Internationale Beziehungen (ZIB)* – on communicative interaction in international negotiations can be of great help in further clarifying the role of deliberation within Eurogroup discussions. This debate was mainly conducted between constructivist scholars focusing on arguing and deliberation in international negotiations, and advocates of game theoretical models of communicative action. The discussion reflected the general constructivist-rationalist divide over ontology regarding the motivation and preference formation of actors in international negotiations (see on the constructivist-rationalist divide Pollack 2001; Risse and Wiener 1999). As an advocate of game theoretical approaches on communicative interaction Otto Keck (1997, 1995) rejected the criticism voiced by Müller and Risse's research on the role of arguing and deliberation in international negotiations (see above discussion on the definition of deliberation) that game theoretical models are per se inadequate to account for a change in actors' positions as a result of persuasion through reasoned argumentation. Reflecting his rationalist ontology, Keck understands arguing and deliberation as processes which comprise essentially the common definition of the situation and the common definition of regulations in social life. Actors try to persuade their counterparts that the latter have ignored certain consequences of their intended action or are unclear about the interests of the other parties involved in the negotiation process. While this approach can indeed demonstrate that the rationalist agenda goes beyond the analysis of 'hard bargaining' situations, Keck's notion of arguing and deliberation does not transcend the logic of exogenously given preferences in the sense that it still assumes that these preferences are not scrutinised in terms of truth-seeking.

Departing from this debate over ontology the book seeks to make productive use of the opposition between the two camps. The term *deliberation* is exclusively used in a very restrictive way, as has been outlined above. In addition, the term *information exchange* is used to refer to the mode of communication conceptualised by Keck. In the latter mode actors do not change their basic motivations with regard to the interaction process. However, they try to realise or maximise their own interests by exchanging information with other parties. For example, as regards the interdependent euro area economies the mutual exchange of information on the economic situation and the policy preferences of national governments can be beneficial for all involved actors. The precise knowledge about the strategies and intentions of the others enhances one's own ability to adapt to the respective situation. Indeed this mode of interaction has also been identified with mechanisms of 'soft', i.e. non-binding coordination, as in the context of the OMC which includes the transfer of knowledge and technical assistance (Culpepper 2002).

In this way, finally, the ('hard') *bargaining* mode is the easy part in the categorisation of communication modes used in Eurogroup discussions. This mode is the exact mirror image of policy deliberation. It is characterised by pure strategic interaction of actors advocating exogenously given preferences. In practice, all three modes of communication occur simultaneously in a given negotiation context. Furthermore, the actual mode used in a given situation is sometimes difficult to specify since redistributive claims, for example, are often made in the form of argumentative intervention.[3] However, as has been demonstrated above, only policy deliberation can lead to the political commitment required to govern informally, i.e. through the commitment of all involved parties to the group consensus in the absence of neutral enforcement mechanisms. The empirical analysis therefore has to focus on deliberation and on how the results of such discussion processes frame the occurrence of the two other modes.

The conditions of policy deliberation

So, does the Eurogroup provide a particularly good context for policy deliberation? In other words, what are known conditions of policy deliberation and how far do they apply to the context of the Eurogroup? In order to answer these questions the discussion is organised around two separate aspects of the negotiation process. The first aspect is the *setting* of negotiations. This is constituted by, for example, the number and political profile of participants, the degree of confidentiality of the discussions, the time frame of the meetings or the way the group meetings are prepared. The second aspect concerns the *content* of the discussions. Debates may centre on economic policy ideas or shared problems such as the reaction to a price shock. Discussions may focus on conflicts between euro area countries or may be characterised by general uncertainty with regard to particular policy developments. The following review of the conditions of policy deliberation constituted by the negotiation *setting* deals with the question of who negotiates in what kind of environment? The discussion of the possible effects of the *content* of negotiations deals with the question of what is negotiated and how this influences communication behaviour within the Eurogroup. This distinction will not only allow for a better account of individual factors. It is also important with regard to the aim of assessing the applicability of the Eurogroup's informal working method in other policy areas of EU governance, as Chapter 7 will discuss in greater detail.

The setting

Some of the studies, which have already been mentioned in the above discussions, implicitly or explicitly, specify conditions of policy deliberation. The sociological institutionalist analysis of the Council and COREPER provides indications on the role of culture and routinised practices in EU negotiations (Lewis 2000, 1998a, 1998b; but see also Wiener 1998). A more explicit attempt to formulate concrete hypotheses on the occurrence of deliberation in the context of international negotiations has been made in connection with the research projects directed by Müller and Risse (see in particular Müller and Risse 1999; Risse and Ulbert 2001). Moreover, perhaps the most important basis for the construction of a framework for the analysis of informal governance within the Eurogroup is provided by the literature on policy learning. This literature focuses on the creative element of collective decision-making (see Bennett and Howlett 1992; Haas 1992). Negotiations are treated as an independent source of policy change. As Adler and Haas (1992: 385) have summarised:

> The sources of collective learning in international relations can be found in the evolutionary process characterized by the diffusion, selection, and persistence of political innovations. Thus, changes in the epistemological assumptions and interpretations that help frame and structure collective understanding and action constitute the most meaningful notion of learning in international relations. This definition implies that national policymakers can absorb new meanings and interpretations of reality, as generated in intellectual, bureaucratic, and political institutions, and therefore can

change their interests and adjust their willingness to consider new courses of action.

While there are different conceptions of learning (see for an overview Hall 1993; Kissling-Näf and Knoepfel 1998), in essence most of the contributions deal with learning in a way which is fully compatible with what is called here the process of policy deliberation. In the area of international relations theory policy learning has been studied within the context of the literature on epistemic communities (Adler and Haas 1992; Haas 1992, 1989; Verdun 1999) and norm compliance (Checkel 2001a, 2001b; Susskind, Chayes and Martinez 1996). Like the literature on COREPER and the occurrence of arguing and deliberation in international negotiations, Haas's (1992, 1989) contributions on epistemic communities deal with negotiation settings composed of (senior) civil servants and technical experts who negotiate on behalf and under the instruction of their governments. Consequently, particular attention needs to be paid to the conditions under which these findings apply to an informal circle of ministers.

However, the greatest number of studies referring to the process of policy learning have emerged in the area of public policy analysis (Bennett and Howlett 1992; Benz 1990; Hall 1993; Jenkins-Smith and Sabatier, 1993; Kissling-Näf and Knoepfel 1998; Majone 1993; Sabatier 1998, 1993, 1988). They are part of a new turn in public policy analysis which gathered considerable momentum in the mid-1980s and throughout the 1990s (Héritier 1993). This development brought about the analytical turn towards interactive processes of policy formation within negotiation settings. In addition, it also reflected a normative concern with regard to state–society relations. This leads back to what has been said above on the importance of the deliberative principle in democratic theory and political philosophy. In contrast to a state-centric perspective, which focuses on the hierarchical imposition of policy objectives, the approaches discussed here understand learning as a collective process emerging from the challenge to address a shared problem. This interactive process involves both government representatives and societal actors such as interest groups and independent experts. The learning process is reciprocal. Pre-defined positions are reviewed and adapted, thus making 'solutions possible without concessions on the part of any of the participants' (Benz 1990: 98). Again, the set of actors studied by these approaches differs from the Eurogroup which is composed only of the most senior decision-makers of the euro area. In addition, the focus has been on formal institutionalisation as the outcome of learning processes (Kissling-Näf and Knoepfel 1998) whereas the Eurogroup lacks the capacity to conclude formal decisions. Nonetheless, the focus of the learning literature is on distinct learning networks involving a limited number of individuals. Furthermore the aspect of inter-institutional learning processes is discussed extensively in this literature. The similarity between learning networks and informal policy deliberation within the Eurogroup is very well summarised with the following definition of learning processes in policy networks:

> In contrast to the classical organisation, networks do not have monolithic power and decision-making centres. Moreover, they are less formalised than organisations. Among the typical features of such networks is informal interaction which results from reciprocal dependencies and which also contributes to the decentralised processing of problems. A central feature of the network is the shared problem. (Kissling-Näf and Knoepfel 1998: 347)

The 'shared problem' as the central feature of the learning network leads directly into the discussion of the relation between the negotiation *setting* and the occurrence of policy deliberation and learning. Deliberation should particularly occur in settings in which *the discussion process is organised around one or several clearly identified shared problems*. In this case a strong interest among participants to engage in deliberation and learning can be expected (see also Checkel 2001b). The *size of a group* and its impact on the interaction process within the group have already been analysed by the sociologist Georg Simmel (1992). He emphasised that small and closed circles develop patterns of interaction among their members which cannot be found in larger groups. Although it is difficult to specify a definite figure for the maximum size of a small group, the mere organisational constraint of meetings, which last a few hours rather than a day or more, is obvious. In other words, the smaller the circle of participants the better. The main criterion is whether the number of participants allows for the spread of an argument or position throughout the group, i.e. the active participation of each member of the group in this argumentation – be it through oral interventions or internal reflection of the argument. Hank Jenkins-Smith and Paul Sabatier (1993: 42) have called this phenomenon the 'rate of turnover'.

In addition to the absolute time restrictions another factor influencing the consensus formation process is the *flexibility* of the group's agenda. As Antje Wiener (2003) has argued in her analysis of discourses on EU constitutional norms among British and German elites working on EU related affairs, the discourse over norms is unlikely to be a one-off event. Ignoring this specific feature of the norm discourse can result in backlash and policy failure. Friction can only be avoided where the participants in the norm discourse engage in a continuing process of norm contestation and the common definition of meaning. This is particularly important in the context of the EU where participants in the norm discourse come from different cultural and societal backgrounds often associating different meanings with what are perceived to be shared norms and principles. This view is also echoed by the learning literature with regard to the instrumental level of policy enforcement (Kissling-Näf and Knoepfel 1998). The degree of flexibility in the composition of the Eurogroup's agenda will therefore be an important indicator showing the group's ability to adapt to these requirements of norm discourse. Another factor related to the organisation of the agenda and the preparation of the meetings concerns the existence of 'formalised arrangements for the production and dissemination of knowledge' (Kissling-Näf and Knoepfel 1998: 361). In the absence of these arrangements the learning process is likely to be of a rather casual and unsteady nature. Finally, the availability of new information has been identified as a trigger of learning processes (Hall 1993). Beside the timing and the flexibility of the agenda another structural precondition for deliberation is *equal access to the dialogue*. For example, where power structures prevent interventions deliberation is at risk (Müller 1994).

As has been already mentioned, policy deliberation has been studied so far only in senior civil servant and expert settings. For both categories of negotiators it can be said that deliberation is facilitated by the fact that the participants share a great deal of *technical knowledge*. This knowledge is likely to function as a common ground or reference point in discussions. Moreover, these two groups of negotiators are more likely to approach negotiations from a technical or analytical point of view than from a straightforward political or strategic point of view. Both observations might indeed indicate the difficulties of policy deliberation among ministers. It is for the empirical analysis to see whether there are any similar factors within the Eurogroup setting. However, seen from a different perspective, the *seniority of Eurogroup participants* is likely to have a very positive effect on the process of deliberation. Civil servants and technical experts lack the political competence to agree on positions deviating from their relatively narrowly defined negotiation position. This makes discussions involving genuinely political decisions more or less impossible. Lawrence Susskind, Abram Chayes and Janet Martinez (1996) have pointed to the fact that in international negotiations senior government officials are quite often already instructed not to explore certain options in the discussion. This often leads to sub-optimal outcomes with negative consequences for all sides. In this respect, an informal circle of ministers opens up new opportunities for intergovernmental policy deliberation.

Another crucial factor concerning the composition of the group of negotiators is the degree of *ideational affinity among group members*. This phenomenon has been conceptualised in different ways. However, there is general agreement in the literature about its relevance. The central assumption made by all approaches is that in order to make progress in finding a consensus among advocates of diverging views a kind of common ground or shared underlying conviction is necessary. In their reference to Habermas's (1995) theory of communicative action Müller

(1994) and Risse (2000) have called this condition of successful consensus formation the common lifeworld of negotiators. This common lifeworld includes shared interpretations to which group members can refer. The lifeworld is reproduced 'through the innumerable interactions of the social actors through which historical tradition, culture, values etc. are transferred and altered'[4] (Müller 1994: 27). Alternatively, Paul Sabatier has conceptualised this pre-condition of policy learning or deliberation as the 'middle ground for informed conflict' (Sabatier 1993: 140) which must be shared among group participants. Similarly Peter Haas (1992) has pointed to a shared set of normative and causal beliefs as a pre-condition for learning. The existence of common notions of validity with regard to the existing knowledge within an area of expertise characterises what Haas calls an epistemic community.

As a general rule, consensus orientated negotiations are thought to be more successful in a *confidential negotiation atmosphere* than in a more public or open environment (Checkel 2001b; Zürn 2000). The literature has also pointed repeatedly to the role of personal attributes of participants – such as *credibility, professional reputation and respectability* – in the deliberation process (Adler and Haas 1992; Sabatier 1993). A negotiation setting composed of individuals who fulfil these criteria is more likely to trigger policy deliberation. Moreover, it is unlikely that all group participants fulfil these criteria to the same extent at a given stage within the discussion process. These attributes are often associated with individuals as a result of shared working experiences. Therefore, the second criterion is in how far the negotiation setting allows actors to assess the personality of their counterparts. Here, the total time of shared discussion experience and the frequency of meetings are important factors.

The content

The discussion now turns to the *content* of negotiations as the second factor influencing communication behaviour. The content of Eurogroup negotiations is determined by the task of coordinating the economic policies of the euro area member states. The following discussion of the relevant literature is essentially based on three arguments. They concern the general nature of a discourse over economic policy, the material self-interests of the participants in the negotiation process and the quality and degree of economic policy coordination.

As Peter Hall (1989) has noted, constraint as well as creation determine economic policy-making. Substantial discussions on economic policy decisions go beyond the clarification of empirical facts and the countering of misunderstandings. Kathleen McNamara has linked this observation to the particular nature of economic ideas. These ideas are beliefs about causal relations in macro-economics:

> Ideas are critical in the monetary realm because of continuing uncertainty over the basic workings of the macroeconomy, the difficulties of collecting and interpreting signals from macroeconomic data about the effects of policy, and the lack of agreement over what constitutes 'correct' macro-economic policy. (McNamara 1998: 57–58)

Consequently, economic ideas are permanently open to challenge by competing beliefs and ideas. This rejection of explanatory models in which either material constraints, competing interests or institutional constraints function as determinants of the course of economic policy making is also echoed by Otto Singer (1993: 169). He characterises the role of ideas in economic policy formation as 'independent factors, which cannot be simply reduced to the respective interests of the actors in the political process'.[5]

On the basis of his study of the relation between core economic science and the formation of economic policy in the Western world, Singer emphasises the role of non-scientific experts. The latter influence policy formation through pathways other than those pursued by academics. Consequently, the attachment or detachment of the group's discussions to the science discourse and the non-scientific spin are crucial criteria. In general, one can assume that discourse over economic policy inevitably leads into policy deliberation. Even hard material interests are defined against the background of causal beliefs about the functioning of the economy and the relation between policy definition and market perform-ance. *Economic policy ideas are contestable ideational entities*, thus provoking discourse. In fact, such an endeavour can be beneficial to all involved participants.

Irrespective of the particular role of economic ideas, the literature has sought to specify material constraints on and catalysts for learning and deliberation. Giandomenico Majone (1993) has argued that policy deliberation is most likely to occur in situations in which policy formation results in a *cooperative positive sum game*. Majone relates the absence of a theoretical interest in processes of policy deliberation back to the preoccupation of political scientists with redistributive conflicts in connection with the consolidation of the Western welfare states. This preoccupation has resulted in 'pluralistic reductionism' (Majone 1993: 100). However, policy formation is fundamentally concerned with the correction of market failure and the creation of efficient institutions, which are able to improve the situation of the vast majority of the involved actors. Such a policy objective highlights the importance of rationale argumentation and reasoning in developing optimal solutions. The positive sum character of the game implies that participation in the deliberation process is in the interest of all concerned actors since it potentially improves the finally chosen policy to the benefit of everyone. The generally perceived tendency of a growing complexity of policy problems further adds to the demand for policy deliberation. By contrast, Majone expects little or no willingness to engage in deliberative processes in situations in which the redistribution of resources is at stake. Zero sum games do not constitute a suitable environment for policy deliberation. However, Majone acknowledges that both processes, the correction of market failure and the reallocation of resources between different social actors, can be intertwined.

Finally, contributions from the literature on international and European political economy can help to better understand the main features of economic policy coordination and the role of policy deliberation in such a context. Michael Webb has defined economic policy coordination as 'negotiated mutual adjustment that causes states to pursue different policies than they would have chosen had policy-making been unilateral' (Webb 1995: 11). This definition reflects what Helen Milner (1992) had already identified in her seminal review of theories of international cooperation as the prevailing consensus in the literature. The definition encompasses the *political as well as the economic dimension of international policy cooperation*. In some instances the literature uses the term 'cooperation' to characterise forms of interaction that are less strict than the negotiation of immediate policy adjustments (see Mooslechner and Schuerz 2001). However, as with many other authors, this book uses the terms interchangeably in order to characterise the general content of Eurogroup negotiations. The focus is on how economic interdependencies are addressed through intergovernmental discussions on appropriate policy responses. Finally, this use of the term 'coordination' is also compatible with the language applied by the EU itself, thus facilitating the reference to documents and interviews.

Nonetheless, as is demonstrated in the following, policy coordination in the euro area can take many different forms. It is, therefore, helpful to briefly relate the most common forms of policy coordination to the respective modes of communication or negotiation behaviour which they are likely to trigger. Here, Randall Henning and Robert Putnam's (1989) categorisation of the different modes of coordination is relevant. It was developed by the two authors in the context of their case study of the Group of Seven's (G7) 1978 Bonn summit. Henning and Putnam distinguish between unilateral adjustment, consultation, reinforcement, package deals and supranational integration as the five different forms of coordination (see Table 1.1 below). Unilateral adjustment occurs as the result of information exchange between international decision-makers. Knowing the policy objectives and instruments of their counterparts enables decision-makers to adjust their own policies in order to counter adverse effects and optimise the economic performance of their country. Unilateral adjustment policies are particularly important for small and open economies, which tend to be reactive rather than proactive with regard to external economic developments. Consultation implies that the national analysis of the economic situation, as well as the policy preferences derived from this analysis, are subject to challenge in international deliberations. Consultation is indeed the most common mode of coordination in the global context:

> In practice much of what actually happens in international economic discussions falls under the rubric of consultation, as officials try to persuade one another that their respective analyses or preference schedules are confused or mistaken. Talk of 'peer pressure' in the context of the current Group of Seven (G-7) arrangements for international economic policy discussions seems to refer to this type of cooperation. (Henning and Putnam 1989: 15)

Reinforcement of national policies takes place where international agreement leads to a strengthening of the position of a national government in pursuing a certain set of policies. Although the respective policies are not a result of international deliberations their enforcement is speeded up or facilitated by international support. Package deals (or 'genuine coordination' in the terminology of some authors) involve internationally negotiated policy adjustment on the part of all involved actors. Such arrangements can react to particular interdependencies and involve the balancing of costs and benefits among the involved parties. The negotiations can either be restricted to one specific field of economic policy or can involve package deals linking different sectors, e.g. budgetary and structural issues. Finally, supranational integration is the most advanced form of international cooperation. Policies are set at the supranational level through a pre-defined procedure, for example qualified majority decisions in the Council, or a single authority, for example the Commission. The deliberation over policies, the sharing of information and the balancing of the costs and benefits are regulated through established procedures. Since economic policy coordination through package deals and supranational integration requires formal agreement, coordination through consultation and reinforcement will be the main catalyst for processes of policy deliberation in informal settings.

Generating informal resources

The above discussion has laid the theoretical foundations for an analysis of the Eurogroup's ability to foster consensus-oriented discussions among independent decision-makers. However, the question of how to conceptualise the outcome of informal policy deliberation remains. The creation of consensus among euro area ministers can manifest itself in many different forms. The common discussions may lead to clearly identifiable *de facto* decisions on mutual policy adjustment. Euro area ministers might also coordinate their positions prior to official Council meetings.

Table 1.1 Negotiation behaviour triggered by the different modes of economic policy coordination

Coordination mode	Unilateral adjustment	Consultation	Reinforcement	Package deal	Supranational integration
Negotiation mode		Deliberation	Deliberation	Deliberation	Deliberation
	Information exchange	Information exchange			Information exchange
				Bargaining	Bargaining

Alternatively, discussions may lead to the establishment of policy guidelines and assessment criteria, which reappear within the discussion at a later point or are applied by ministers in domestic processes of policy formation. The more subtle manifestations of the group consensus in particular require additional reflection. In her work on the 'embedded *acquis communautaire*' Antje Wiener (1998) has demonstrated that the establishment of the formal resources of EU decision-making, such as treaty provisions and directives, is essentially linked to an existing set of so-called *informal resources*, such as shared norms and established practices. The day-to-day business in the EU is understood as a constructive or constitutive process. This perspective accounts for a dualism of the policy process. On the one hand, policy-making within the EU is the execution of the principles and policies laid down in the formal *acquis communautaire*. On the other hand, the daily routine of the application of these principles and policies becomes in itself a source of the alteration of the formal resources. The results of this practical process are so-called informal resources. The latter structure the application of formal rules and procedures and influence future legislation or decisions without having been formally adopted. In order to characterise the often subtle nature of the way Eurogroup discussions influence the formal decision-making process it is possible to conceptualise the Eurogroup as a generator of such informal resources (Puetter 2001). Constructivist research programmes have already contributed significantly to the analysis of the structuring effects of informal resources, as for example in the context of the literature on international norm compliance (see for example Chayes and Chayes 1993; Finnemore and Sikkink 1998; Katzenstein 1996). However, the question of norm construction and alteration has still to be addressed more thoroughly (Wiener 2001). Here, the in-depth analysis of informal policy deliberation within the context of the Eurogroup can make an important contribution to the wider debate on norm construction.

The literature on the nature and evolution of policy ideas, which partly overlaps with the contributions on policy learning, provides another valuable access point for the conceptualisation of the results of orientation debates or the evolution of a particular working consensus within a group. A much-discussed approach on the relation between policy learning and policy change has been Paul Sabatier's (1998, 1993, 1988) advocacy coalition approach. As already indicated above, the set of actors and the scope of the research agenda are distinctively different compared to the analysis of a circle of ministers. The focus is on political subsystems or issue areas in which so-called 'advocacy coalitions' (Sabatier 1998: 121) struggle for policy change. Policy change in general is attributed to the altered 'belief systems' (Sabatier 1998: 123) of decision-makers. These belief systems comprise core political values and convictions as well as assumptions on the prevailing causal relations within a given policy area and the effectiveness of specific policy instruments. The 'core beliefs' (Sabatier 1998: 122), around which an advocacy coalition assembles itself, are relatively stable over time. Sabatier assumes that changes within a belief system require a period of approximately ten years. Differences within an advocacy coalition are considered to centre on secondary aspects. Actors are more likely to give in when struggling over such secondary aspects than to risk the erosion of the core beliefs of their coalition. In addition, Sabatier assumes that changes in this underlying consensus occur only in connection with external events. These events may include changing power-relations or economic developments. The assumption that a stable ideological core and a more flexible periphery are characteristic to a learning or deliberation network is also echoed by Peter Hall (1993). His often cited distinction between first, second and third order policy changes centres on a similar idea.

According to Hall a framework of ideas and standards, a 'policy paradigm' (Hall 1993: 279), guides decision-makers whenever they choose policy instruments or recognise problems in their application. This framework is stable over a longer period of time. Consequently, third order changes go hand in hand with paradigm changes. The Eurogroup's ability to govern informally through forging a consensus among its participants will therefore depend on whether the discussions are based on an underlying working consensus, which is stable over time.

Hypotheses

The central argument is that the Eurogroup's influence over economic policy-making within the euro area will depend on the voluntary commitment of group members to commonly agreed policy objectives. This commitment is only likely to occur if agreement on common policy objectives is truly consensual. Genuine consensus can only emerge from policy deliberation. The aim of this chapter, therefore, has been to construct a framework for analysis, which allows assessing the ability of the Eurogroup's informal working method to foster processes of policy deliberation among finance ministers. The review of the literature on empirically similar institutional contexts and styles of governance within the EU system has produced valuable insights on individual aspects of informal governance within the Eurogroup. However, this literature could not provide the basis for the construction of a coherent analytical framework. These deficiencies have been addressed through reviewing legal approaches to EU comitology, the literature on policy learning, and research on the role of arguing and deliberation in international negotiations, which can offer useful analytical tools for the empirical assessment of the Eurogroup's informal working method. The results of the previous discussion can be summarised in three interrelated working hypotheses:

Firstly, the Eurogroup's ability to influence decision-making within EMU will depend on the occurrence of policy deliberation as the prevailing mode of communication within the group. Only policy deliberation can generate voluntary commitment to common policy objectives.

Secondly, the particular setting of negotiations among ministers, the Eurogroup's informal working method, will function as a catalyst for processes of consensus formation through policy deliberation.

Finally, the particular content of the discussions among the euro area's top decision-makers matters. In general, issues related to economic policy coordination should be conducive towards policy deliberation.

Methodology and data collection

The following analysis builds on methodological considerations known from the literature on international negotiations. However, the analytical focus of this book is not on the analysis of a particular negotiation process or a series of negotiations. The point of departure is the question of how far the Eurogroup's informal working method generates a particular negotiation environment. In other words, the focus is on the context of negotiations rather than on individual negotiation episodes. To this end, the following empirical analysis is based on the methodological concept of an analytical case study. This perspective is complemented by a focused comparison, which comprises the evolution of four negotiation episodes over time. The main advantage of an analytical case study is that it emphasises the role of the negotiation context. Moreover, this research strategy represents a middle way between a merely descriptive case study and a research design aimed at the falsification of theoretical propositions (Druckman 2002).

The following presentation of the empirical information on the Eurogroup is split into two parts. Chapter 2 provides a full description of the historical and political background of the Eurogroup's creation and Chapter 3 introduces the features of its informal working method. This description is selective in the sense that it is organised around the theoretical argument presented in Chapter 1. The focus is on those features of the informal working method and the particular content of negotiations, which were identified as conducive towards policy deliberation. Chapters 4 and 5 turn to the actual process of negotiating the coordination of economic policies in the euro area. They show the Eurogroup in action. Chapter 4 reviews the key negotiation topics. Chapter 5 then focuses on one particular discourse over policy in the fashion of a focused comparison. Four similar negotiation episodes are compared. The episodes are presented in chronological order. This complementary perspective allows the control of particular aspects of the negotiation process – which are difficult to grasp through an essentially non-comparative research strategy – such as the impact of the negotiation attitude of individual participants and the intergovernmental bargaining power of a country on the informal negotiations. As in the case of the review of the Eurogroup's agenda points, the case penetration of the focused comparisons is thick. Moreover, the analysis of the negotiation process follows the concept of process tracing and seeks to identify specific turning points in the negotiation process (Druckman 2001).

The data collection followed two main criteria. Firstly, it was necessary to obtain detailed information on both the features of the Eurogroup's informal working method and the actual negotiations. The latter aspect in particular required data collection over a longer period of time. Secondly, the organisation of the data collection had to address the particular challenges posed by the informal and highly secretive character of the negotiation environment. Discussions among ministers within the Eurogroup take place behind closed doors and no official minutes or protocols of the debates exist. The only way of obtaining information on what is going on within the Eurogroup is by talking to the participants of the meetings and their closest advisers. Therefore, a series of structured expert interviews was carried out between December 2001 and May 2003. The group of interviewees comprises members of the Economic and Financial Committee (EFC) and officials in the national finance ministries and the Community institutions in charge of the preparation of Eurogroup negotiations. A case study on a small and secretive group, such as the Eurogroup, inevitably has to rely on a relatively small number of interviewees. Nevertheless, the existing sample of interviewees ensures diversity as regards the following criteria: members of European and national institutions; representatives from smaller and from bigger member states; members of institutions with different ideational preferences. The questions concerned the views of the interviewees on the conduct and quality of the discussions, the assessment of the negotiation setting and the political relevance of the group's work. In addition, the Europe-by-satellite (EbS) online archive, the Agence Europe news bulletins and leading European newspapers were scanned for the documentation of Eurogroup negotiations and related events. Finally, the analysis of official EU documents, such as the Treaty, the presidency conclusions of European Council meetings and the documentation of the work of the ECOFIN Council provided the necessary information on the formal framework of economic governance in EMU.

In order to preserve the anonymity of the interviewees, quotations from interview transcripts follow an anonymised format. The sample has been split into two categories of interviewees. The first category comprises all interviewees who have attended (or still attend) Eurogroup meetings in person. The second category comprises all interviewees who are in charge of the preparation of Eurogroup delegations but do not participate in person. All transcripts have been numbered in consecutive order as A, B, C, D, and so forth. The individual letters have been allocated in a random fashion. Throughout the text anonymous interview quotations are marked as '(Anonymous interview, participant X)' or '(Anonymous interview, official Y)' respectively. A list of the interviewees can be found in the References.

Notes

1   The name OMC was attributed to this particular style of coordination in the area of economic policy by the Lisbon European Council in March 2000 (European Council 2000).
2   For an excellent overview of the different legal problems and the various normative positions see De Búrca and Scott (2000).
3   In his analysis of international negotiations and state interaction Frank Schimmelfennig has used the term 'rhetorical action' to characterise argumentative behaviour, which lacks the potential for truly deliberative interaction because it simply disguises irrevocably defined self-interest (Schimmelfennig 2001; 1997; 1995).
4   My translation.
5   My translation.

2

Why does EMU require informal governance?

So, one might ask what is then the function of the Eurogroup? Obviously the function of the Eurogroup is, while this system [of economic governance in EMU] on paper looks clear enough and does not necessitate anything like the Eurogroup, nevertheless it is quite clear that there is scope for some kind of, I do not know if coordination is a good word, I think dialogue is a better word, in order to avoid misunderstandings, in order to have people more or less to see the things in the same light. (Anonymous interview, participant F)

In contrast to an official Council formation the Eurogroup governs informally. The group operates outside the framework of Community institutions and has no decision-making power. It can only influence policy through informal agreement among its members. Moreover, the group's influence depends on whether individual ministers advocate the group consensus while acting in formal decision-making contexts. This procedure, which is defined here as *informal governance*, can take different forms. The effects of informal governance can be as direct as in the case of coordinated position-taking by euro area ministers in the ECOFIN Council. In this case the Eurogroup pre-agrees pending Council decisions informally. Given that euro area member states command the vast majority of the votes in the ECOFIN Council, agreement there is only a formality. In a similar way the Eurogroup can coordinate decisions by national governments. The latter scenario of course implies that the respective finance ministers enjoy the political authority to enact the agreed measures at the domestic level. However, informal governance also takes more subtle forms. The discussions within the Eurogroup encourage individual ministers to advocate particular policies when they are facing pressure from cabinet colleagues, parliament or interest groups. Nevertheless, the question of why the EMU requires such a parallel system of informal governance remains.

For analysing the work of the Eurogroup it is crucial to understand the institutional constraints and political coordinates within which the group operates. This chapter, therefore, explains the institutional and historical background of the Eurogroup's creation. It points to the potential sources of informal governance implicit in EMU's formal constitutional framework. Moreover, the discussion recalls the most important steps in the negotiation process leading to the foundation of the Eurogroup.

At first glance, EMU's economic governance set-up as it is foreseen in the Maastricht Treaty does not seem to require an additional – if even only informal – decision-making institution. Political authority is clearly allocated and detailed procedures for the definition of common policy objectives and their implementation exist. So, what is left for the Eurogroup? Is the informal group a mere reflection of the fact that the euro area countries are an avant-garde within the EU, which is eager to exclude the other member states from the decision-making process? In that scenario the Eurogroup would essentially function as the solution to a particular problem of differentiated integration (Tuytschaever 2000). However, given that the Maastricht Treaty already envisages exclusive voting rights for euro area countries in the Council it is not entirely clear what the value-added nature of the Eurogroup would be. Or, finally, is the Eurogroup the result of a simple trade-off between France and Germany? In other words, did the Germans give in to French demands for the creation of a European *gouvernement économique* (economic government) or political counterweight to the ECB in return for the French approval of a *Teutonic* SGP? Such a view would be compatible with a strategic interactionist perspective, which sees the Eurogroup wrestling with the ECB over political superiority in EMU (Campanella 2000). However, the latter interpretation seems in discordance with the Eurogroup's status as a merely informal forum for discussion among ministers.

However, answering the question of why EMU produces a need for something like an informal circle of ministers is not an easy task. In fact, a variety of factors were responsible for the emergence of informal governance structures. As demonstrated in the following discussion, it is essential to understand the interplay of these diverse sources of informal governance. By combining legal and economic considerations, on the one hand, and a historical-descriptive perspective on the other, this chapter argues that the Eurogroup is both the product of political compromise and an innovative attempt to establish a new working method for enhanced policy coordination in Stage 3.

EMU's institutional architecture was set up with the provisions of the Maastricht Treaty on economic and monetary policy. These provisions defined the legal and technical coordinates within which European governments were preparing their countries for the final phase of the EMU project in the second half of the 1990s. Notwithstanding the creation of the *informal* Eurogroup the Treaty provisions on EMU also still represent the valid *formal* framework for economic governance in the euro area. Not surprisingly, the Maastricht provisions largely inform the current understanding of EMU's policies and processes. However, as the following discussion will demonstrate, EMU's constitutional framework became in itself the most important source of informal governance. The inherent contradictions and dynamics of EMU's institutional architecture triggered the emergence of parallel informal governance structures. The following discussion briefly introduces the key features of this architecture and relates them to the process of informal governance. EMU is based on a two-pillar architecture consisting of an essentially intergovernmental economic pillar and a genuinely supranational monetary pillar (see Figure 2.1 below). The discussion first focuses on the economic pillar, which constitutes the main area of Eurogroup activities. In a second step the relationship between the monetary pillar and the economic pillar is addressed. Finally, the review of EMU's constitutional framework turns to the differentiated nature of the process of European monetary and economic integration.

EMU's evolving institutions and policies

Economic policy in EMU is based on a decentralised system of governance. The member states remain fully responsible for policy implementation. The definition of policy objectives follows the principle of subsidiarity. The course of economic policy is defined at the national level. However, national decision-making has to be in accordance with a set of common rules. These rules comprise the general demand to formulate policies in accordance with the general policy framework of the Community (Articles 2-4, TEC)[1] and 'with the principle of an open market economy with free competition' (Article 98, TEC). Most importantly, the Treaty requires the member states to 'avoid excessive government deficits' (Article 104.1, TEC). A separate protocol annexed to the Treaty[2] specifies that this deficit rule implies sustaining the ratio of the actual or planned government deficit below 3 per cent of the gross domestic product (GDP) and to restrict the total government debt to not more than 60 per cent of the GDP.

The deficit rule reflects the concern of the authors of the Maastricht Treaty with sound public finances. This European 'stability consciousness' (Stark 2001: 78) had emerged against the background of deteriorating public finances across Europe throughout the 1980s and at the beginning of the 1990s. The definition of an explicit safeguard mechanism and strict entry criteria for participation in the single currency sought to revise this trend and was aimed at creating confidence in the new currency among European citizens and within international financial markets. In principle, budgetary consolidation increases the potential to

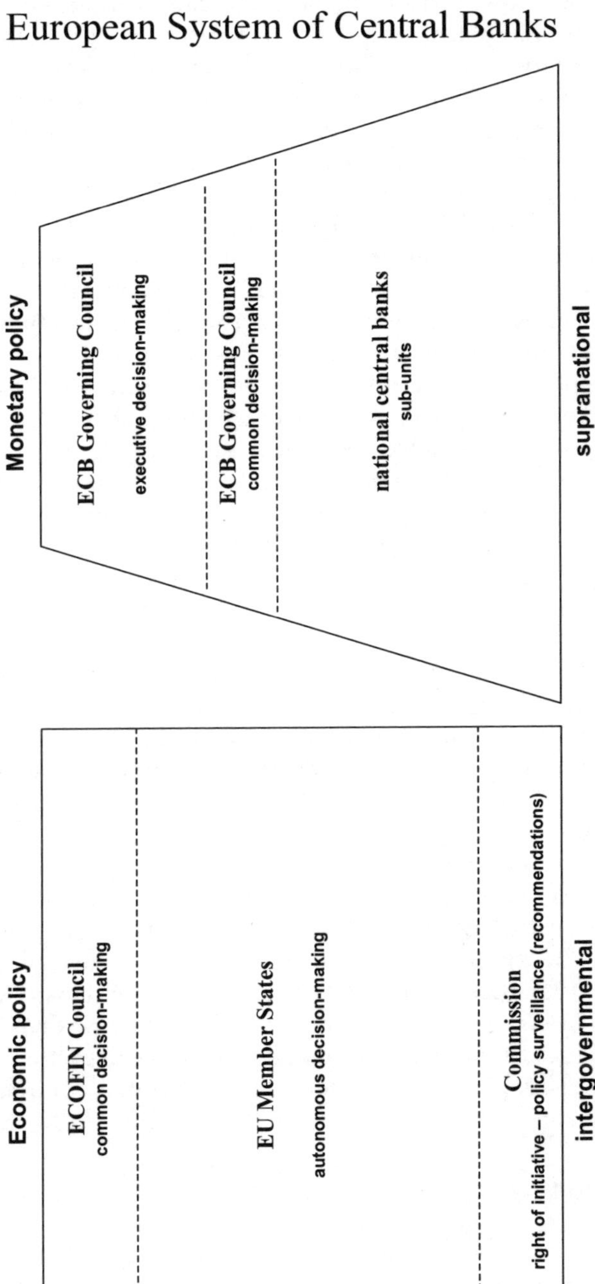

Figure 2.1   The two-pillar architecture of EMU

weather economic downturns through the so-called process of automatic stabilisation. This mechanism implies that governments are able to sustain spending in the downturn because of the financial resources which they have accumulated during economically more favourable periods. Moreover, sound public finances reduce the burden of monetary policy in maintaining price stability because they reduce the inflationary pressure stemming from government deficits. As a result of this strategy the economy benefits from falling interest rates. However, this strategy can only be maintained if all members of the single currency equally respect it. Otherwise, non-simultaneous or unequal consolidation leads to free-riding by a member who has chosen to consolidate less while others shoulder the double burden of higher interest rates and more restrictive spending. In a political sense the deficit rule therefore also constitutes a solidarity mechanism. Individual free-riding attempts can easily trigger general disrespect of the deficit rule because of rising mutual mistrust among the members of the single currency zone. The smaller member states of the euro area are especially vulnerable to attempts by bigger member states, which account for most of the euro area's economic activity, to circumvent the deficit mechanism. It is because of this political dimension of the deficit rule that the latter has the status of a constitutional provision.

In addition, the Treaty makes the national economic policies subject to a common coordination process within the Council (Article 99.1, TEC). While the deficit rule specifies a particular policy objective the Treaty does not pre-define the content and scope of policy coordination within EMU. The reluctance of the architects of the Maastricht Treaty to specify further supranational rules or to force member states to regularly conclude coordination agreements on pre-defined policy areas has two main rationales. The first rationale lies in the particular set of liberal economic policy ideas behind EMU's institutional architecture. It was the conviction of the authors of the Treaty provisions that, in principle, monetary union was possible without far-reaching coordination of the economic policies of the involved member states. Moreover, close coordination was considered to be counterproductive as it might reduce the incentives for individual member states to adapt economic policy to the specific requirements of a single currency zone (Glomb 1998). As Sixtén Korkman[3] (2001, pp. 281-290) observes:

> This set-up reflects the view that close coordination of discretionary economic policies would be extremely complex, might reduce the transparency of the policy regime, could create uncertainty with regard to policy assignments, and would thereby risk undermining the credibility of policies. EMU is, by and large, based on respect for national discretion within a framework of supranational rules.

However, this economic conviction also matched a particular political reality. By the time EMU was created member states were simply not prepared to surrender sovereignty over the definition and implementation of economic policy to the supranational level. This view is still valid. Economic policy is a highly sensitive area when it comes to exercising sovereignty. Decisions often seal the fate of governments. Moreover, the national executive frequently shares responsibilities with parliament and federal or regional authorities (Webb 1995), thus limiting, for example, the scope for formally negotiated amendments to national budget drafts. As long as the EU does not transform itself into a federal state there is hardly a way around this situation. EMU's economic pillar will therefore remain largely decentralised (Brouhns 1999). However, as debates within the economics literature on the future institutional development of EMU demonstrate, the degree of centralisation and the patterns of political authority might change over time (see for example Collignon, 2001; Jacquet and Pisani-Ferry 2001). In other words, if the actual operation of EMU demonstrates the technical need for closer coordination, a debate over the appropriate political structures might resurface. In turn, a change in the political coordinates of European integration towards a more federal system might open up new opportunities for the organisation of the coordination set-up. However, with regard to the short- and medium-term development of EMU these speculations do not seem to match the reality. More precisely, attempts to concentrate greater authority over economic policy at the supranational level might turn out to be counter-productive in political terms. Therefore, Nigel Wicks (1999: 9)[4] argues that

> it is right that the member-states retain responsibility for matters which often reflect deeply entrenched national cultures and ways of doing things, and which go to the heart of member-state identity. So running the economic union on a decentralised basis is the only way of proceeding efficiently without provoking tensions. ... For these issues, anyone who ignores Europe's diversity in designing its future economic governance risks a botched job.

The unambiguous assignment of sole responsibility for economic policy to national governments clearly limits the scope for coordination. It is therefore unlikely that economic policy coordination in EMU takes the form of formally negotiated package deals among national governments (see the definition by Henning and Putnam introduced in chapter 1). However, there is also a second rationale behind the reluctance of the authors of the Maastricht provisions to further regulate the scope and content of the coordination process through constitutional provisions. From the beginning a certain degree of uncertainty among decision-makers was a characteristic feature of the EMU process. By the time the constitutional framework was drafted it was not entirely clear how the coordination process would evolve after the effective creation of the single currency. Grégoire Brouhns (1999: 9)[5] recalls that

> this dynamic of EMU's economic pillar did not impose itself right away in the course of the negotiations leading to the Maastricht Treaty. The Treaty provisions relating to EMU indeed had to be edited in a way allowing in legal terms the absorption of an inevitable and predictable maturation of ideas in an area which has been without precedent in economic and monetary history.[6]

Consequently, economic governance has an evolutionary element and requires a considerable degree of flexibility with regard to the development and adaptation of policy objectives, instruments and procedures. After having discussed the overall institutional framework of economic governance the discussion now turns to the instruments and procedures regulating the coordination of economic policies and the enforcement of the supranational deficit rule. The central coordination instruments are the so-called broad economic policy guidelines (BEPGs) which are a compendium of commonly agreed policy objectives (Article 99.2, TEC). The BEPGs are generated through a complex and essentially intergovernmental procedure. The Commission presents a draft to the European Council which formulates a conclusion. This conclusion in turn functions as the basis for the final legal act – a formal Council decision adopting the BEPGs in the form of a recommendation to the member states. Consequently, the policy guidelines generated through this procedure are not legally binding. Nevertheless, the Treaty foresees a specific backup mechanism aimed at increasing the pressure on individual member states to comply with the BEPGs – the so-called multilateral surveillance procedure (Article 99.3, TEC). The Commission monitors the economic situation and the compliance of national policies with the commonly agreed guidelines. However, the role of the Commission is restricted to the provision of policy guidance and the initiation of Council action. In cases of non-compliance with the BEPGs the Commission recommends that the Council addresses a recommendation to the respective member state. In its recommendation the Council demands the correction of the diagnosed policy failure. In a second step the Council can decide to make this recommendation public. Consequently, both the adoption of common policy objectives and the control of compliance with these objectives require a consensual form of decision-making. Although the Council *de jure* takes all formal decisions in connection with the above procedures by qualified majority it is *de facto* inconceivable to conclude a set of non-binding policy guidelines against the will of one or even several individual countries since persistent or multiple non-compliance would easily compromise the moral authority of the instrument.

The enforcement mechanism associated with the excessive deficit rule follows a very similar pattern. Again, the Commission plays the role of a watchdog. However, the Commission cannot sanction non-compliance. Even the declaration of the mere existence of an excessive deficit is subject to a discretionary decision by the Council. After this first step in the initiation of an excessive deficit procedure the Council follows a carefully differentiated catalogue of further options in its attempts to respond to continued non-compliance. This catalogue comprises, among other options, the publication of the initial recommendation demanding the correction of policy failure, the request of a specific timetable for action on the part of the non-complying country and, finally, the option to impose financial sanctions (Article 104, TEC). Although the deficit rule of the Treaty can be considered as a hard or legally binding rule compared to the soft nature of the non-binding BEPGs, the related enforcement procedure provides considerable room for political discretion on the part of the Council. Moreover, the Treaty does not specify a particular time frame for the completion of the procedure or its individual stages. In theory, this makes it possible to delay the effective sanctioning of non-complying countries indefinitely.

It was this fragility of both the excessive deficit rule and the BEPG mechanism which led to the first refinement of EMU's coordination regime through the adoption of the SGP in 1997 (see on the main aspects of the pact Cabral 2001, 1999; Fischer and Giudice 2001). Consisting of a European Council resolution and two Council regulations (Council of the European Union 1999) the pact seeks to strengthen the coordination process and the enforcement of the deficit rule. The SGP further specifies the objective of budgetary discipline and formalises the exercise of the discretionary powers of the Council, in the context of the surveillance and response procedures. In this the pact fully respects EMU's constitutional framework and its assignment of responsibilities. Moreover, the pact directs the overall coordination process towards the question of budgetary discipline through emphasising a particular hierarchy of policy objectives:

> The European Council underlines the importance of safeguarding sound government finances as a means to strengthening the conditions for price stability and for strong sustainable growth conducive to employment creation. It is also necessary to ensure that national budgetary policies support stability oriented monetary policies. Adherence to the objective of sound budgetary positions close to balance or in surplus will allow all Member States to deal with normal cyclical fluctuations while keeping the government deficit within the reference value of 3 % of GDP. (Resolution of the European Council on the Stability and Growth Pact, Amsterdam, 17 June 1997 (97/C 236/01))[7]

The original package constituting the SGP was supplemented and partially amended in March 2005 when the European Council endorsed a report by the ECOFIN Council on 'Improving the implementation of the Stability and Growth Pact' (European Council 2005). The changes did not affect the key features of the pact but led to a further specification of conditions under which member states can get more time to correct national budgets which are in danger of breaching the deficit rule or have already done so.[8] Many observers interpreted these changes essentially as a weakening of the pact in the light of the difficulties of a number of countries to comply with its provisions. Widely unnoticed, the revision of the pact, however, also took stock of and sought to correct a number of difficulties concerning its implementation which had been encountered up to that stage. As will be demonstrated in Chapter 5 the revision of the pact is also in many ways the expression of a long and informal consensus-building process on the nature and appropriate use of the SGP as a key policy instrument in Stage 3.

Through the means of secondary legislation the SGP puts the so-called 'medium-term objective'[9] of bringing the budgetary positions of the member states close to balance or in surplus in the centre of the coordination process. This means that the SGP seeks to actively influence the process of budgetary consolidation over the economic cycle. The provisions are aimed at avoiding the occurrence of excessive deficits through enhanced consolidation efforts during economically favourable periods. The medium-term objective of the SGP also implies a more complex and closer surveillance procedure than the one originally specified by the Treaty. The budgetary positions of the member states are now subject to a continuing reviewing process. Changes in the economic situation require the periodic adjustment of consolidation efforts. The SGP therefore further develops the Treaty's surveillance regime through the specification of procedures and the definition of time frames. At the heart of these mechanisms is the so-called 'early warning system'.[10] Under this system the Council is required to alert a member state in a pre-emptive manner prior to the actual occurrence of an excessive deficit, or a case of non-compliance with the BEPGs, to the need for corrective action. This surveillance mechanism is complemented by the submission of national 'stability programmes'.[11] These publicly available programmes, which are updated on an annual basis, contain information on the actual medium-term objective of a member state and the adjustment path which the respective country intends to pursue. In short, the programmes outline the overall course of national policy and relate it to the set of common rules and policy objectives. The programmes are subject to a common examination procedure. The Commission and the Council scrutinise the envisaged policy objectives for their compliance with the common objectives and discuss the sustainability of the economic expectations on which national planning is based. Consequently, the annual adoption of stability programme updates in the Council constitutes a periodic renewal of the self-commitment of member states to EMU's stability framework. Jürgen Kröger (2002: 200)[12] points out that 'the pact is political in nature. It must be seen as an instrument for coordinating fiscal policy, which is still a national responsibility. The stability programmes are adopted by the ECOFIN Council and provide a practical framework, a sort of benchmark, for subsequent reviews.'

Finally, with regard to cases of effective non-compliance with the deficit rule the SGP seeks to strengthen the Treaty's response and sanctioning procedure through setting up time frames for the imposition of sanctions and the definition of potential exemptions.[13] Contrary to its popular image the SGP is neither identical with the deficit rule nor does it represent a genuinely supranational mechanism which circumvents national discretion. In this respect, the problem that EMU's credibility is built on a fragile intergovernmental framework reproduces itself with the pact. The role of the pact as a 'disciplining device' (Schelkle 2002) depends essentially on the political environment in which it is applied. In other words, the SGP very much reflects the dualism of coordinated action and national sovereignty, which is characteristic of EMU's governance framework. Designed to make EMU's stability and multilateral surveillance architecture operational and to further discipline national budgetary policies, the application of the pact has often serious consequences for national budgetary policy. Consequently, the stability mechanism attracts political opposition from those governments which are not prepared to sacrifice their often already heavily restricted room for manoeuvre at the domestic level. In such a situation the room for political discretion within the Council, which is reserved by the Treaty provisions and the SGP alike, can become problematic. Consequently, the credibility of the pact as a rigorous safeguard mechanism against lax budgetary policies, which is promptly applied by decision-makers, is not a foregone conclusion (Sutter 2000).

EMU's economic governance set-up limits the scope for policy coordination. Nevertheless, as the discussion of EMU's existing coordination instruments has shown, the fragility of the set of common rules and policy objectives clearly leaves room for complementary coordination activity. Notably, the implementation of the deficit rule and the exercise of multilateral surveillance in the context of the BEPGs and the SGP procedures, can be optimised through further activities. EMU's coordination instruments particularly depend on the organisation of consensus among national decision-makers. Finally, there also remains room for collective action agreed on a case-by-case basis, for example, in reaction to ad hoc situations such as price shocks or market turbulences. Korkman (2001: 290) characterises such complementary activity as 'close policy dialogue':

> The assignment principle [the clear allocation of decision-making competences in EMU] limits the scope for discretionary coordination but does not preclude policy dialogue, or even some genuine coordination, between policy actors so as to improve the compatibility of decisions on timing and the size of policy changes. A close policy dialogue is indeed essential to avoid communication failures and to strengthen mutual understanding and confidence of decision-makers.

In contrast to the exercise of legislative functions within the context of the ECOFIN Council a close policy dialogue requires a different working method. The emphasis is on a continuous and confidential exchange of views and information – not on the negotiation of immediate decisions. Consequently, the format of the ECOFIN Council might not be sufficient for the task of operating EMU's coordination regime in Stage 3. As Benoît Coeuré (2002: 72)[14] explains:

> Within the European legal framework the ECOFIN Council exercises the legislative functions, such as the adoption of European regulations and directives, which call for the regulation through specific procedures. Whereas issues such as the budgetary strategy or the dialogue on growth developments do not call for an immediate decision but require often the regular and informal exchange of views, which enables each minister to elaborate in full confidentiality on the situation of her/his country and the choices she/he has to face.[15]

The interplay with the monetary pillar

In contrast to the intergovernmental coordination set-up in the area of economic policy, monetary policy is organised within the supranational framework of the European System of Central Banks (ESCB). The ECB is at the top of this system while the formerly independent national central banks function as its sub-units. Monetary policy is an exclusive competence of the Community. The monetary pillar comprises all relevant decision-making competences in this policy area such as the definition and implementation of monetary policy, the conduct of foreign exchange operations, the holding and management of the foreign reserves of the member states and the surveillance of the operation of the payment systems (Article 105.2, TEC). The ECB is the only institution with the right to authorise the issuing of banknotes (Article 106.1, TEC). As regards the economic pillar, the authors of the Maastricht Treaty were reluctant to pre-define any common policy objectives except the deficit rule. In contrast, the objectives of monetary policy in EMU are clearly spelled out by the Treaty provisions:

> The primary objective of the ESCB shall be to maintain price stability. Without prejudice to the objective of price stability, the ESCB shall support the general economic policies in the Community. (Article 105.1, TEC)

This formulation also points to the particular relation between the monetary and the economic pillar. In the sense that monetary policy is aimed at supporting economic policy, the monetary pillar is subordinated to the economic pillar. The part of political discretion falls to the economic pillar and monetary policy is determined by technocratic considerations. However, this subordination is made conditional on the achievement of the 'primary objective' of monetary policy – that is, the maintenance of price stability. In this sense monetary policy follows an autonomous policy objective. Pursuing this objective can even imply tensions with the economic policy authorities. The potential for political conflict between the economic and the monetary pillar is further highlighted by the assignment of full political independence to the monetary institutions with regard to their task of implementing the constitutionally defined objectives of monetary policy:

> When exercising the powers and carrying out the tasks and duties conferred upon them by this Treaty and the Statute of the ESCB, neither the ECB, nor a national central bank, nor any member of their decision-making bodies shall seek or take instructions from Community institutions or bodies, from any government of a Member State or from any other body. (Article 108, TEC)

Following these provisions the ECB and its national sub-units enjoy an even higher degree of political independence than the German Bundesbank did prior to EMU. The institutional template of the European version of central bank independence never enjoyed the protection of its status by constitutional provisions. Consequently, the relationship between monetary policy and economic policy is reversed. Whatever direction economic policy takes, the ECB will defend price stability, regardless of what the motivations were behind the conduct of economic policies. At first glance, this characteristic clear-cut division of political competences between EMU's monetary and economic pillar seems to prevent any communication between the economic and the monetary institutions since the scope for genuine policy coordination is virtually non-existent. Actual coordination would imply that the ECB had to promise a specific stance of monetary policy under the condition that economic policy fulfils pre-agreed objectives. For example, a reduction in interest rates by a pre-agreed margin would be offered in response to the adoption of spending cuts. Such an explicit deal would clearly compromise the ECB's independence. However, as a closer look at the arrangements reveals, a lack of communication between the two poles can in fact lead to sub-optimal outcomes with regard to the interplay of economic and monetary policy. As Brouhns (1999: 5) points out:

> Because of their irritation at their asymmetry the two pillars of EMU cannot look upon each other in a hostile way. On the contrary, they represent the

two led horses of the same carriage – the one of EMU. In fact, the permanent search for the appropriate policy-mix of the euro zone is their common
task. Here lies their essential common dynamic from which the success of a
lasting EMU will depend. This permanent search for an appropriate policy-
mix is conducted through a continuing dialogue between the two poles.[16]

Seen from the perspective of the ECB, the bank is committed to the
objective of price stability but it does not have an interest in tightening
monetary policy more than necessary, as this would have adverse effects
on economic activity. Consequently, the bank is likely to pursue two main
purposes when communicating with economic policy-makers. On the one
hand, the central bank will seek to gather information on the conduct of
national economic policies and future planning. This knowledge will
enable the ECB to draw the necessary conclusions for its own behaviour
in a pre-emptive manner. On the other hand, in response to the require-
ment to support economic policy, the central bank will have a strong
interest in communicating its own policy to the key decision-makers in the
area of economic policy. For example, the ECB will wish that the latter
are aware that in a given situation an expansionary spending policy is
likely to trigger a more restrictive stance of monetary policy. Similarly,
economic policy-makers will take an active interest in the conduct of ECB
policies because they will want to enquire about their own room for
manoeuvre and consider their alternative policy options. Finally, decision-
makers in the area of economic policy will have a strong interest in
scrutinising the ECB in order to find the right balance between the two
policy objectives of maintaining price stability and supporting economic
policy. As indicated above, the ECB is likely to reject any attempt by
economic policy-makers to pre-define its own decisions. Therefore, the
latter can only scrutinise the ECB through the contestation (or substanti-
ation) of information about economic or budgetary developments and
through the discussion of the technical appropriateness of certain policy
responses in a given situation.

In consequence, one should expect a strong interest in communication
on the part of both the monetary and the economic policy authorities.
Communication is likely to be concentrated on an exchange of information and deliberations on the appropriate policy-mix with a view to the
two constitutionally defined objectives of monetary policy. However, this
kind of communication is in any case politically delicate because the line
between communicating with the ECB and influencing the ECB is easily
crossed. It is therefore preferable that communication between economic
and monetary policy authorities in EMU essentially takes place through
informal dialogue. In fact, the Treaty already acknowledges the need for
communication between the ECB and the institutions of the economic
pillar, notably the Council and the Commission. However, the existence
of formal procedures for communication between the ECB and the

Council is unlikely to change the above assumption that economic and monetary policy-makers in EMU would prefer informal dialogue as the main means of communication. The respective president of the Council and a member of the Commission have the right to participate without being entitled to vote in the meetings of the Governing Council of the ECB (Article 113.1, TEC) which is the central decision-making body within the monetary pillar. In return, the Council is asked to invite the president of the ECB to participate in its meetings whenever issues related to monetary policy are discussed (Article 113.2, TEC). However, the official format of Council meetings implies that the scope for communication between the two pillars is in fact very limited. The ECB will be rather cautious if not entirely unwilling to engage in a more detailed discussion of its preferred policy options within a formal decision-making body from which it has been granted political independence by the Treaty. As a result, the official lines of communication envisaged by the Treaty are not of much practical use with regard to a close dialogue between the ECB and decision-makers in the area of economic policy. In practice, one should, therefore, expect that the involved actors would try to circumvent these formal lines of communication.

Another aspect of the interplay between the institutions of the economic and the monetary pillar is the external representation of the single currency. The Treaty provisions on monetary policy only define a complex procedure for the conclusion of exchange rate agreements with third countries and the definition of exchange rate policy guidelines (Article 111, TEC). The question of the political representation of the euro area within international financial institutions such as the G7, the IMF and the World Bank is not addressed at all. Technically, each institution with competences in the area of EMU, i.e. the Council, the Commission and the ECB, are involved in these international affairs in some way or another. Consequently, the question of the hierarchy of the decision-making process and the allocation of specific competences arises. In this respect, a lead role for the ECOFIN Council in this area seems difficult as long as not all EU member states have adopted the single currency. In this situation, the presiding minister who is supposed to attend, for example a G7 meeting, might come from a country outside the euro area. This leads to the third and final characteristic feature of EMU's institutional architecture, which is considered here in its relation to the emergence of informal governance structures – the non-simultaneous development of economic and monetary policy integration.

The flexibility regime

As has been discussed above, according to the Maastricht provisions, the ECOFIN Council is the central decision-making institution within EMU's economic pillar. Like every other EU Council formation the ECOFIN Council assembles the ministers and the delegations of all member states. In effect, however, not all member states equally participate in the EMU framework. Some are members of a single currency zone and others are not. Nevertheless, all take part in the decision-making process within the Council. In other words, the architects of EMU sought to combine the preservation of the unity of the Council with a flexible regime for the transition of individual member states to the single European currency.

In fact, the Maastricht Treaty contains not only one but two different flexibility regimes for the area of EMU. The first is enshrined in the Treaty's core provisions on economic and monetary policy. Through the definition of detailed procedural provisions the Treaty makes full participation in the EMU process conditional on the fulfilment of a set of legal and economic criteria. In principle, all member states are required to fully participate in EMU and to adopt the single currency. In order to achieve this goal the member states have to adjust their economic policies and national legislation in a way that allows them to comply with EMU's so-called entry criteria. In this sense the first flexibility regime can be seen as an automatic entry mechanism. Once a member state fulfils the necessary criteria it proceeds automatically to the single currency. In contrast the second flexibility regime exempts member states from this automatism and makes it subject to the political discretion of a member state when it wants to apply for membership of the single currency. This flexibility regime applies only to two EU member states – Denmark and the United Kingdom. It finds its expression in two protocols annexed to the Treaty, each of them relating to one of the two countries. Both regimes are quite often confused because technically Denmark and the UK are treated, in many ways, in the same manner as those countries not yet fulfilling the economic and legal requirements for the adoption of the euro. However, the two flexibility mechanisms have very different political implications. As Tuytschaever (2000: 175) observes, the first flexibility regime, the automatic entry mechanism, already represents a radical alternative to the usual pattern of integration known from the EU context:

> From the outset, proposals for EMU have espoused views on European integration which partially abandoned traditional dogmas about the universality of EC law and the uniformity of its application, and which, inspired by a good dose of common sense (it is after all impossible to ignore differences in the Member States' levels of socio-economic development), have opted in favour of a more gradual approach to integration.

The political delicacy of the automatic entry regime lies in its contradictory nature. On the one hand, the introduction of the single currency is a project of constitutional nature. It requires all member states to be fully committed to the EMU process which is seen to be at the heart of

European integration. On the other hand, some member states are, although in principle only temporarily, excluded from the single currency. The main dilemma here is that every attempt to exclude the out-group from the decision-making process would risk compromising the 'centripetal forces to pull the outs towards participation in those very same activities' (Tuytschaever 2000: 186). At the same time, however, it is obvious that the actual participation in the single currency implies a higher degree of commitment to the common rules of the EMU framework than is the case for those countries only preparing for the fulfilment of EMU's entry criteria. The current constitutional framework seeks to find a compromise between the two extremes by assembling all member states regardless of their actual status of participation in the single currency within the same decision-making body. However, the Treaty provisions suspend the voting rights of the countries belonging to the out-group with regard to a number of crucial decisions (see Table 2.1 below).

The political delicacy of this flexibility regime is further expressed by the fact that the procedural provisions concerning the transition to the single currency are defined within the Treaty, rather than through secondary legislation. The authors obviously feared that the issue of economic and monetary integration could be reopened at every critical stage of the EMU project. Consequently, the Treaty provisions try to legitimise a two-class Community membership through the temporary nature of the exclusion of some member states from the single currency. In addition, the active participation of all member states in the decision-making process, even if some have only limited voting rights, is aimed at preserving the unity of the Council. As a result of its inevitable institutional ambiguity the automatic entry mechanism is not designed to deal with a two-tier integration process over a longer period of time or with larger proportions of member states not participating in the euro area. In fact, the architects of the Maastricht provisions did not consider this to be a likely scenario, as interviews with former negotiators suggest.

This finally leads to the Treaty's second flexibility regime which was introduced above. The granting of opting-out clauses from the automatic entry mechanism is by definition a contradiction in itself. Since the architects of the Treaty wanted to make the EMU project irrevocable they never considered an exit option as a viable alternative to the automatic procedure. Nonetheless, the political reality of the Intergovernmental Conference (IGC) leading to the Maastricht Treaty and the following ratification procedure left the authors of the EMU provisions with little choice. Not surprisingly the solution, which was reached in order to respond to the categorical rejection of an automatic entry mechanism by Denmark and the United Kingdom, is, once again, of an ambiguous nature. The two protocols granting the exemptions from the automatic

Table 2.1   Euro area restricted decision-making in the Council

Treaty article	Suspended voting rights of the out-group
99.2 broad economic policy guidelines	
99.4 multilateral surveillance	
100.1 and 2 financial assistance	
104.6–8 excessive deficits	
104.9 notification on measures for the deficit reduction within a specified time-limit	×
104.11 sanctions in case of non-compliance with 104(9) procedure	×
104.12 Abrogation of decisions taken under 104.6-9 and 11	
104.14 provisions replacing the Protocol on excessive deficits	
105.6 conferring certain tasks to the ECB in supervision	
106.2 specifications for coins	×
107.5 amendment of the specified ESCB statutes' articles	
107.6 adoption of provisions referred to in the specified ESCB statutes' articles	
111 exchange-rate policy	×
114.3 composition of the Economic and Financial Committee	
112.2b appointment of members of the ECB's Executive Board	×

Treaty article	Suspended voting rights of the out-group
122.2 abrogating a derogation	
123.4 adoption of conversion rates at the beginning of stage III	×
123.5 adoption of the euro rate	×

entry mechanism are part of the Treaty but do not have the legal status of Treaty provisions. By using the back door of constitutional agreement the authors of the Maastricht provisions sought to avoid anything which would have come close to a general enabling clause for countries willing to remain outside the single currency for an indefinite period of time. However, this compromise was the first step towards making obsolete the concept of a temporary and limited use of the instrument of flexibility in the area of EMU.

When Sweden joined the EU in 1995 it became the first member state to interpret the opt-outs for Denmark and the UK in its own way. Sweden decided to deliberately delay the fulfilment of some of the technical criteria for accession to the euro area in order to avoid participation. For the first time an accession country had demonstrated that EMU's non-negotiable automatic entry mechanism was in fact not as strict as suggested by the Treaty provisions. Moreover, it became clear that for the time being three out of fifteen member states would not join the euro area regardless of their actual ability to fulfil the entry criteria in a technical sense. As a result of the coexistence of the two conflicting flexibility regimes the role of the ECOFIN Council as the sole and unitary decision-making body in the area of EMU becomes questionable. Finally, when ten new member states joined the EU in 2004 the balance between participants and non-participants in the single currency was adjusted to an extent which had not been envisaged by the architects of the Maastricht Treaty. Again, the viability of the concept of a unitary decision-making body for the economic pillar becomes questionable. However, a solution to these problems through an adjustment of the constitutional framework seems not to be an option. The dilemma of the coexistence of two conflicting flexibility regimes is simply difficult to solve. In fact, this is the main reason why finance ministers have categorically rejected proposals to subsume EMU under a general mechanism for enhanced cooperation within the EU. This issue was raised in connection with the IGCs leading to the Amsterdam and Nice Treaties. The vast majority of EU member states simply consider EMU to be far too important a policy area to make it subject to an *à la carte* entry mechanism. In addition, the creation of a separate euro area Council formation seems almost inconceivable. Given the important role of the ECOFIN Council in the overall Council structure such a step would be likely to mark the end of the principle of the unity of the Council, which is one of the cornerstones of the EU's constitutional order. Again a characteristic feature of EMU's institutional framework can be associated with a demand for informal solutions. The coexistence of member states participating in the euro area and those remaining outside of it for an indefinite period of time makes it unlikely that the current euro area countries will refrain from establishing closer coordination structures among themselves. However, because of the above institutional sensitivities, closer ties among euro area countries can only emerge within the informal realm.

Negotiating the creation of an exclusive euro area forum

The discussion now turns to the political process of the creation of the Eurogroup in the run-up to Stage 3 of EMU. The above argumentation pointed to the institutional dynamics inherent to EMU's economic governance set-up, as it is specified in the Treaty. It could be demonstrated that the formal institutional framework has a dual quality. It provokes the emergence of informal governance structures but at the same time represents also the set of valid formal rules within which the Eurogroup has to operate and which needs to be respected by all actors. However, this discussion remained essentially theoretical. It could only highlight tendencies or constraints inherent in the formal institutional framework of EMU. In the end, whether or not policy-makers actually decide to opt in favour of particular institutional alternatives is an empirical question. Moreover, the actual historical and political process leading to the creation of governance structures is generally considered to be an independent source of constraints and lock-in effects shaping an institution in its further development (Pierson 1998). The reconstruction of the most decisive steps in the negotiations leading to the foundation of the Eurogroup also implies that the discussion has to rely almost exclusively on the empirical research conducted in connection with this study. As indicated in Chapter 1 neither the creation nor the actual work of the Eurogroup have so far been subject to detailed empirical analysis.

In the run-up to Stage 3 in the second half of the 1990s, policy-makers became increasingly aware of new challenges to economic governance within EMU to which the Maastricht provisions did not provide ready-to-use solutions. As already indicated the negotiation, of the SGP framework was the first major development in this context. The creation of the

Eurogroup and the issuing of further political guidance by the European Council followed quickly. This renewed initiative on the development and enhancement of economic policy coordination in EMU reignited the struggle over the exercise of political control over the new structures of economic governance. The three countries which had decided not to apply for participation in the single currency for the time being, found themselves at odds with the rest of the EU.

In order to trace back the history of the creation of the Eurogroup it is necessary to briefly return to the negotiations of the Maastricht Treaty in 1991. This is not to say that the Eurogroup or a similar arrangement was already on the negotiating table by this time. On the contrary, the negotiations centred on the construction of the formal constitutional framework of economic governance in EMU. It was perhaps during and shortly before these negotiations that the antagonism between two different concepts of economic governance was most clearly pronounced. This antagonism concerned the preferences of France and Germany. Together, the two countries were the driving force behind the EMU project. However, each of them was attached to a different model of European economic governance. Germany was mainly concerned with the guarantee of central bank independence. This had to do not only with the intrinsic value of this economic idea but was also motivated by a certain degree of German mistrust with regard to the other European partners. The fear was that central bank independence and the orientation towards price stability could be easily compromised once EMU had come into being. In contrast, France raised concerns that the German model would lead to a situation in which economic policy-makers were deprived of the possibility of discretionary action. As the then French finance minister Pierre Bérégovoy explained with a view to the German demand for strict central bank independence:

> Of course! I am in favour of monetary policy independence within economic policy independence. Within the framework of economic policy guidelines for which a political authority is responsible, which is constituted by the European Council, the central bank should be able to run independently the monetary policy of the Community.[17]

In both cases the respective national position was routed in core policy traditions (see Dyson and Featherstone 1999; Howarth 1999). The emphasis on price stability had been one of the cornerstones of the macro-economic policy framework of the Federal Republic after World War II. The scepticism with regard to central bank independence was anchored in the French republican tradition. This Franco-German row found its expression in the Maastricht Treaty. The German model became enshrined in the unambiguous provisions on central bank independence and the avoidance of excessive deficits. Nonetheless, the expansive room for political discretion, which is enjoyed by the Council with regard to the control of compliance with the set of common rules, was derived from the French model and followed Paris's draft provisions for the IGC. Against this background it is not surprising that any further refinements of the economic governance framework were a sensitive issue for the two countries. It was in the context of the debates on the creation of the SGP, which were initiated by German finance minister Theo Waigel in the second half of 1995, that the question of an exclusive coordination forum for the future members of the single currency zone was raised. By this time it was not clear which countries would be among the first to adopt the single currency. Nevertheless, there was little doubt that it would be only a limited number of EU member states. From the beginning the debate over a new coordination forum was one about parallel structures of decision-making which would exclude the non-participating countries. The French government reiterated its demand for the creation of a European economic government which it had previously advocated during the IGC (see Colomb 1998). Negative reactions from the German finance ministry and the Bundesbank followed swiftly. The Germans warned the French to respect the Treaty. Despite this opposition the first draft of a European stability pact by the German finance ministry from November 1995 also proposed the creation of additional coordination structures. The then German deputy finance minister Jürgen Stark (2001: 88) summarises the draft provisions as follows:

> The member states form a European Stability Council within the ECOFIN Council, which decides on whether these self-imposed restraints have been violated and, if necessary, enforces them. It meets at least biannually, either on presentation of the deficit figures by the Commission or at the request of a member state.

The idea of a stability council was later dropped and the management of the SGP was firmly anchored within the ECOFIN Council (see above). Nevertheless, the draft of the German finance ministry had demonstrated that the issue of an exclusive euro area forum was debated on both sides of the river Rhine. The idea of the creation of a new venue for policy coordination in Stage 3 was not only popular among French politicians. The actual political conflict rather concerned the specific format and status, as well as the precise tasks of such a forum. Meanwhile the SGP negotiations were in full swing. The negotiations evolved over a period of nearly two years. Despite a relatively swift agreement between France and Germany on the general objectives of a European stability pact the two countries disagreed on several occasions on the degree of intergovernmental discretion reserved by the SGP procedures. The Germans preferred an unambiguous and automatic procedure for the imposition of sanctions in cases of non-compliance with the deficit rule. In contrast, the French were anxious to avoid a further restriction of national sovereignty through the pact. In this respect the finally agreed SGP 'represents in a way a compromise between the initial provisions of the Maastricht Treaty and the rigorous demands of Waigel' (Sutter 2000: 31).[18] As outlined at the beginning of this chapter, the pact further strengthens the stability orientation of the EMU system through the means of secondary legislation but still leaves considerable room for political discretion. In this, the result of the SGP negotiations clearly reflected the concerns raised by France and other countries. Moreover, during the final phase of negotiations other obvious concessions to the French concerns were made. The decision that the official terminology should refer to a 'Stability *and* Growth Pact' rather than to a 'Stability Pact' incorporated the continuous claim that the stability orientation of EMU should not compromise growth. This rhetoric was further substantiated by the introduction of a separate 'Resolution on growth and employment' in addition to the 'Resolution on the Stability and Growth Pact' in the Amsterdam European Council conclusions (European Council 1997a), which marked the end of the SGP negotiations. Finally, following a French initiative the Amsterdam Treaty contained the additional Title VIII on employment. However, as the findings of the empirical research conducted in connection with this study suggest, the creation of a new coordination forum for Stage 3 was in no way part of the negotiations on the SGP. It was in the context of the debates over the SGP that the issue of a euro area forum came to the surface. However, neither did the French make the outcome of the negotiations conditional on the creation of such a forum, nor did the Germans suggest such a body as a kind of compensation for the approval of the SGP.

With the negotiations on the SGP approaching closure, the debate over an exclusive euro area forum intensified in the first half of 1997. In particular, the French continued to draw attention to the issue. The French prime minister Alain Juppé even claimed that he had secured general agreement on a 'Euro-Council' at the Dublin European Council in December 1996 (Howarth and Loedel 2003: 74). In January 1997 the president of the German Bundesbank Hans Tietmeyer reminded the French government to respect the Treaty's provisions on central bank independence and warned against the creation of a political counterweight to the ECB. However, the public debate continued. During its campaign in the run-up to the French parliamentary elections in June the French socialist party under Lionel Jospin further pushed the issue of the creation of a European *gouvernement économique*. In this context it is noteworthy that the term 'economic government' is used in France in many different ways. The different concepts attributed to the term range from a strengthened EMU stability regime, over a coordination mechanism between the ECOFIN Council and the ECB, to proposals for EU involvement in job creation policies.[19] In a contribution to a conference in Brussels on 27 May 1997 the Belgian finance minister Philippe Maystadt (1997: 37) pointed to a possible line of compromise. While he embraced the French demand for a 'Council for stability and growth' he did not question the role of the ECB. Instead Maystadt stressed that the ECB would only be able to support economic policies on the basis of a 'credible and effective coordination of the economic policies of the member states' (ibid.). He highlighted the fact that it would be necessary for the ECB to 'have a clear and precise idea of the general economic policy orientations of the member states' (ibid.). Moreover, the Belgian finance minister suggested an informal format for the envisaged coordination forum which should not question the role of ECOFIN. Participants should comprise the finance ministers, the Commission and the ECB. As a key topic for discussion Maystadt saw the question of the appropriate policy-mix in the euro area, i.e. the interplay of national economic policies and the common monetary policy. Finally, the minister underlined the necessity to find a solution for the external representation of the euro area.

The Amsterdam European Council meeting in June 1997 can be seen as a turning point in the developments leading to the creation of an exclusive euro area forum. So far the discussion was mainly conducted through the media and within expert circles. Now the Community institutions became officially involved. The Amsterdam presidency conclusions explicitly requested the Commission and the Council 'to examine and indicate how to improve the processes of economic co-ordination in stage three of Economic and Monetary Union consistent with the principles and practices of the Treaty' (European Council 1997a). In July the Monetary Committee studied the possibility of a closer dialogue between ministers and the ECB. The Committee also discussed the question of whether the format of informal ECOFIN meetings, which are only attended by one minister and one adviser per country, was a potential institutional framework for such discussions. At the occasion of an informal ECOFIN Council meeting in Mondorf in Luxembourg in mid-August 1997 the first serious political discussion on the creation of an exclusive euro area forum took place. The French idea of a formal euro area Council for policy coordination was on the table. Suspicious of French ambitions to create a political counterweight to the ECB the German deputy finance minister Stark reportedly (according to anonymous interviews) rejected the French demands in a long statement. He emphasised that the asymmetry in the Treaty provisions with regard to the emphasis of central bank independence and the maintenance of price stability was intentional and needed to be respected. Ironically, the German rebuff received the greatest support from the UK government. The latter emphasised that coordination of economic policies was a matter for all member states. The British were anxious to prevent the emergence of new governance structures outside the ECOFIN Council. Nonetheless, this picture was soon revised when the Germans took the initiative using the intimate bilateral atmosphere of the Franco-German economic council meeting in Münster in Germany, only two months later on 14 October. The French delegation was surprised to learn about the new German flexibility with regard to an exclusive euro area forum. In fact, the Germans themselves were interested in strengthening policy coordination among euro area countries. To evade institutional conflict they suggested the format of an informal group with a clear mandate. Moreover, reference to the group as a 'Council' should be avoided. The bilateral Münster meeting can be seen as a breakthrough on the way towards the creation of the Eurogroup. It marked the end of the Franco-German row about the potential role of parallel coordination structures in Stage 3.

As the accounts of senior officials who were involved in the negotiations suggest, the debates among ministers and officials over the creation of an exclusive euro area forum reproduced a pattern well known from the SGP discussions. Principal agreement between France and Germany on the necessity of such a coordination forum in Stage 3 existed from the beginning. However, the issue of the right balance between an automatic stabilisation regime based on unambiguous central bank independence, on the one hand, and the need for political discretion, on the other, had held up a final agreement. As a participant in Eurogroup meetings explains:

> Germany and France needed a long time to agree on the Eurogroup this was essentially related to the old French idea of a political counterpart to the ECB. Conversely, the Germans were anxious to agree something similar. The French readiness to agree on an informal body was the key to a compromise. (Anonymous interview, participant D)

And another Eurogroup participant emphasises:

> Although there were differences between France and Germany regarding the name and the relevance of such a group the basic idea was always clear and uncontested. The finance ministers should have the opportunity to meet in a small group together with the ECB and the Commission for discussion. (Anonymous interview, participant A)

At the ECOFIN Council meeting on 17 November it became clear that the idea of an informal group was well received among most of the other EU countries (see ECOFIN Council 1997a). The end of the Franco-German row had paved the way for the participation of the ECB in the new coordination structures. The fact that an informal venue had been found for the dialogue between ministers and the ECB was particularly welcomed by smaller member states. The latter particularly feared that in the absence of such a venue they might have been excluded from any informal communication with the ECB in Stage 3. As a participant in Eurogroup meetings recalls:

> To say it ... bluntly, the first two tasks I just have talked about [the dialogue with the ECB and the coordination of budgetary policy] cannot be fulfilled in the regular ECOFIN – even if it meets in restricted sessions. This would be quite difficult for the ECB because ECOFIN is a Community institution. Without the Eurogroup the dialogue with the ECB would probably take place behind the scenes involving only the big countries of the euro zone. In the absence of the Eurogroup we would be unable to involve all member states in the dialogue with the ECB. The Eurogroup made this possible, so nobody is excluded. We had quite some problems with our foreign affairs colleagues when we wanted to create the Eurogroup. They were very concerned about the idea of an informal forum for ministers, saying that we were weakening the Community institutions. But this is not true. On the contrary! We tried to explain them that it wouldn't be possible to involve all member states in the dialogue [with the ECB] otherwise. (Anonymous interview, participant C)

However, the creation of a euro area forum was not yet a done deal. Another problem moved to the centre of discussions. The idea of an exclusive euro area forum provoked fierce opposition on the part of those countries which were likely to remain outside the group. The main question was how the future forum would be reconnected with the ECOFIN Council. Moreover, fears were raised at the November ECOFIN meeting that the creation of the new forum could render decision-making in EMU opaque (IEA 1997). This situation did not change very much at the next ECOFIN Council at the beginning of December 1997 – the final meeting before the Luxembourg European Council. The negotiations were stalled (see ECOFIN Council 1997b). The creation of an exclusive euro area forum had developed into an issue of high politics. The ministers were not able to solve this issue and referred it to the heads of state and government. As a participant in Eurogroup meetings recalls:

> At the time when the 'Luxembourg conclusions' were formulated, the format of the Eurogroup was heavily contested. At this time it was also unclear how many member states would participate in the first wave. However, the Swedes and the British were very much aware that they would not be part of this first group of countries. Especially the British made sure that the mandate of the Eurogroup would be narrow and that they would have the opportunity to participate in this group in its enlarged version. However, the countries which were in no doubt that they would be part of the euro zone were absolutely in agreement that the new era would require a special forum in which only the ministers would meet. (Anonymous interview, participant A)

At the Luxembourg European Council meeting on 12 December the British prime minister Tony Blair proved to be 'the last major opponent' (according to an anonymous interview) to the creation of an exclusive euro area forum. Apart from the Swedish government, which supported the fundamental opposition of the British, all other countries welcomed the idea or had no further objections. This was also true for Denmark, which had decided to opt out of the single currency, and for Greece which already knew that it would not immediately qualify for participation. Only after lengthy and difficult negotiations with Blair who fundamentally opposed the idea of a separate euro area forum besides the ECOFIN Council, was an agreement reached. The great pro-euro majority of EU countries had been reluctant to make any significant concessions to the British and Swedish objections. It is reported that the French finance minister Dominique Strauss-Kahn rejected a compromise on the exclusion of non-euro countries by saying that 'married couples don't want anybody else in their bedroom' (as quoted in Tuytschaever 2000: 188). As a Eurogroup participant who was present at the summit meeting explains:

> The founding of the Eurogroup was also, one has to bear this in mind, a clear signal to the others that they have to pay for opting-out – for not being part of the euro. That is also why it was so difficult to convince Blair. (Anonymous interview, participant D)

Finally, the Luxembourg European Council concluded a decision on the issue and the practical preparations of the creation of the new informal euro area forum began.

Notes

1　Reference to Treaty articles follows the updated numbering of the Amsterdam Treaty.
2　See Protocol No. 5 on the excessive deficit procedure annexed to the TEC, reproduced in: Council of the European Union 1999: 75.
3　Sixtén Korkman is director general of the Social and Economic Affairs Directorate General of the Council Secretariat and a senior practioner working on EMU affairs.
4　Sir Nigel Wicks was the president of the EU Monetary Committee until the beginning of Stage 3 of EMU when the committee was transformed into the EFC.
5　Grégoire Brouhns is secretary general in the Belgian ministry of finance and a senior practioner working on EMU affairs.
6　My translation.
7　Reproduced in Council Secretariat (1999: 27).
8　See Council Regulations (EC) No. 1055/2005 and 1056/2005 of 27 June 2005, Official Journal (7 July 2005).
9　Council Regulation (EC) No. 1466/97 of 7 July 1997 on the strengthening of the surveillance of budgetary positions and the surveillance and coordination of economic policies, paragraph 4; reproduced in Council Secretariat (1999: 32).

10   Ibid., paragraph 5.
11   Ibid., section 2.
12   Jürgen Kröger is director of the economic studies and research directorate of the Commission's Directorate General for Economic and Financial Affairs (DG ECFIN).
13   See Council Regulation (EC) No. 1467/97 of 7 July 1997 on speeding up and clarifying the implementation of the excessive deficit procedure, reproduced in Council Secretariat (1999: 43-57), and No. 1056/2005 of 27 June 2005, Official Journal (7 July 2005).
14   Benoît Coeuré is economic counsellor to the director of the Treasury Department in the French Ministry of Economics, Finance and Industry.
15   My translation.
16   My translation.
17   Interview with *Les Echos*, 19 November 1990; reproduced in Krägenau and Wetter (1993: 341). My translation.
18   My translation.
19   For a typology of the term in the context of French debates see Howarth and Loedel (2003: 75-77).

3

The informal working method

Against the background of the account on the institutional and historical-political sources of informal governance this chapter introduces the features of the Eurogroup's peculiar working method. It is within this institutional setting that the euro area's top decision-makers address the challenges to economic governance in Stage 3. The actual work of the group is not regulated through legal provisions. Informal governance within the Eurogroup is built on a set of routinised practices and shared rules. Although the process of informal governance is often fluid and has been adjusted over time, nonetheless some characteristic patterns have evolved over the last six years. They deserve particular attention.

Creating the structures of informal governance

By definition the structures of informal governance can neither be the product of a merely formal or legal process, nor the product of an entirely self-referential process. The Eurogroup operates in relation to and in competition with the official Community institutions. It is not possible that this activity can evolve without the consent of the Community institutions. As regards the evolution of the Eurogroup's informal working method, two factors can therefore be distinguished. One is external and refers to the formal Community institutions. The other is internal and refers to informal agreements among Eurogroup participants. In this respect, the Luxembourg European Council conclusions contain the formal source of informal governance in EMU. The document *formally* enables the ministers of the euro area member states to meet *informally*:

> By virtue of the Treaty, the ECOFIN Council is the centre for the coordination of the Member States' economic policies and is empowered to act in the relevant areas. In particular, the ECOFIN Council is the only body empowered to formulate and adopt the broad economic policy guidelines which constitute the main instrument of economic coordination.
>
> The defining position of the ECOFIN Council at the centre of the

economic coordination and decision-making process affirms the unity and cohesion of the Community.

The Ministers of the States participating in the euro area may meet informally among themselves to discuss issues connected with their shared specific responsibilities for the single currency. The Commission, and the European Central Bank when appropriate, will be invited to take part in the meetings.

Whenever matters of common interest are concerned they will be discussed by Ministers of all Member States.

Decisions will in all cases be taken by the ECOFIN Council in accordance with the procedures laid down in the Treaty. (European Council 1997c, paragraph 44)

The wording of the presidency conclusions reflects very well the difficulties in achieving an agreement, thus expressing the institutional delicacy of informal meetings among euro area ministers. Even before the actual novelty of the establishment of informal discussions among euro area ministers is announced the text reaffirms the role of the ECOFIN Council. Obviously, the negotiated arrangement constitutes, or comes at least very close to constituting, an amendment of EMU's constitutional framework. However, this is not the official reading of the Luxembourg conclusions. According to its mandate the European Council issues policy guidance on EU policies to the Community institutions and national governments. The summit meetings of the heads of state and government do not conclude official EU legislation. The latter is the prerogative of the Council of Ministers. This legal detail is the first characteristic feature of the Eurogroup's informal working method. The group does not have a legal basis in terms of either secondary legislation or a Treaty provision. Thus, the group is not an official Community institution and does not belong to the Council structure. However, since the presidency conclusions of European Council meetings have the status of an official EU document, a link between the formal Community structures and the informal meetings of euro area finance ministers is created nonetheless.

This procedural ambiguity is complemented by the lack of a detailed definition of the tasks of the Eurogroup. The Luxembourg presidency conclusions defined an enabling clause rather than a precise mandate for the Eurogroup. Apart from the very general characterisation of the content of discussions as 'shared specific responsibilities' the document issued no guidance with regard to the group's work. More precisely, the conclusions did not refer to a 'group' of ministers – let alone a 'Eurogroup'. Everything which could point to the creation of an actual institution, i.e. a name, a statute or the assignment of responsibilities, was avoided. Neither the European Council nor the ECOFIN Council further specified a mandate for the new body at a later stage. Only a few exemptions were made with regard to individual aspects of the Eurogroup's work. Six months after the first Eurogroup meeting the Vienna European Council defined the first statutory task for the informal group. The presidency conclusions stated that the 'President of the Euro 11' represents the EU at G7 meetings (European Council 1998b, paragraph 14). (Euro 11 was the name by which the Eurogroup was known at the time.) Moreover, the related report of the ECOFIN Council explicitly assigned the preparation of EMU affairs for G7 meetings to the Eurogroup. A further twelve months later the Helsinki European Council conclusions, and the annexed ECOFIN Council report on policy coordination in EMU, explicitly acknowledged the work of the Eurogroup and encouraged a further development of cooperation inside this framework. From then on the European Council has repeatedly referred to the Eurogroup's work in the area of economic policy coordination. However, this practice does not constitute a change of the group's informal status.

This leads to the second factor influencing the evolution of the Eurogroup's informal working method – the Eurogroup's internal discussion process. It is here where the 'shared specific responsibilities' (European Council 1997c, paragraph 44) of the euro area countries are defined and further developed. In this respect the Eurogroup's first meeting was perhaps as important for the development of the group as the Luxembourg presidency conclusions. The founding meeting provided the context for the informal affirmation of political agreement among euro area ministers on the central features of the Eurogroup's working method and its agenda. The meeting concluded a process of extensive preparatory discussions within the Monetary Committee. Within this expert committee the future format and the agenda of the Eurogroup had been discussed in greater detail ever since the idea of a new euro area forum had come on the agenda of the ECOFIN Council in the second half of 1997 (see Chapter 2). As explained below the first informal discussion among euro area ministers settled the relations of the Eurogroup with the formal Community institutions which have competences in the area of EMU, i.e. the ECOFIN Council, the Commission and the ECB. As stated above the Luxembourg conclusions avoided the specification of a name for the envisaged discussions among the ministers of the euro area. In fact, various names have been attributed to the Eurogroup at the different stages of its history. Early proposals for an exclusive euro area forum talked of a European 'Stability Council' (Stark 2001). The term 'Euro Council' was used in working papers and found its way into the media reports of the time. Then, in the run-up to the Luxembourg European Council and during the short period before euro area ministers met for the first time within the new framework, the group was named 'Euro X'. The name reflected the necessity to avoid the term 'Council' as this could have suggested that the envisaged discussions were part of the official Council structure. From the first meeting on the ministers from the eleven euro area countries referred to their discussions as meetings of the 'Euro 11'. This term was used until the beginning of the French presidency in summer 2000 when the Greek finance minister joined the gatherings because the southern European country had fulfilled the entry criteria. From then on the term 'Eurogroup' was used in order to avoid further changes in the group's name on the occasion of each enlargement of the euro area.

Who's who: the small circle of participants

Six months after the Luxembourg European Council in December 1997 euro area ministers met for the first time. The beginning of Stage 3 of EMU, the date for the legal creation of the single currency, was only a further six months away. A line-up of limousines in front of Chateau de Senningen in Luxembourg during the evening hours of Thursday 4 June, indicated that something important was going on inside the historical building. The locality was normally used by the military secret service of the Grand Duchy, as one participant recalls (anonymous interview). Even outside the conference room the activities and the limousine traffic did not stop. The first Eurogroup meeting had attracted more visitors than foreseen on the guest list. Together with the ministers, the permanent representatives of the prospective euro area member states had arrived from Brussels. This was not unusual. This group of ambassadors always accompanies the ministers on the occasion of Council meetings. However, the gathering inside Chateau de Senning was different, and the host of the meeting, Austrian finance minister Rudolph Edlinger, had not invited the ambassadors. The minister took no chances and a senior ministerial official had to pose as the doorman, watching out for the diplomats at the entry. To continue the analogy with the exclusive club scene, half an hour after the meeting had started another guest was forced to leave and vanished in his limousine. This time it was the British finance minister Gordon Brown who was spotted in his car.

Indeed, this scene demonstrated very well what the first meeting of the Eurogroup was about. Euro area ministers for the first time took *de facto* decisions among themselves. They decided on how to organise the work of the new group. One of the most important issues here was the definition of the circle of participants in the gatherings (see Figure 3.1 below). The selection process underlined that the Eurogroup was not only the result of a delicate political compromise but also represented an attempt to find new working methods for coordinating economic policy among euro area member states. The emphasis was put on face-to-face discussion among ministers or, to be more precise, finance ministers. Only in exceptional circumstances are ministers responsible for other portfolios spotted in the Eurogroup. For example, when the German finance minister Oskar

Lafontaine resigned from office in March 1999 during the German EU presidency, the Eurogroup meeting was chaired by the German economics minister Werner Müller. However, under no circumstances it is permissible for more than one minister per country to join the meetings. This restrictive participation regime is one of the most important features of the Eurogroup's informal working method. As one of the driving forces behind the Eurogroup's creation, the French finance minister Strauss-Kahn, once pointed out:

> There was a clear need to create something more informal than ECOFIN where there are as many as 100 people between ministers and officials. With the Euro-11 there are only 22 members: each minister and one adviser. This means we can have a real exchange of views.[1]

While the ECOFIN Council is essentially concerned with the finalisation of formal decisions, the rationale behind Eurogroup meetings was the need for a close policy dialogue among the euro area's top decision-makers. The Eurogroup removes a simple technical obstacle to such a dialogue. The dramatic reduction of the number of participants leaves more time for interventions, which is an essential precondition for a real and meaningful debate. As a participant in Eurogroup discussions observes:

> The discussions are quite different from ECOFIN. There are arguments and counter-arguments. Ministers do not read out prepared statements. They have a real debate. I think there is a better exchange of views now in the Eurogroup than we ever had before. (Anonymous interview, participant B)

And another participant remarks:

> And yes, the atmosphere in the Eurogroup is quite relevant. You can say what you want. It is an interactive process. Ministers do not read out prepared statements – if you want to put it this way. There is a real conversation. They really react to what their colleagues say and they are very frank and quite direct. This is not to say that in ECOFIN there is no substantial debate. Ministers can be quite frank there as well with regard to criticism and appraisal but it is less interactive because it is not that restricted. (Anonymous interview, participant C)

In analogy to the format of informal ECOFIN meetings this aspect of the Eurogroup's informal working method is called the 'minister plus one approach'. The Luxembourg conclusions already acknowledged the suitability of this particular working method for the final phase of EMU. However, they avoided explicit reference to the Eurogroup setting:

> Monitoring of the economic situation and policy discussions should become a regular item on the agenda of informal ECOFIN sessions. In order to stimulate an open and frank debate, the ECOFIN Council should from time to time meet in restricted sessions (minister plus one), particularly when

conducting multilateral surveillance. (European Council 1997c, resolution
on economic policy coordination in stage 3 of EMU, paragraph 5)

The choice of the 'one' who accompanies the minister also reflects the
orientation of the Eurogroup's work towards substantial discussions over
policies. Alongside each minister one of their most senior civil servants
participates in the meetings. Depending on the administrative organisation of the respective national finance ministry this person has the rank of
a deputy finance minister (secretary of state in the terminology of some
member states) or director general in charge of budgetary policy and/or
European affairs. In several cases this person is also the representative of
the respective finance ministry in the Economic and Financial Committee
(EFC) which is the influential expert committee for EMU affairs in Stage
3 (see below). This implies the exclusion of another important group of
top officials who usually take a seat right beside the ministers – the permanent representatives (see above). Whenever issues of EU decision-making
are discussed at an intergovernmental level these ambassadors of the
member states play an important role in the decision-making system of the
EU. They are involved in the pre-negotiation of all official agreements and
attend the various Council meetings. The permanent representatives function as a kind of administrative memory and ensure the coherence and
continuity of the decision-making process (see Hayes-Renshaw and
Wallace 1997; Lewis 2003; Wallace and Wallace 2000). This official role
makes the participation of the diplomats in Eurogroup meetings difficult.
Their presence could lend an official character to the group.
    Moreover, the fact that ministers prefer their own finance ministry offi-
cials to the top-ranking diplomats is not only a matter of etiquette with
regard to the political sensibilities of the non-euro countries. The permanent representatives are policy generalists because of their simultaneous
engagement in the various areas of EU decision-making. In contrast, their
colleagues from the finance ministries are experts in the day-to-day issues
of European economic governance. The latter focus on the narrow objectives of finance ministries, whereas EU ambassadors tend to emphasise the
compromise between different policy areas and the conflicting preferences
of individual countries. This accentuation in the composition of the
Eurogroup further underlines the ambition of euro area finance ministers
to create their own independent forum in the canon of EU institutions.
    Similar to the Council structure the meetings among ministers are
chaired by one minister. The presidency of the group changes each semester in accordance with the general EU system of rotating presidencies.
Each time a minister takes over the Eurogroup presidency they are accompanied by two additional officials who assist the minister in their
presidential tasks. However, since not all EU member states participate in
Eurogroup gatherings the cycle of Eurogroup presidencies is adapted

whenever a country from outside the euro area takes over the EU chair. As in the case of the first meeting of the Eurogroup, which took place under the British EU presidency, the finance minister from the incoming EU presidency presides over Eurogroup meetings. Therefore, the British minister had to leave the inaugural meeting of the Eurogroup only moments after he had read out a statement on its foundation. Apart from the meetings of the so-called enlarged Eurogroup (see below) this was the only time that a minister from a country outside the euro area had been given the opportunity to address the group.

Besides the composition of national delegations the other important issue with regard to the definition of a participation regime for the Eurogroup concerns the involvement of members from other Community institutions. Again, the first meeting of the Eurogroup proved pivotal in settling these relations. Since the Eurogroup is not an official Community institution but an informal group of ministers the Luxembourg conclusions foresaw a particular procedural hierarchy in the Eurogroup's relations to the Community institutions with responsibilities in the area of EMU. Euro area ministers *invite* other guests to join their debates:

> The Commission, and the European Central Bank when appropriate, will be invited to take part in the meetings. (European Council 1997c, paragraph 44)

For the first meeting of the Eurogroup the president of the Commission Jacques Santer had arrived together with the commissioner responsible for economic and financial affairs Yves-Thibault de Silguy. The discussions on the organisational structure of Eurogroup meetings showed a strong mutual interest in a close working relationship between the Eurogroup and the Commission. Ministers also agreed on a proposal by their French colleague Strauss-Kahn to improve the statistical information provided by the Commission for the euro area. As will be demonstrated in Chapter 4, the provision of statistical and analytical background information allows the Commission to play a pivotal role in the discussion process. While the presence of the Commission president in the first meeting was aimed at demonstrating political commitment to the informal dialogue within the Eurogroup, the actual practice is that the Commission president only occasionally joins the group of ministers. The key Commission representative is the current economic and financial affairs commissioner. The commissioner is accompanied by the director general of the Commission's Directorate General for Economic and Financial Affairs (DG ECFIN).

The first meeting of the Eurogroup also led to a specification of the relationship with the ECB. Eurogroup president Edlinger was charged by his colleagues with inviting the ECB's president Wim Duisenberg to the following gatherings. As Edlinger explained after the Luxembourg meeting participation of an ECB representative would 'not be necessary every time'[2]. However, the effective creation of the single currency has led to a change of these plans and the ECB is now represented at all Eurogroup gatherings. The EU's most senior central banker attends the Eurogroup frequently in person. The ECB president is replaced by the bank's vice-president in nearly every second meeting. Sometimes the two bankers arrive together at the meetings. If only the vice-president attends it is sometimes the case that the chief economist of the ECB also joins the informal gatherings.

The Luxembourg meeting also led to the permanent invitation of the president and the secretary of the Monetary Committee. This committee became the EFC with the beginning of Stage 3. The president of the EFC is considered to be one of the most respected figures among the group of senior experts from the national finance ministries and vice-presidents of the EU's central banks who gather in the EFC. As outlined in greater detail below, both the EFC and its secretariat play a pivotal role in the preparation of the Eurogroup's agenda. Finally, the director general of the economic and financial affairs directorate general of the Council's General Secretariat attends the Eurogroup meetings together with two members of the Council's legal services. This link to the organisational infrastructure of the Council is important in order to ensure coherence of the Eurogroup's work with the legal and procedural framework of decision-making within EMU. This applies in particular to the activities of the ECOFIN Council. Figure 3.1 illustrates what the meeting table of a regular Eurogroup meeting looks like.

Preparation of the meetings

Even an informal group outside the regular Community structure needs to entertain some relations with the regular EU infrastructure. The various links with the Brussels infrastructure are vital lifelines for the Eurogroup, particularly with regard to the preparation of its meetings. Unlike the Council the Eurogroup does not have a self-administrating infrastructure. There is neither a secretariat nor a Eurogroup post box in Brussels. Consequently, the functioning of the Eurogroup relies on informal arrangements with the formal EU institutions (see Figure 3.2 on page 75). Instead of being treated as shareholders, euro area ministers literally have to cadge their cup of coffee from an administration which is under different circumstances at their full disposal. Before the Eurogroup could start to meet on a regular basis very practical issues needed to be solved. As a participant in Eurogroup meetings recalls:

> The decision in Luxembourg was based on the compromise to set up an informal institution implying that no organisational and technical structure would be established. Even the allowance that the Eurogroup can meet in the Council building in Brussels – this means interpreters and coffee – was

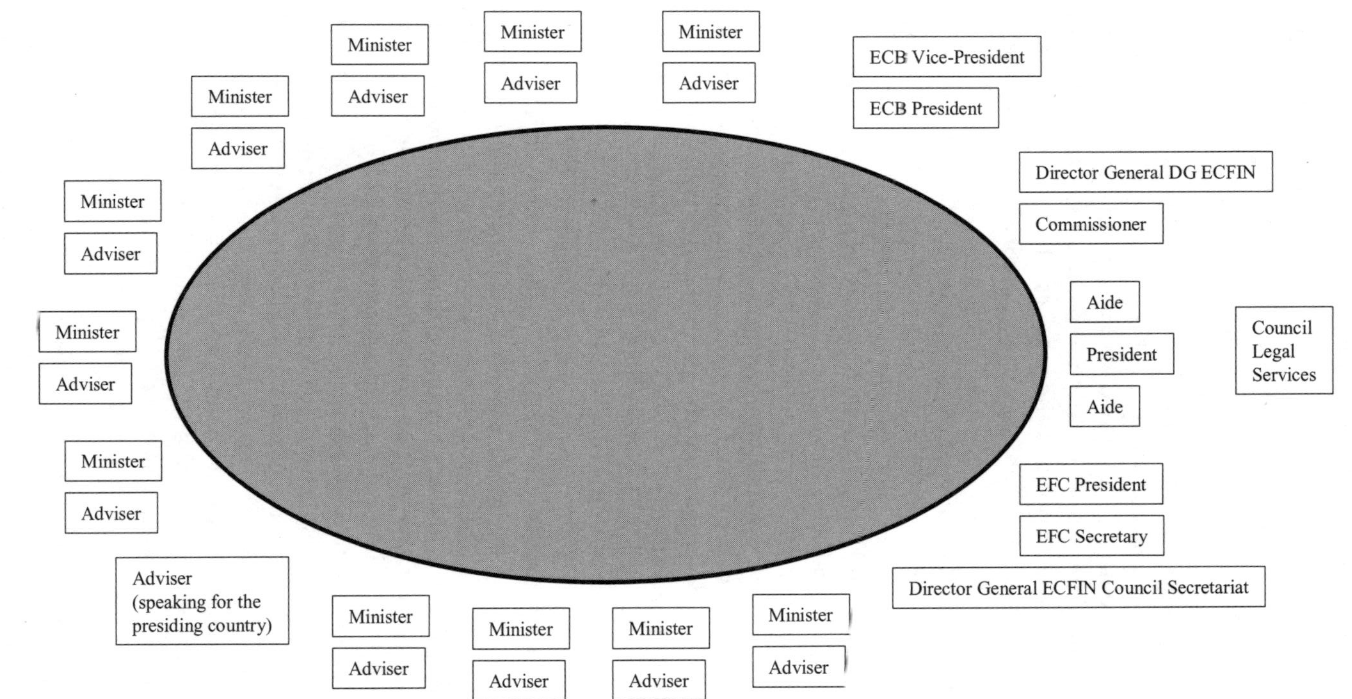

Figure 3.1   Eurogroup meeting table

only agreed informally given the mildness of the Brits, Danes and Swedes on that issue. (Anonymous interview, participant D)

The access to the Council building solves most of the practical problems. It also means that the Eurogroup can gather easily the night or even the morning before regular ECOFIN meetings, for which ministers travel to Brussels each month. Moreover, the meeting place inside the Justus-Lipsius building allows the application of the full EU language regime. Ministers can follow and contribute to the discussion in their mother tongue if they wish to do so. Only once the Eurogroup has to meet outside Brussels is the language regime usually restricted to English, French and German. The Eurogroup also uses the services of the Council's General Secretariat as regards the coordination of all practical aspects of the gatherings.

However, the bulk of the preparatory work for the Eurogroup concerns more substantial questions such as the preparation of the agenda, briefings on individual issues and working documents. Without these preparations there would not be much to discuss. Here the EFC, the EFC's secretariat, the Commission and the respective presidency of the Eurogroup share the work. According to their constitutional mandate neither the EFC nor the Commission have any particular responsibilities with regard to the work of the Eurogroup. Nonetheless, the i formal arrangement to provide support for the group's gatherings does not necessarily constitute a violation of formal rules. The EFC as well as the Commission are required by the Treaty to provide expertise and policy guidance on issues related to the final stage of the EMU process. It is only that the Eurogroup does not appear as the recipient of this preparatory work in the Treaty provisions. Therefore, the actual communication between the informal Eurogroup and the two Community institutions takes a particular form. The most delicate relationship is the one with the Commission because it is one of the three official decision-making bodies of the EU. In contrast to its relations with the Council, the Commission therefore avoids concluding collective decisions over its contributions to the work of the Eurogroup. Instead, the Commission input takes the form of a document of the Commission services which is transmitted to the EFC. Through the EFC the document then finds its way into the briefing boxes of Eurogroup ministers. Its particular structure as a committee of national experts makes the EFC the most important interface between the formal Community institutions and the informal Eurogroup. This implies that the committee exercises considerable influence over the agenda of Eurogroup discussions. As a participant in Eurogroup meetings explains:

> If, for example, the Commission wants to push an issue in the Eurogroup it has to bring it first into the EFC. If you don't discuss it here you can forget it. It is not sufficient that the commissioner presents the issue in the

> Eurogroup. Ministers will simply forget it afterwards or will talk about something else if it was not in their briefing boxes. (Anonymous interview, participant D)

The EFC is the EU's expert committee for EMU affairs. Following the Treaty provisions it is charged with supporting the work of the Commission and the Council in this policy area from the beginning of Stage 3 of EMU. The EFC's mandate comprises the permanent review of the economic and financial situation in the member states and the Community. In addition, the committee has to carry out regular examinations of the movement of capital and the freedom of payment. The Commission and the Council can ask the EFC to provide opinions, or advisory or preparatory support whenever they deem this necessary (see Article 114.2, TEC). In addition, the EFC can act on its own initiative and issue opinions to the two Community institutions. Despite its pivotal role within EMU the EFC keeps a low public profile. Its statutes demand strict confidentiality.[3] The committee is composed of representatives from the national finance ministries, the Commission and the ECB. Before the 2004 enlargement of the EU the vice-presidents of the national central banks of the EU also always participated in EFC meetings.[4] The EFC members from the national finance ministries are senior officials in charge of EMU affairs and the preparation of their respective ministers. Some of them have the status of a deputy finance minister or secretary of state. EFC members are usually also part of the national delegations which attend the ECOFIN Council sessions. The most senior civil servants among them actively participate in the discussion when they replace their minister in a meeting or are asked to provide additional input. The seniority of this group of finance ministry officials is of particular importance for the functioning of the Eurogroup. This has not only to do with the fact that some of them actually participate in the meetings. Most importantly, these senior civil servants are the masterminds of the briefing notes used by their respective ministers in preparation for Eurogroup discussions. The discussion in the EFC can be seen as a microcosm of the big world of discussions among ministers. The committee is an important forum for exploring topics for collective discussion. Here the officials try to solve as many technical problems as they can and prepare the more political questions for the discussions among their ministers.

Both the flexible mandate of the EFC and the direct link between its members and the finance ministers make it the natural interface between the formal and informal governance processes. Unlike the Commission, which has to respect its formal obligations under the Treaty when supporting the Eurogroup, the EFC evades these institutional delicacies much more easily through the simple fact that its members, i.e. those from the national finance ministries, are by definition subordinates of the national finance ministers. There is no need for the EFC to discuss issues related to the Eurogroup agenda in coded language. All this implies of course the consent of those EU member states which do not participate in the euro area. Agreement on the central role of the EFC in the preparations of Eurogroup meetings with the non-euro countries was possible not least because this arrangement lends a certain degree of transparency to the informal discussions. Finance ministry officials from outside the euro area participate in the preparation. The pivotal role of the EFC in the preparation of Eurogroup meetings and the scope of the work are further illustrated by the fact that the EFC has established a so-called Eurogroup working party. Here the officials from the national finance ministries and representatives from the Commission and the ECB can meet without the presence of the vice-presidents of the national central banks. The working party further prepares the results of the EFC's more substantial deliberations for discussion among ministers. Working party meetings focus on the structure of individual agenda items and consider time constraints and the relative weight of the individual issues in the overall agenda. Officials also seek to put specific questions to the ministers in order to kick off and structure the debate during the actual meeting. This refinement of the preparation process is the outcome of an internal learning process.

In turn, Eurogroup ministers ask the EFC to carry out further work on specific topics or to prepare background material for future discussions. These close links between the EFC and the Eurogroup resemble in many ways the committee's formal mandate to support the work of the ECOFIN Council. *De facto* much of the committee's work is now carried out with a view to Eurogroup discussions. Moreover, the EFC's ties with the Eurogroup are in many ways closer than those with the ECOFIN Council. In connection with the work of the ECOFIN Council the EFC is not the only preparatory body. It shares competences with COREPER. The agenda of the ECOFIN Council covers areas in which the EFC has no mandate, for example the important field of taxation. Questions that concern the introduction or amendment of legislation are automatically a matter for COREPER. The EFC might be asked to contribute but it does not control the entire preparation process. In other words, the EFC largely functions as an expert committee providing economic advice and policy guidance. In relation to the Eurogroup these discrepancies do not exist. There is no gap between the Eurogroup's focus on a close and informal policy dialogue and the EFC's expert-oriented character and its concentration on economic policy coordination and supervision. Finally, as regards the Eurogroup the EFC actually has the opportunity to turn the outcome of its own work into a more political agenda for discussion among ministers. This is something which the committee finds much more difficult with regard to its work for the ECOFIN Council. The compatibility between the informal setting of Eurogroup discussions and the

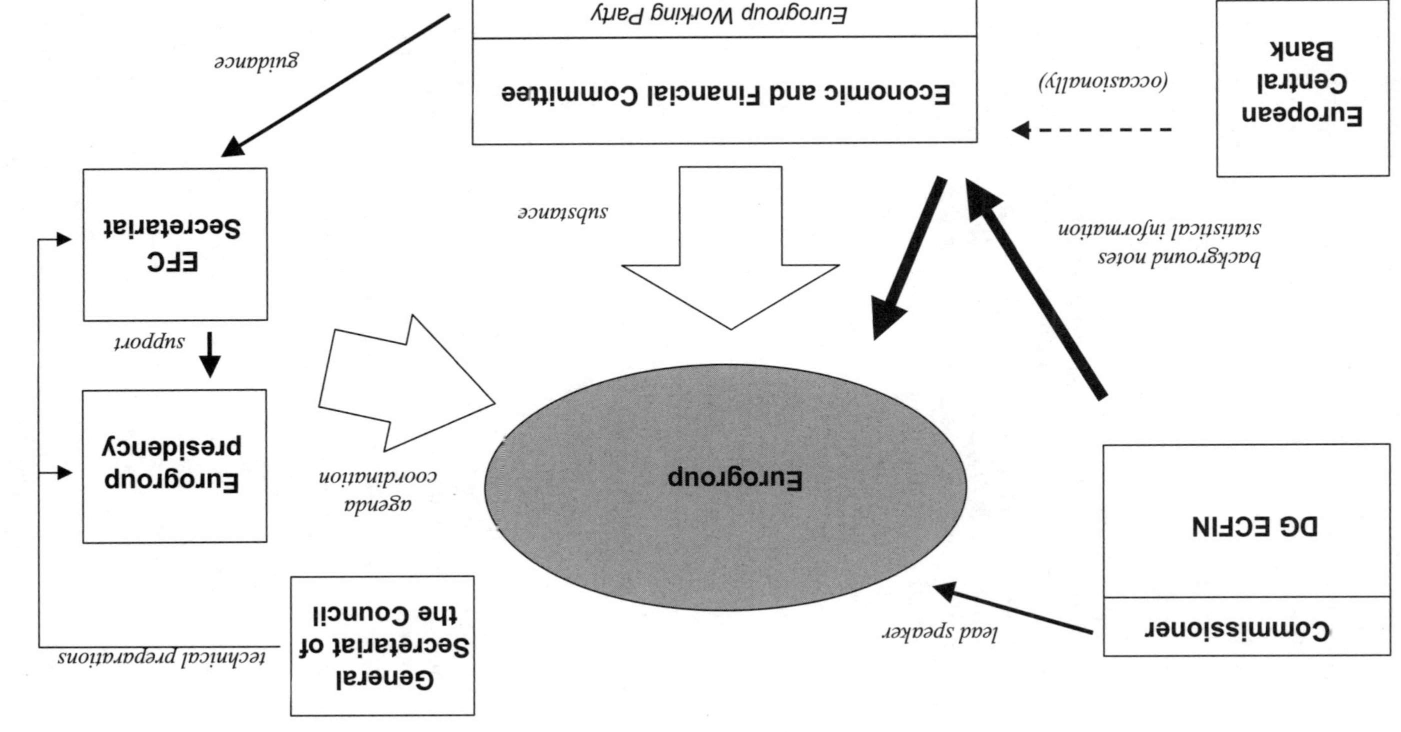

Figure 3.2   The preparation network

working method of an expert committee are also reflected in the way EFC advice is received by ministers. As an EFC member and participant in Eurogroup discussions explains:

> For the EFC it is much more stimulating to present our analysis in such an informal forum because people react more frankly and more directly to what you say. If you do it in ECOFIN you never know what the ministers think about it. You rarely get any direct reactions to what you say. In the Eurogroup it is different. (Anonymous interview, participant B)

The establishment of procedures in an informal environment

In its preparatory work the EFC can rely on its own administrative infrastructure – the EFC Secretariat. Financed by the Commission, this small unit of less than ten people operates from the Brussels headquarters of the Commission's DG ECFIN. The EFC's secretary, who has the rank of a director in the Commission's internal hierarchy, is directly responsible to the EFC and does not take instructions from the Commission. Literally, besides its regular work for the EFC, the secretariat has taken on the function of an invisible Eurogroup secretariat. It provides the vital infrastructure for the day-to-day coordination in the run-up to and in the aftermath of Eurogroup meetings. The officials are in permanent contact with the national finance ministries, the EFC president and the respective Eurogroup presidency. Most importantly, the secretariat's role as the technical centre of the preparation process lends a certain degree of continuity to the fluid informal process. Before the Eurogroup decided to elect its own president for a period of two years (see below) the presidency of the group rotated every six months, or twelve months in the case of a non-euro country holding the EU presidency. In this context the tiny secretariat provided and still provides vital continuity to the preparatory process. The former EFC secretary Günter Grosche worked in this position right from the beginning of the Eurogroup's gatherings and accompanied the group's work until he retired in 2004. Moreover, each presidency of the Eurogroup has its own priorities. This affects not only the agenda but also the working method itself. As demonstrated below this can imply changes in the way the group communicates with the media or approaches the discussion of specific agenda points.

Given the limited administrative resources of the secretariat its influence over the preparation of the agenda can vary over time. Personal factors, workload, a lack of administrative capabilities and the political objectives of the respective presidency can influence the process. In addition to the experience of the secretariat officials, the use of non-papers or secretariat notes, which are circulated among EFC members, are an important instrument for the routinisation of procedures and practices governing the Eurogroup's work and the preparations of the meetings. It is only through such papers and notes that procedural arrangements for the preparation and conduct of Eurogroup meetings exist in a written form. However, these documents are in no way legally binding. They derive their practical authority only from the fact that they refer to already established practices and the results of pivotal EFC discussions on the Eurogroup's working method. In addition, much depends on the active use of these notes as reference documents in the preparatory process. Reflection exercises have been carried out several times within the EFC context on the functioning of the Eurogroup's working method since the foundation of the circle of ministers in 1998. In general, the attempts to further improve the preparations of the debates follow the insight that informal discussions are very sensitive to deficiencies in the preparation regime. As the examples discussed in Chapter 4 will demonstrate, there is a high risk that debates will become unfocused because there is no formal constraint to conclude final decisions. At the same time, participants quite often do not immediately have a sense of discussion failure.[5]

However, the preparatory work is not the only important factor; much also depends on the conduct of the debate. Here, the respective presidency of the Eurogroup plays a crucial role. The presidency formally invites ministers for each meeting and sends out the final draft of the agenda. The presidency can also ask individual ministers to act as lead speakers on a particular topic. During the discussion the minister in the chair may structure the debate through putting specific questions to their colleagues. The president may also orally summarise the group consensus after the discussion. Since the Eurogroup concludes no formal decisions these interventions by the president can be highly significant for the degree of commitment which emerges among participants as a result of the discussions. Another practice which has evolved as a result of the experiences made with the work of the Eurogroup, is the circulation of a letter by the president among participants after each Eurogroup meeting. First applied at the start of the Finnish Eurogroup presidency in July 1999, the procedure uses once more the technique of a written informal understanding. In a personal letter to their colleagues the president summarises the main results of the discussion, singles out particular contributions or highlights issues for further consideration. In addition, each presidency seeks to structure the Eurogroup's work through the presentation of a work programme at the beginning of its term. However, the influence of this instrument depends essentially on whether such a programme is compatible with the prevailing group consensus. In this context psychological factors, such as the personality of the president, can also play a pivotal role (see below).

Confidentiality versus visibility

The confidentiality of the discussions among ministers is another important feature of the Eurogroup's informal working method. The rationale
behind the demand for confidentiality lies essentially in the nature of
economic policy decisions. Ministers are eager to avoid damage to the
credibility of the overall economic governance set-up by displaying their
differences in public. The behaviour of market participants is very sensitive to changes in the area of budgetary and exchange-rate policy. The
tendency to create informal forums for discussion is therefore not a new
phenomenon in the context of European monetary integration. In addition, the relationship between budgetary and monetary authorities is not
without delicacy given the assignment of responsibilities within the EMU
framework. As one participant in Eurogroup meetings points out:

> Confidentiality is a precondition for crucial negotiations in the area of
> economic policy. That is why ECOFIN has seen regular luncheons and
> informal meetings. Especially exchange-rate and budgetary coordination
> require these settings. Regarding the interplay between monetary and budg-
> etary policy we had informal coordination between central banks and
> budgetary authorities also before EMU. Except for the Eurogroup there is
> no such body within the framework of EMU. (Anonymous interview, partic-
> ipant E)

Another important aspect of the demand for strict confidentiality is of a
more political nature. Decisions by finance ministers are generally subject
to severe scrutiny within the domestic arena, ranging from the demands of
cabinet colleagues to public pressure. Moreover, the finance minister
often shares competences with parliament or federal and regional authorities. Whenever a finance minister starts to think aloud about their
options they can easily antagonise decision-makers or constituencies at
home. Moreover, budgetary planning is by definition tight. Ministers are
reluctant to admit downside risks in the economic situation at an early
stage because this would bring into question carefully negotiated compromises over national budgets. Nevertheless, these are the topics of
particular interest to a common review of national policies. Only if ministers trust each other that nothing will emerge from such discussions will
they be prepared to debate worst case scenarios and envisaged policy
responses. However, mutual trust cannot evolve through a simple agreement that confidentiality will be kept. The question of confidentiality is
also one of personal relationship. Again the restricted number of participants proves to be a vital instrument of the Eurogroup's informal working
method, as a participant in the debates explains:

> Let me add a general point, the Eurogroup simply functions well because it
> is so small. That is the decisive difference. The Eurogroup is the smallest
> group in Brussels. With thirty people in the room this is an unusually small

setting. Everybody knows everybody. And everybody can normally rely on the others that nothing emerges from the discussion to the outside. That creates an atmosphere where everybody is relatively frank. (Anonymous interview, participant A)

At the occasion of ECOFIN meetings each minister is not only framed by the most senior officials of the respective finance ministry; in addition, there are dozens of officials from the different branches of national ministries floating in and out of the room. Depending on the respective agenda point they take a seat in the second row behind their national delegation. Others follow the discussion on large video screens in separate meeting rooms. Debates on the conclusion of legislative issues are now also open to the public through video coverage. However, even during debates to which the public has no direct access the risks of leaks in such an environment is much higher. Moreover, ministers do not only mistrust their ministerial officials with regard to the possibility of leaks; they simply do not like the idea of discussing matters of substance in the presence of their subordinates who might have advised them to act in a different way. In addition, many Eurogroup participants tend to be very selective in their debriefings on Eurogroup meetings when they return to their national capitals. As an official, who does not attend Eurogroup meetings in person but is involved in their preparation, remarks:

> Ministers can be very frank and have the opportunity to criticise colleagues in a way which they would not do officially in ECOFIN. They have the opportunity to talk off the record. ... On the other hand, these features [of the Eurogroup's informal working method] imply a disadvantage. The Eurogroup meetings are confidential, only attended by the ministers, and there is no debriefing in the end. Consequently, the feed-back from the Eurogroup appears to be rather sparse. ... Related to the issue of confidentiality is the fact that one rarely gets information on what ministers have said in the Eurogroup. Perhaps a minister says something when leaving the room on who said what and which decisions have been made. (Anonymous interview, official E)

In fact, officials in the national finance ministries and the Commission who do not take part in Eurogroup meetings often appear to be uncertain about the actual role of the informal meetings. While they inevitably take note of the *de facto* decisions of the Eurogroup in the run-up to ECOFIN meetings they are less aware of the more subtle effects of informal governance. What is true for the internal communication within finance ministries, is even more obvious with regard to the communication with the markets and the wider public. Concealment from public attention implies that the Eurogroup is hardly recognised as a pivotal player in EMU's economic governance set-up outside Brussels. As one participant in Eurogroup meetings points out:

> I think that the Eurogroup is completely underestimated by the public. That is understandable – the strength of the Eurogroup is its confidentiality. There are also not many leaks. This ensures effectiveness but means at the same time that the rest of the world cannot know what good is being done there. This is a conflict which I do not know how to solve. If we made it more transparent – as discussed by some – then the discussion would not be so frank. (Anonymous interview, participant A)

Not surprisingly the Eurogroup needed some time to find its own communication strategy. The basic problem for the group is to convey the results of pivotal debates to the public without revealing details on the actual discussion process. The Eurogroup's president and the commissioner for economic and financial affairs frequently talk to the press when leaving a Eurogroup meeting. The two also use the general press conference following each ECOFIN meeting to comment on Eurogroup discussions. These statements rarely reflect the actual structure of the debate, let alone individual interventions by ministers. For example, the wording 'we touched briefly on' can conceal the fact that there was a veritable debate. Other agenda items are not mentioned at all. However, Eurogroup ministers also frequently agree on common positions with regard to communication with the outside world. It is then the task of the president to convey the message to the press. In addition, the press briefings of the president also represent a personal assessment of the political priorities emerging from a Eurogroup meeting. Depending on the president in office the accentuation can change. On the initiative of the French Eurogroup presidency in the second half of 2000 the Eurogroup created its own regular press conference. Throughout the year 2001 the Belgian Eurogroup president Didier Reynders pursued this approach. However, his attempt to strengthen the Eurogroup's visibility through the instrument of a regular press conference was not very well received by the majority of Eurogroup participants. It was feared that the pressure to present results to the media would compromise the informal atmosphere and the confidentiality of the meetings. Separate Eurogroup press conferences are now only convened on special occasions. Similarly, the use of written public statements is reserved for exceptional circumstances. However, since the beginning of the Belgian presidency a draft agenda for Eurogroup meetings is released on a special Eurogroup website of the respective presidency. It is unnecessary to add that the actual agenda may deviate from the published draft.

However, it is not only the fear that interventions of individual participants might become public which constitutes a difficulty in the Eurogroup's relationship with the outside world. The Eurogroup has to represent the euro area as a political entity. This is of particular importance with regard to the international financial markets. In addition, the single monetary policy shifts political attention in the domestic arena to the European level. This is of particular importance with regard to the interplay of monetary and economic policy. Some of the biggest problems during the first years of Eurogroup discussions were the numerous public interventions by individual euro area ministers on issues which were still under discussion within the group. In addition, ministers spoke in the name of the euro area while their statements did not reflect the existing group consensus. As participants admit, it is only in the last two years that the discipline among group members, with regard to communication with the press, has considerably improved. As a general rule communication with the media is now exclusively left to the respective Eurogroup president. Given that the Eurogroup agrees explicit terms of reference for communication with the media only on a very limited number of agenda points, much depends on the ability and willingness of the respective president to convey the actual group consensus.

The intimate atmosphere: personality and group dynamic

Individual and psychological factors such as personality and group dynamics are crucial in the context of the Eurogroup's informal working method. The example of the president's role in the Eurogroup's communication with the outside world demonstrates how much the discussion process relies on individual characters. The president is central to the discussion process. Without a chairperson, who is able to point to the group consensus in a fluid and often complex discussion process, results are easily lost. This constitutes not only a problem with regard to the presentation of the results of the Eurogroup's work to the media, but the internal organisation of the discussion process also suffers. As a participant in Eurogroup meetings observes:

> Informal groups without a formal institutional basis depend on particular persons or characters. The quality of the debate largely depends on the particular persons taking part in the debate or chairing it. For example, the ability to present the conclusions of the deliberations is important with regard to the impact of the debate on decision-making within the euro-zone. Policy-makers want to know what has been discussed, what the results are and what do we tell the public and the media. The fear that something inappropriate can be said in the media can destroy the atmosphere. (Anonymous interview, participant D)

As outlined, it is one of the key features of informal governance that the participants in informal discussions act as advocates of the results of these debates in formal contexts of decision-making. Consequently, awareness among participants of the key results of a debate is an essential pre-condition for the Eurogroup's ability to influence policy formation at the national and European level. Moreover, the reliance on the president's ability to speak on behalf of the group raises particularly high expectations among the participants. Eurogroup members suspiciously watch the president's handling of communication with the media. The success of a Eurogroup presidency very much depends on the evolution of an atmosphere of trust and respect vis-à-vis the president. Participants report that the evolution of such an atmosphere is not a foregone conclusion. Not all presidencies of the Eurogroup were well received. It is part of the curiosities of the secretive character of the group's discussions that the media image of individual Eurogroup presidents can deviate significantly from the role of the respective person in the actual discussion process. Someone can be perceived as a strong and active leader of the group of euro area countries in the media without commanding much respect inside the group. Not surprisingly, many participants favoured the idea of an elected president who handles the affairs of the Eurogroup for a more prolonged period of time. The template for these considerations was the EFC. The expert committee usually elects its chairperson from the group of the most respected participants in the discussion process for a period of two years. Therefore, the initiatives in the context of the European Convention to change the EU's system of rotating presidencies have been particularly well received among Eurogroup participants, as one of them explains:

> The style of the chairmanship of course plays a role. You can't underestimate this. I think the idea to have a two-year chairmanship is a good idea. This will not only help the representation of the Eurogroup. It is important internally as well. You can better organise the debate. (Anonymous interview, participant C)

The group implemented the two-year presidency scheme unilaterally in September 2004. At the beginning of 2005 the mandate of the first elected Eurogroup president, Luxembourg's prime minister and finance minister Jean-Claude Juncker, began.

Personality also matters with regard to the role individual ministers play in the discussion process. It is one of the characteristic features of the Eurogroup's informal working method that the nationality of a minister is less important than individual qualities as regards the role of a person in the discussion process. In this respect, the absence of formal decision-making mechanisms and the room the Eurogroup's working method leaves for substantial and technical considerations are crucial. As a participant in the discussions examines:

> Personality, yes I do think that it is one of the unavoidable characteristics of both the Council work in general – I mean in all work here I would say personalities have a certain role to play – but in the Eurogroup even more so. Perhaps because the Eurogroup is a forum for discussion and what you have is that around the table in the Eurogroup you have two representatives of each member state and one of them, the minister, who typically speaks. And that has one interesting aspect that the 'smalls' are as big as the 'bigs'

> while in the Council there is of course a differentiation of voting rights. ...
> There is absolutely no doubt that somebody can carry more weight than
> others and that the way they are able to articulate the arguments and their
> experience is something which influences the role they can play.
> (Anonymous interview, participant F)

The technical knowledge and personal experience of individual ministers
are often the basis for their ability to lead the discussions. However, the
ability to refer to the group consensus and to react to previous debates are
also considered to be important factors in determining the role of an individual participant within the group. Despite the fact that individual
participants differ with regard to their ability to influence the discussions
the general threshold to intervene is considered to be relatively low. As
another Eurogroup participant explains:

> Some simply say more than others. Some like to take an active part in the
> discussions and do not have a problem with that while others tend more to
> read out their speaking notes – but this is similar in every forum.
> Nevertheless, in the Eurogroup, because the people know each other very
> well, discussions are relatively broad. (Anonymous interview, participant A)

The intimate atmosphere of the discussions facilitates the access to the
dialogue. This group of finance ministers and senior policy advisers generally works together over a longer period of time. Many of them are
veterans in EMU affairs. Some have survived several parliamentary elections in their home countries or have served in varying coalition
governments. They also meet in the context of ECOFIN Council meetings
and EFC gatherings. In addition, many of them stay in permanent tele-
phone contact and consult each other on numerous issues. Nonetheless,
the intimate setting of Eurogroup discussions does not necessarily imply
an unqualified relationship of mutual trust among participants. The close-
ness of the group has also enabled ministers to carefully sense the
credibility of statements made by individual colleagues. Participants in
Eurogroup meetings report that for them the discussions are a touchstone
for the reliability of individual colleagues, with regard to the commitment
to commonly agreed policy objectives.

Other informal groups in the context of EMU

The Eurogroup is not the only place for informal discussion among
finance ministers within the context of EMU. There are three other
forums in which finance ministers regularly gather for an informal
exchange of views. They all follow the restricted format of Eurogroup
meetings. The following briefly introduces the three forums in order to
avoid confusion of the different settings. Before the beginning of Stage 3
the ECOFIN Council had already convened so-called informal meetings.

As in the context of other Council formations these meetings are intended to provide a particular framework for programmatic reflection on individual policy areas, debates on institutional issues or the in-depth discussion of areas in which the decision-making process has stalled. There is at least one informal ECOFIN Council meeting per semester. No formal decisions are concluded at these meetings. The informal meetings cover the whole ECOFIN agenda. For example, questions related to the negotiation of new legislation in the field of taxation are regularly a topic at informal ECOFIN meetings. Agreement on the harmonisation of national taxation regimes has repeatedly proven to be particularly difficult. In this context, informal ECOFIN meetings are seen as an opportunity to break the deadlock in the negotiation process in face-to-face discussions among ministers. The restricted format of informal ECOFIN meetings is also used to agree on candidates for important positions in the context of the EU or international financial institutions. For example, the composition of the ECB's Governing Council or the appointment of a new EFC president are discussed in this context. Also institutional issues, as in the case of the negotiations on the creation of an exclusive euro area forum in 1997, are regularly on the agenda of informal ECOFIN meetings. Moreover, these meetings provide the framework for the dialogue with the international financial institutions and the preparation of the summit meetings of the G7, IMF and the World Bank. In this context overlap with the Eurogroup's agenda can hardly be avoided as the EU pursues common interests in these institutions which are not restricted to those of the euro area countries. Since the beginning of Stage 3 informal ECOFIN meetings also focus on another topic which is known from the Eurogroup context. Ministers regularly review the economic and budgetary situation in the member states. This overlap reflects the fact that EMU's core coordination instruments, the BEPGs and the multilateral surveillance procedure, formally comprise the economic policies of all fifteen member states.

Another curiosity in the context of the multi-speed process of European monetary integration is the so-called enlarged Eurogroup. During the negotiations leading to the creation of the Eurogroup it was agreed that the ministers from non-euro countries should join Eurogroup meetings from time to time in order to discuss issues of common concern. This arrangement was intended to counter the impression that the Eurogroup would operate entirely beyond the control of the out-group. Enlarged Eurogroup meetings originally took place once a semester but this frequency could not be maintained. As a general rule meetings of the enlarged Eurogroup focus on economic policy coordination in Stage 3 while informal ECOFIN meetings are reserved for issues related to formal decision-making in the ECOFIN Council. Nonetheless, overlap between the two formats certainly exists, as the example of the EU's representation in international financial institutions and the multilateral surveillance debates demonstrate.

Finally, at the occasion of each ECOFIN meeting EU finance ministers meet briefly to discuss individual aspects of the Council work and current affairs in strict confidentiality. It is on the occasion of these so-called ECOFIN luncheons that ministers seek to overcome deadlock on pending Council decisions through 'backroom deals'. Moreover, the president of the Eurogroup uses the gathering to debrief the ministers of the non-euro countries on the Eurogroup meeting of the night before. ECOFIN luncheons are also the preferred place to discuss delicate institutional or personal issues.

It would be beyond the scope of this book to further discuss the particularities of those forums in comparison with the Eurogroup. However, what is perhaps the most striking difference between these forums and the Eurogroup is the fact that they lack the steadiness and the scope of the Eurogroup discussions. Consequently, many aspects of the Eurogroup's informal working method are not that clearly pronounced in these settings. In addition, the agenda of ECOFIN luncheons and informal ECOFIN meetings essentially follows the decision-making agenda of the Council and does not develop its own dynamics, as it is the case with regard to the Eurogroup.

Notes

1   Interview with the *Financial Times* (12 February 1999).
2   *Agence Europe*, Bulletin (5 June 1998).
3   See *Official Journal* (9 January 1999).
4   The vice-presidents of the national central bank now only join EFC meetings when their expertise is of particular relevance to the deliberations. This change in the participation regime was intended to deal with the drastic increase in the number of participants in the wake of the 2004 EU enlargement. For the changed statutes of the EFC see *Official Journal* (2003, L 158/59).
5   Anonymous interviews.

4

The agenda

The necessity and the advantages [of informal discussions within the Eurogroup] are obvious. If one shares a single currency there are problems and issues which are of interest for this group of finance ministers only. The finances ministers who do not belong to this group might also have an interest but they are not directly concerned. And so we have a community bound together by shared interests – or a community bound together by fate – depending on the degree of dramatisation you wish to apply. (Anonymous interview, participant A)

The Eurogroup's informal working method provides the context for the discussion of a wide range of issues. The following two chapters analyse the functioning of the Eurogroup's negotiation setting in the context of the particular *content* of the discussions. The individual items on the group's agenda pose very different challenges to the informal dialogue. Analytical debates on economic developments can precede controversies over policy responses. The discussion of a tenth of a percentage point in the deficit figures of a member state can shift suddenly to fundamental economic policy ideas. Some agenda points might comprise broad orientation debates, while others demand an immediate decision on a common euro area position. This chapter gives an overview of the Eurogroup's agenda. It outlines the main characteristics of each agenda item and points to crucial developments. This perspective is intended to demonstrate the role of informal policy deliberation with regard to different aspects of economic policy coordination in the euro area.

When the Eurogroup gathered for its first meeting in June 1998 the participants were not fully aware of what the priorities of the group's discussions would be. Some even doubted that there was enough to talk about in order to justify a schedule of monthly meetings. Moreover, the thin legal basis of the Eurogroup's work implied that there was no formal guidance with regard to the choice of topics and the frequency and duration of the meetings (see Chapter 3). The Eurogroup's agenda evolved over time. Changes in the structure of individual agenda items (see Table

4.1 below) and the occurrence of new topics for discussion very much reflect the fact that euro area ministers engage in a collective learning process when they are gathering for Eurogroup meetings. The discussion in Chapter 2 showed that the foundation of the Eurogroup responded to specific institutional dynamics which emerged with the beginning of Stage 3. In this sense, the Eurogroup's work did not start from scratch. The first informal discussions were embedded in a wider political and economic discourse on the transition towards the final stage of EMU. Notably, the definition of the euro area's policy-mix and the political representation of the new European currency in international financial forums were considered to be uppermost on the agenda. However, the practice of informal discussions among finance ministers led to the correction of some of the initial expectations on what the work of the euro area forum might be. The first one to two years particularly were crucial in the evolution of the Eurogroup's main agenda items.

Initially, Eurogroup meetings were squeezed into the early morning hours before ECOFIN Council meetings, which usually start between ten and eleven o'clock. This practice has been changed and the Eurogroup now usually meets the night before ECOFIN Council sessions. This adjustment also reflects the fact that Eurogroup meetings now last longer than initially foreseen. Ministers normally gather for two to three hours.

Table 4.1 Schematic Eurogroup agenda

Time frame	Agenda item	Frequency
45'–90'	Economic situation (common analysis, euro exchange rate, external representation)	Always
45'–90'	Budgetary situation (SGP, surveillance, price developments)	Always
30'–45'	Structural policies	Twice a semester
15'–30'	Changeover to the euro	Always (only from October 2002 to March 2003)
30'–60'	Reflection exercises	Once or twice a semester
5'–15'	Miscellaneous	Always

Source: Anonymous interviews; *Agence Europe*, Bulletins 1998–2002; Eurogroup presidency websites.

However, in reaction to current events or whenever immediate decisions have to be reached a meeting can last for up to four hours or more. For the same reason the discussion of individual agenda items is frequently rescheduled. For example, a debate on aspects of structural reform might be postponed because of a pending early warning decision by the ECOFIN Council or the Commission. The schedule of monthly meetings implies that the Eurogroup convenes as often as the most important Council formations within the EU – the General Affairs Council and the ECOFIN Council.

Common analysis of the economic situation

Usually each Eurogroup meeting starts off with a discussion about the economic situation. The debates are a mixture of an exchange of information and a common understanding-building process on the most significant developments. In this respect the common analysis of the economic situation lays the basis for the following discussions on appropriate policy responses. This applies particularly to the area of budgetary policy. The commissioner for economic and financial affairs acts as a lead speaker and introduces the main developments and prospects for the euro area and the wider global economy. The presentation is based on the most recent statistical and economic analysis prepared by the Commission's DG ECFIN. Central to the Commission analysis are the so-called key indicators for the euro area. This statistical information on core economic developments in the euro area, such as industrial output, consumption, investment and employment is updated on a monthly basis. Moreover, DG ECFIN prepares specific background notes for Eurogroup discussions which elaborate and comment on individual indicators and point to crucial developments. Participants describe the scope and the quality of the Commission analysis as excellent and regard it as the most important basis for further debate on euro area developments. This gives the Commission significant influence over the structure of the discussions among ministers. In this respect the creation of the Eurogroup has provided the Commission with an additional forum where it can voice its concerns over economic developments and policy reactions. This is of particular importance since the Commission has no decision-making authority in the area of EMU (see Chapter 2). Its role essentially depends on whether ministers follow its policy recommendations. Although the Commission is officially only invited to Eurogroup meetings (see Chapter 3) the example of the discussion on the economic situation illustrates its *de facto* role in the discussion process. As a participant in Eurogroup gatherings explains:

> The Commission has in this area [of EMU] no own decision-making competencies but can of course prepare some of the issues. The status of the

Commission is very similar to the one of the ECB. If you look at Luxembourg [the European Council conclusions], it says that the Commission and the ECB 'can be invited'. However, *de facto* they were always invited, and *de facto* the Commission introduces every item on the agenda, and usually the agenda items are prepared through papers provided by the Commission. Thus the Commission plays an important role because it can lay the basis regarding the different issues. Additionally, the Commission takes part in the debate: answers questions and asks questions. This depends, however, on the subject. (Anonymous interview, participant A)

After the commissioner's presentation the president of the EFC briefly reports on the discussions within the committee and comments on crucial economic developments. Then the president of the ECB concludes the round of introductory presentations with a longer statement. The presentation of the central bank's analysis is in many ways complementary to the information provided by the Commission. Usually the two supranational institutions converge in their assessment of the core developments. The ECB president continues the presentation with an explanation of the reactions of monetary policy. Finally, the central banker comments on the euro exchange rate and the currency's role in international financial markets. Only then is the floor opened to the ministers. The scope and the duration of the following debate on economic developments can vary significantly. Much depends on whether fundamentally new information on specific developments has emerged as a result of the lead presentations.

A crucial aspect of the interventions by individual ministers is the assessment of important economic developments in their respective home countries. Moreover, due to the administrative capabilities of the bigger member states ministers from these countries might contribute valuable additional information on the global economy. Smaller member states with limited administrative resources particularly benefit from such information, as an official from a smaller member state explains:

For us as a small member state the idea of having a group such as the Eurogroup, where all the ministers of the bigger member states are present, is quite important. This gives us great information on the international economy. And this is frank information. Our minister takes it seriously if Hans Eichel says that there is a fall in German tax revenues and these sorts of things. Also the background papers provided by the EFC and the Commission are quite important. We are only a small administration and we would never get this information ourselves. (Anonymous interview, official G)

However, routine analysis does not exclusively dominate the introductory point on the Eurogroup's agenda. This item also sees debriefings and discussions in connection with the meetings of the international financial forums. Following the Vienna European Council conclusions of December

1998, the Eurogroup presidency represents the EU in the G7 and the IMF. However, this arrangement did change the role of individual euro area countries as independent members of the G7 or the IMF. For example, at the occasion of G7 meetings the Eurogroup's president participates alongside the finance ministers of France, Germany and Italy – the three G7 member countries in the euro area. The task of the preparatory discussions in the Eurogroup is therefore twofold. On the one hand, the debates are intended to prepare the interventions of the Eurogroup's president, as in the case of the G7 meetings, or of the representative of the Eurogroup's presidency at the IMF's Executive Board. On the other hand, the discussions are aimed at enhancing the consistency of the different national positions in the respective forums. To this end common euro area positions are drafted in writing prior to Eurogroup meetings. Ministers then comment on individual aspects of the speaking notes for their president. In addition, the formulation of so-called common understandings on particular developments or country specific situations is an important instrument in the coordination of national positions. The members of the Eurogroup also evaluate the outcome of the international gatherings at the following Eurogroup meeting. The president and individual ministers debrief their colleagues on the discussions. Afterwards, ministers give their assessment of the results.

Another important topic for the first round of discussions at each Eurogroup meeting regards communication with the markets and the wider public. Such debates are intended to avoid conflicting public statements by individual euro area ministers on significant economic developments or crisis situations. Again the instrument of the formulation of common positions with the help of written drafts is used. On the basis of a draft, participants discuss so-called terms of reference for the public presentation of Eurogroup positions. A good example of the importance of a coordinated communication strategy for the euro area, is the year 2000. At the time the euro's continuing fall against the dollar provoked a series of conflicting public statements by members of the Eurogroup. The different remarks on the relevance of the exchange rate developments and on the possibility of interventions by the ECB further undermined confidence in the single currency. It was not least because of these events that the Eurogroup put a greater emphasis on the discussion of communication behaviour in relation to key economic and monetary developments. As a participant in Eurogroup meetings recalls, the establishment of a communication strategy for the euro area was one of the key problems which had emerged with the beginning of Stage 3:

> Another big debate was the image problem and the lack of discipline in connection with the fall of the euro exchange rate. We had to find out how we do it and who can speak for us. This was a learning process. Once the unorganised behaviour had appeared we had to restore confidence and to

establish a new strategy. But this has clearly improved. (Anonymous interview, participant D)

The difficulties in restoring confidence were reflected in an unusual move by euro area ministers. In September 2000 the Eurogroup agreed for the first time ever on the publication of a written press statement. However, the use of this instrument remains the exception in the Eurogroup's communication with the press.

Reviewing budgetary policy in the euro area

The second key topic on the Eurogroup's agenda is the review of budgetary policy in the euro area. This agenda item usually sees the longest and the liveliest debates. The general pattern of the debate follows that of the discussion on the economic situation. The commissioner initiates the debate with an introductory statement. The presentation comprises crucial analytical information on the budgetary situation and critically points to problematic policy developments in individual member states. Again, background notes prepared by the Commission for the Eurogroup discussions elaborate on specific developments or introduce the topic of the subsequent discussion. Afterwards, the intervention by the ECB president focuses on price developments in the euro area and the budgetary situation as such. Frequently the ECB president uses the presentation for critical remarks on the policies of individual countries and points to the adverse effects for monetary policy. Finally, the president of the EFC refers to the discussion in the expert committee and comments on the budgetary situation. The interventions by the commissioner and the ECB president usually focus on analytical background information, peer review and the explanation of the policies of the two supranational bodies. In contrast, the EFC president concentrates on pointing to different policy options and asks ministers to indicate their preferences. The statement alerts ministers to future challenges for decision-making and asks for guidance with regard to the further work of the committee. The EFC president also points to possible inconsistencies between the results of different discussions and recalls previous decisions of relevance to the current debate. The style of the statement largely reflects the preparatory and advisory functions of the EFC.

A recurrent topic of the debates is the monitoring of the budgetary situation in the euro area. This exercise can be seen as the Eurogroup's core business. The debates combine the analysis of the situation with a discussion on policy responses. In order to structure the debate and to allow more in-depth analysis of country specific situations the discussions are organised around specific questions. One Eurogroup meeting might see an orientation debate on the budgetary outlook for the next two years whereas the following meeting is exclusively devoted to the review of budgetary policy in individual member states. For example, in preparation for the meetings the Eurogroup's president might ask three or four colleagues to prepare a presentation on the situation in their respective home countries for the next meeting. In addition, the Commission is invited to prepare comments or background analysis. During the meeting the individual ministers start off the discussion on their own country with an introductory statement. They elaborate on budgetary developments, point to risks and explain the stance of national fiscal policy. After each presentation the commissioner comments on the suggested course of policy. In the following open debate the other participants ask questions, critically point to perceived policy failure or express their support for the positions of individual ministers in domestic debates. As an official in charge of Eurogroup affairs explains, the continuing review of national policies in the Eurogroup can be quite important for individual ministers even if they are already committed to the core principles of the EMU framework such as budgetary consolidation:

> There is no doubt that consistent pressure from Brussels forces one to stick to the own objectives and it reminds one of the short-term objectives for the budget. ... Given all the voices, which are raised in the national context, demand for tax cuts etc., it is very helpful to hear all these things in which one believes from the colleagues within the Eurogroup. One feels supported that the own plans are correct in technical terms and reasonable in the medium term perspective. The discussions in Brussels, which are sometimes very frank and harsh, can function as a backing. When in times of crisis the pressure from the street becomes too strong well-known political wisdoms about the time lag, the negative consequences of subsidies, the public deficit are easily forgotten. (Anonymous interview, official E)

The fact that in the context of these debates the commissioner regularly acts as a lead commentator underlines once again the key role of the Commission in Eurogroup discussions. The Commission not only structures the debate through its technical input; ministers also accept its role as a *primus inter pares* in the peer review process. While initial country reviews in the early years of Eurogroup meetings occasionally saw individual ministers acting as the lead commentators, that job is now exclusively left to the commissioner. Given that the Commission has been assigned the role of permanently opposing national policies, this is not an easy task for the commissioner. As a participant in Eurogroup meetings explains:

> There is occasionally a tension between the Commission and ministers which is unavoidable because it is the role of the Commission to be the watchdog. And I think it is not always a grateful role as we have seen in the discussions. ... It is fully understandable that those ministers who then get the negative message in a way – that they are concerned. Clearly, they may

be facing elections. It is never particularly pleasant to be the subject of criticism. Still I would say that one should keep in mind here that it is still the role of the Commission to draw attention to issues and to give information but then it is really for ministers to put peer pressure on each other. And they do! ... I guess, here we are in the area of peer pressure. Here, we are precisely at what corresponds with the idea of the SGP. And I see it being implemented reasonably. Perhaps, it could be better but still in my view it does function reasonably well. (Anonymous interview, participant F)

Depending on the difficulties identified with the policies of an individual country the debates on country specific situations can easily jeopardise the schedule of a Eurogroup meeting. Quite often the planned reviews are continued at the following meeting or the discussion of other issues is postponed. The routine monitoring generally covers all euro area countries in consecutive meetings. In addition, discussions on country specific situations are put on the agenda whenever unforeseen developments might require it. It is in the context of this continuing policy review that the Eurogroup discussions have led to common standards and reference points with regard to the assessment of budgetary policy. Moreover, these informal discussions on budgetary policy developments complement EMU's formal multilateral surveillance procedures regulated by the SGP. How the interaction between informal dialogue and formal surveillance procedures unfolds over time is illustrated in greater detail in Chapter 5.

In addition, the Eurogroup also intervenes in the process of the formulation of formal policy guidelines in the context of the BEPGs and the SGP procedures. Formally, the Commission and the ECOFIN Council are exclusively responsible for operating these coordination instruments. The Eurogroup cannot directly participate in the decision-making process leading to the adoption of formal policy guidelines. It can, however, pre-discuss the decisions of the ECOFIN Council with regard to issues of particular relevance to the euro area. In addition, the Commission consults the Eurogroup when it is exercising its own responsibilities with regard to the drafting of new policy guidelines. In this the Commission acknowledges the leading role of euro area countries in the Council. Nevertheless, the Eurogroup's role in the drafting of new formal policy guidelines has not only the strategic aspect that the euro area countries seek to pre-agree important formal decisions in the area of EMU among themselves. The Eurogroup's involvement in the operation of EMU's core coordination instruments and procedures also affects the quality of the decision-making process.

For example, with regard to the adoption of a new set of BEPGs Eurogroup discussions supplement the ECOFIN Council debates. The Eurogroup setting allows for restricted discussions and the allocation of additional time to the consultation process prior to the formal adoption of a set of BEPGs. Moreover, these discussions are embedded in the

Eurogroup's regular activity of reviewing and coordinating budgetary policies. In other words, the Eurogroup's involvement in the drafting process increases the feedback of information on past experiences. In addition, the greater involvement of ministers in the drafting process enhances the commitment to the policy guidelines. The BEPGs have the legal status of a non-binding Council recommendation. Consequently, their impact on policy formation largely depends on whether they are recognised as authoritative at the national level. To use the language of officials in Brussels, the member states must 'own' the guidelines in order to respect them. The Eurogroup intervenes at all stages of the decision-making process. During the months of February and March the Eurogroup usually sees initial orientation debates prior to the finalisation of the official Commission recommendation on a new set of BEPGs. Participants discuss the euro area's fiscal stance with a view to the definition of policy priorities in the new guidelines. The Eurogroup also reflects on the outline and organisation of the BEPGs. For example, this includes the question of how the text of the BEPGs will address the specific needs of the single currency zone. In turn, the results of these orientation debates feed into the Commission's internal drafting process. After the publication of the official Commission recommendation on the BEPGs the Eurogroup discusses aspects of the final draft again ahead of the ECOFIN Council meeting in May, which finally adopts the guidelines.

The Eurogroup also discusses the formulation of formal policy objectives under the SGP procedures. The SGP requires member states to prepare so-called stability programmes. These programmes contain information on the intended course of national budgetary policy. Each year during the month of December the member states submit their stability programmes to the Commission and the ECOFIN Council. The Commission and the Council review the consistency of the programmes with the budgetary criteria of the SGP and the current set of BEPGs. Before member states officially submit their programmes the Eurogroup will have already discussed the individual drafts. These debates scrutinise national planning with a view to the euro area's overall fiscal stance, which would result from the suggested direction of national policies. The discussions also focus on whether the intended course of national policy is compatible with country specific developments, such as strong inflation or the prospect of falling tax revenues. Again the partial communalisation of the drafting process enhances the commitment to the formal coordination instruments and creates additional incentives for policy revision. Commonly formulated policy objectives are crucial normative benchmarks for the monitoring of policy compliance and provide the basis for peer pressure. The continuing discussion of policy options in the context of the regular country reviews and the drafting of formal policy guidelines has contributed to policy learning among euro area finance ministers.

Moreover, the agenda item combines debates on current developments and forward-looking discussions in the context of the formulation of policy guidelines. As a participant in Eurogroup meetings observes:

> The discussion within the group is most important in assessing the policy options. Here progress with regard to a greater convergence of views clearly has been made. I think the group tremendously increased our common understanding of the roles of different policy measures, although it is not necessarily the case that everybody thinks 100 per cent the same way as the others. This will probably never be the case. (Anonymous interview, participant B)

Alongside the regular activities in the context of the collective review of national policies and the discussions related to the operation of EMU's formal coordination instruments, the discussions on budgetary policy also comprise reactions to unforeseen events. In cases of severe price shocks or natural disasters national fiscal authorities might agree ad hoc measures in order to relieve the situation of businesses or industries. However, such measures can have adverse effects on other euro area member states or can threaten the sustainability of commonly agreed consolidation measures. Although the Eurogroup cannot force individual member states to react to unforeseen events in a particular way finance ministers can agree informally on how they will react at the domestic level. There is general agreement among Eurogroup members that ministers inform each other prior to the adoption of ad hoc fiscal measures. The informal coordination of ad hoc measures within the Eurogroup was put to the test for the first time in the second half of 2000. A prolonged rise in oil prices, which was further accelerated by the euro's fall against the dollar, provoked demands to lower taxes for transport businesses throughout Europe.[1] In the context of its regular common reviews of the economic situation the Eurogroup had repeatedly discussed the impact of higher oil prices on economic activity in the euro area. At the beginning of September 2000 when the pressure on national governments reached its highest level so far the Eurogroup started to discuss possible reactions to the demands of the transport sector. When the Eurogroup met again at the end of the month there was wide agreement among finance ministers that the granting of tax benefits would only lead to a distortion of competition. In the light of this discussion on policy options ministers also agreed that individual member states should not consider exceptions from this rule. Ministers feared a round of downward competition with regard to the tax relief measures for transport businesses across the euro area. This view was reiterated at the following ECOFIN Council meeting and the three EU member states outside the euro area gave their consent. However, only hours after the end of the meeting the French government, which was the holder of the Eurogroup's presidency at the time, announced the first round of tax benefits for French hauliers. Other governments followed. The first attempt to coordinate ad hoc measures in the context of unforeseen events had failed. As a finance ministry official in charge of Eurogroup affairs recalls:

> There is the example of the oil price shock in September 2000. The ministers agreed in the Eurogroup and then in ECOFIN that there would be no subsidies. After the ministers went home many did just the opposite following the immense pressure in the domestic arena. This is a coordination deficit. Better coordination and coordination discipline would have let to better results and a distortion of competition could have been avoided. (Anonymous interview, official E)

The incident left many Eurogroup participants frustrated. Dis-appointment was particularly high because the discussions within the group had been promising. The common analysis of the overall situation and the discussion of appropriate policy responses had led to unanimous agreement. Nevertheless, the implementation of the informal agreement failed. Although the incident raised doubts about the personal commitment of some group members the events simply demonstrated another problem. Even in their own area of competence national finance ministers often do not enjoy the authority to negotiate coordination arrangements at the European level on their own initiative.

The dialogue with the ECB

The common analysis of the economic situation and the review of budgetary policy involve exchanges between the ECB president (or vice-president) and ministers. In fact, what is generally called the 'dialogue with the ECB' takes place in the context of these two agenda items. In both cases the interplay between monetary and economic policy, the euro area's policy-mix, is an important aspect of the debate. As was demonstrated in Chapter 2 the creation of a framework for informal discussion among economic and monetary policy authorities was one of the main ideas behind the foundation of the Eurogroup. Moreover, much of the controversy on the institutional status of a euro area forum had centred on the issue of whether the envisaged meetings between ministers and the ECB would compromise the political independence of the central bank. The relationship between the Eurogroup and the ECB is one of the rare aspects of the Eurogroup's work which was discussed in early contributions to the literature on economic governance in Stage 3 (Campanella 2000; Bini Smaghi and Casini 2000). Miriam Campanella (2000) even published her contribution under the title 'The battle between ECOFIN-11 and the European Central Bank'. More recently, Howarth and Loedel (2003) have raised doubts that the dialogue within the Eurogroup has done much to improve the accountability of the bank. In their study on the ECB the two authors warn that national governments need to be able to express their concerns with regard to the policies of the ECB. Otherwise, national decision-makers might question the legitimacy of the bank's independence if they feel that their country is disadvantaged by the ECB's policy (Howarth and Loedel 2003: 124).

In particular, at the time the media coverage suggested that there were continuing tensions between monetary and fiscal authorities during the first years of Stage 3. The first public controversies on the appropriate stance of monetary policy and the necessity of international exchange rate coordination occurred during the second half of 1998 and the first half of 1999. It was the time when euro area ministers gathered for their first meetings within the Eurogroup. One year later several ministers publicly challenged the ECB's policy in connection with the euro's slide against the dollar (see above). Finally, in 2001 the Belgian finance minister Didier Reynders used his position as Eurogroup president to quarrel with ECB president Wim Duisenberg over the right to represent the euro area as a political entity in a series of newspaper articles. Both Duisenberg and Reynders claimed the title 'Mr. Euro'[2] for themselves. However, the interviews with Eurogroup members conducted in connection with this study suggest a different picture with regard to the actual discussions within the Eurogroup. The different accounts of the interviewees unanimously point to a stark contrast between the public statements of individual ministers and discussion behaviour inside the group. As one participant in Eurogroup meetings observes

> There have been instances in the past where ministers have chosen to express themselves more strongly in the press than in the meeting. That is something very unusual but which sometimes has happened. Basically, I still would say that it is not only the purpose of the meeting to foster consensus [between the ECB and ministers] but that it really does this. In my view the debate is usually very constructive. Differences between ministers and the ECB tend to be less than what many people would believe. (Anonymous interview, participant F)

In this sense Campanella's (2000) characterisation of the relation between the ECB and ministers during the first year of Eurogroup discussions as a 'battle between ECOFIN-11 and the European Central Bank' is misleading. What is, however, true is that in particular two members of the Eurogroup publicly campaigned against the ECB's policies in media statements and public speeches. The German and French socialist finance ministers Lafontaine and Strauss-Kahn demanded the negotiation of target zones for the three leading international currencies – the euro, the dollar and the yen. As Campanella (ibid.) rightly observes Lafontaine's preference for Keynesian demand management policies also led him to challenge the ECB on its interest rate policy. Moreover, the rhetoric of the two ministers referred to the Eurogroup as an embryonic European economic government and political counterweight to the ECB. However, the interviews substantiating this study suggest that the two ministers were not able to convey the same message within the group. The German minister Lafontaine particularly, along with his adviser Heiner Flassbeck allegedly offended many Eurogroup participants through their radical opposition to the existing set of policy priorities. As a result the two became increasingly isolated within the group. They were not able to engage other ministers, let alone the president of the ECB, into any significant discussion on positions known from their public statements. Moreover, the axis Lafontaine–Strauss-Kahn was probably less pronounced in Eurogroup meetings than the public activities of the two ministers might have suggested. Strauss-Kahn appealed much more to the group consensus than Lafontaine and embraced EMU's focus on stability oriented budgetary policies. Nevertheless, Campanella's central observation that the ECB decided to categorically resist the discussion of political initiatives, which put its political independence into question, is probably true. Her main conclusion, which was derived from the events during the first year of Eurogroup meetings, seems to be compatible with the experiences made inside the Eurogroup over the following years. During the first years of its existence the ECB reacted particularly cautiously to open demands for closer coordination between monetary and fiscal policy authorities. The bank took this stance not least because it sought to establish its reputation as an independent central bank. However, as long as finance ministers respect the ECB's fundamental competences the bank is prepared to accommodate its policy as far as possible to the needs of fiscal authorities. The current practice of discussions between ministers and the ECB within the Eurogroup confirms this view. There is little doubt that the central bank representatives in the meetings are prepared to fully engage in discussions over policy. As a participant in Eurogroup meetings emphasises:

> I would not say per se that the ECB is not prepared to make concessions on certain issues in the discussion. That depends on what you mean with 'making concessions'. Of course the ECB cannot make concessions in the way: 'After we had this discussion I, the president of the ECB, promise you to reduce interest rates by next week'. ... However, nobody expects this from him. It is already sufficient if he outlines the underlying conditions and explains at which issues the ECB looks at the moment, and what would facilitate or hinder certain decisions. In return the ECB president wants to know from ministers in which direction budgetary policy is going, but also structural policy of course, since both have a hopefully positive impact on growth. (Anonymous interview, participant A)

It is mainly through his introductory statements in the context of the debates on the economic situation and the review of budgetary policies, that the ECB president Wim Duisenberg would communicate the policy of the central bank to the Eurogroup during his term of office. It is in this respect that the Eurogroup is the main forum for the exchange of information on the intended course of monetary policy. In addition, there is little doubt that the statements by Eurogroup ministers on the budgetary situation and the direction of national policy are a key indicator considered by the ECB when it decides on monetary policy in the euro area. Moreover, the ECB president frequently comments on specific policies in individual member states. In this the policy options considered by the ECB are expressed even more plainly. At the same time, the ECB is fully integrated in the debate on appropriate policy responses. Ironically, ministers largely refrain from referring directly to ECB decisions. The active part in this ongoing policy dialogue is played by the ECB. Ministers leave it to the central bank to derive the right conclusions from the individual presentations on the stance of national fiscal policy. In other words, ministers do not scrutinise the ECB for its monetary policy decisions in Eurogroup discussions. The initial fear that a setting such as the Eurogroup would undermine the independence of the ECB through the continuing exercise of political pressure by ministers has not been confirmed. On the contrary, the current situation gives reason for concern because ministers do not critically review the ECB's policy. Instead, it seems that more explicit statements by ministers are only conveyed through media statements. A greater role for ministers in the dialogue with the ECB is therefore necessary, as a participant in Eurogroup meetings warns:

> However, it would be better to have more confrontational discussions within the group and less debate in the media. This really would help things. (Anonymous interview, participant D)

Another indication that ministers are reluctant to actively review ECB policies is the way the participation of the Eurogroup president in ECB Governing Council meetings is prepared. As Lorenzo Bini Smaghi and Claudio Casini (2000) have pointed out, this line of communication has been neglected right from the beginning of Stage 3. According to the Treaty provisions the president of the Council has the right to attend the meetings of the ECB's decision-making forum (see Chapter 2). The respective minister might even demand the discussion of a particular issue. *De facto* the Eurogroup's president exercises this prerogative of the president of the ECOFIN Council. Nevertheless, Eurogroup meetings do not see much preparatory activity with regard to the president's participation in ECB Governing Council meetings.

Finally, the Eurogroup functions as the key forum for the coordination of exchange rate policy decisions between ministers and the ECB. Formally, the Treaty regulates decision-making on the establishment of exchange rate regimes with third countries and the specification of exchange rate policy guidelines through a complex procedure involving all Community institutions with responsibilities in the area of EMU (Article 111, TEC). *De facto* this regime is replaced by informal consultations between ministers, the Commission and the ECB within the context of the Eurogroup. As a participant in Eurogroup meetings explains:

> We simply handle that informally. That is not surprising because when you come to the exchange rate you are talking about a very sensitive area where the idea of having formal proposals and recommendations, initiative of the Commission etc., consulting this and that body is simply rubbish because that is not the way you can deal with these matters. Naturally the Eurogroup has taken over. (Anonymous interview, participant F)

Structural reform

The discussion of the economic situation and the review of budgetary policies account for the bulk of the Eurogroup's work. In addition, the group has also repeatedly focused on the topic of structural reform. During the second half of the 1990s frustration about the continuing failure of EU economies to accelerate economic growth and generate higher employment mounted. At the same time, decision-makers retained their scepticism with regard to the ability of monetary and fiscal policy to provide a stimulus to growth through Keynesian demand management. Consequently, the focus increasingly shifted to new efforts in the area of structural reform. Since the 1994 European Council meeting in Essen, EU leaders have continued to demand greater collective efforts in the area of structural reform. These efforts are seen as crucial in the fight against unemployment. The attempts by EU leaders to draw more attention to the question of employment at the European level, therefore, go hand in hand with a greater emphasis on structural policies. The Dublin European Council highlighted this programmatic link in December 1996. Under the title 'The Jobs Challenge – Dublin Declaration on Employment' (European Council 1996) the role of structural reform in the context of EMU's macro-economic stability framework was spelled out:

> There is no conflict between sound macroeconomic and budget policies on the one hand and strong and sustainable growth in output and employment on the other. The European Council emphasises that the selective restructuring of public expenditure should have a major role to play in promoting growth and employment especially through investment in human resources and active labour market policies. The positive impact of appropriate macroeconomic policies is enhanced where there is greater co-ordination of economic and structural policies as outlined in the Commission's report 'Europe as an Economic Entity'. (Annex II, The Jobs Challenge)

Subsequent European Council meetings laid the basis for enhanced coordination efforts. The formulation of common policy guidelines and the creation of multilateral surveillance mechanisms in the area of employment were in the centre of the so-called Luxembourg process (European Council 1997b). The Cardiff process added the link between employment initiatives and comprehensive structural reform (European Council 1998b). In addition, a regular macro-economic dialogue involving the social partners, the Council, the Commission and the ECB was set up under the Cologne process (European Council 1999). Finally, with the Lisbon Summit in summer 2000 the EU set the task to become the most competitive economy in the world. In programmatic terms the Lisbon presidency conclusions bundled the above processes. It was decided that the BEPGs 'should focus increasingly on the medium- and long-term implications of structural policies and on reforms aimed at promoting economic growth potential, employment and social cohesion, as well as on the transition towards a knowledge-based economy' (European Council 2000, paragraph 35). In addition, the European Council committed itself to devoting an entire summit meeting to economic reform and employment each year in spring. Finally, the Lisbon presidency conclusions summarised this combination of non-binding policy guidelines, increased multilateral surveillance efforts, policy dialogue and regular political guidance by EU leaders under the title 'open method of coordination'. The term was used in order to underline that the collective efforts in this policy area focus on the provision of incentives for further reform and policy learning rather than on a harmonisation of national policies.

As a consequence of the EU-wide emphasis on structural reform the activities of Community institutions and committees in this area have been increased. Senior civil servants from the member states and the representatives of the Commission engage in an ongoing review of national policies within the Economic Policy Committee (EPC). Together with the Commission activities in this area, the work of this committee is a crucial source of peer pressure and provides the basis for the formulation of common policy guidelines in the context of the annual BEPGs. However, the expert discussions within the EPC are less suited to lending political impetus to individual initiatives in the area of structural reform. At the occasion of a gathering of EU finance ministers ahead of the Helsinki European Council meeting in December 1999, the Italian finance minister Vincenzo Visco pleaded for a greater role for finance ministers. He wanted to foster policy learning through restricted discussions among ministers and the Commission in the context of the Eurogroup. As a participant in the relevant meeting recalls, this proposal was enthusiastically received (anonymous interview). However, informal discussions on structural policy are not only in the interest of euro area countries.

Therefore, debates on structural policy also take place among all fifteen EU finance ministers. This has so far been the case in the context of the so-called ECOFIN breakfast meetings. These gatherings take place in the early morning hours prior to Council sessions and constitute an additional opportunity for informal discussions alongside the regular ECOFIN luncheons (see Chapter 3).

In addition, the Eurogroup regularly focuses on the topic. As a general rule informal discussions on structural policy among all fifteen EU finance ministers focus on topics linked to the key EU initiatives in this area. Eurogroup meetings pay particular attention to the interaction between macro-economic and structural policies and evaluate the role of structural policy with regard to the euro area's policy-mix. However, in practice duplication is not entirely avoided. Since the French Eurogroup presidency in the second half of 2000, euro area ministers address the topic of structural reform through country reviews and orientation debates. Discussions centre on labour market reform, national tax systems and administrative structures. Participants compare different national approaches with regard to their impact on unemployment and labour supply. In addition, wage developments and collective bargaining patterns have been discussed in this context. Finally, topics such as the reform of capital markets, the further opening of network industries or the topic of ageing populations are on the agenda. The continuing collective review of different national policy approaches and the common identification of best practices within the euro area aims at creating incentives for further reform. In this respect the style of the discussion on structural policy differs from the way debates on the Eurogroup's main agenda items are conducted. As a participant in Eurogroup meetings explains:

> In many areas, I think, it is important that the ministers see how certain problems are dealt with in other countries without saying we come immediately to the conclusion that this is the valid approach for all of us. However, it can be an eye-opener if one realises that others approach some problems in a completely different way. ... Thus I believe the aim of this structural policy debate is a very different one compared with the economic situation and budgetary policy where the ministers can draw conclusions for their area [of responsibility]. (Anonymous interview, participant A)

Moreover, with regard to most of the topics discussed under the agenda item of structural reform, finance ministers share responsibilities with cabinet colleagues. This significantly reduces the scope for the direct implementation of the results of common discussions. Nonetheless, finance ministers have a common interest in structural reform. As the above discussion of the Eurogroup's main agenda items has shown, the necessity for further efforts in the area of structural reform has been one of the main conclusions of the recurrent policy-mix debates. Therefore, the main objective of the Eurogroup's discussions on structural matters is to strengthen the domestic role of finance ministers as 'transmission belts of structural reform', as one participant in Eurogroup meetings explains (anonymous interview). However, many Eurogroup participants are not satisfied with the way the informal discussions are currently conducted. The main criticism is that discussions fail to generate concrete policy guidance. While there is wide agreement within the group that further reform efforts are necessary, participants find it difficult to formulate responses to specific problems. In this respect the interviewees unanimously identify three factors which participants associate with the difficulties. The fact that finance ministers do not enjoy direct decision-making competences in the identified areas of reform was in many ways underestimated when the Eurogroup decided to address structural matters in greater detail. Finance ministers also find it difficult to act as a 'high-level lobby for the market economy' (anonymous interview) because they are less familiar with the topic than with the usually discussed macro-economic issues. In this respect the preparations of the discussions within the EFC are seen as insufficient. As a participant in the discussions self-critically remarks:

> With regard to structural policy the main problem is that finance ministers have only a few direct competences. Discussions on concrete issues turned out to be a total flop. The other problem is the EFC. We were not able to convey to ministers the politico-economic significance of structural policy discussions within the Eurogroup. (Anonymous interview, participant G)

However, the difficulties in connection with the discussion of structural policies among European finance ministers are not entirely new to those who are involved in the debates. Another participant in the discussions therefore attributes the difficulties to the particularities of the subject area:

> It [the discussion of structural policy] has never succeeded well. I think that is not necessarily because they are not appropriate for the Eurogroup. We have never been able in any forum to deal with structural issues. And I think the reason why we have not been successful is because these issues are inherently so complex. I mean macro-economics is simple – it is the easy part in a way – but structural issues are not only analytically and technically more complex but the institutions are very complex. There are different countries, there are different traditions, and the whole institutional set-up might be very difficult. And perhaps even more important, these matters are in national competence. So, there is not much you can do. (Anonymous interview, participant F)

As EFC members stress, the key challenge with regard to the preparation of structural issues is the definition of concrete problems for decision-making. Analytical and technical aspects need to be framed by a political question. Only where ministers can clearly identify adverse effects of inactivity in a particular issue area will they be able and willing to consider new initiatives or advocate reform in the domestic arena. Moreover, the ability to influence decision-making outside their own cabinet portfolio depends on the progress finance ministers make within their own area of responsibility.

The changeover to the euro

When the Eurogroup was founded in June 1998 the euro did not yet exist. Moreover, Stage 3 began on 1 January 1999 with the irrevocable fixing of the exchange rates of the first wave of euro area countries. In legal terms, the single currency had come into existence. However, the introduction of euro notes and coins was still a further three years away. According to the Treaty provisions on EMU the Council now had to take all 'the other measures necessary for the introduction of the ECU [i.e. the euro] as the single currency in the Member States concerned' (Article 123.4, TEC). Despite the role of the ECOFIN Council in agreeing on the necessary legal steps in connection with the changeover to euro notes and coins the Eurogroup functioned as the virtual organisational centre of the preparatory work. In comparison with the other agenda items discussed in this chapter, the preparation of the euro changeover occupied the Eurogroup only for a limited period of time. Apart from occasional debates over practical aspects of the circulation of euro notes and coins the topic is no longer on the group's agenda. This situation is unlikely to change until new members join the euro club. Nevertheless, for a period of more than one and a half years the group focused regularly on the practical aspects of the introduction of euro notes and coins. Deviating from the content of the discussions in the context of the other agenda items the changeover debates mainly focused on technical issues.

The Eurogroup's regular discussions on the topic were preceded by an orientation debate within the context of an informal ECOFIN meeting in Versailles on 9 September 2000. For the first time, ministers briefed each other on the state of preparations in their home countries. Moreover, ministers expressed different preferences and concerns with regard to the concrete organisation of the changeover. For example, some were in favour of bringing coins into circulation prior to the official date of the changeover while others rejected this idea. Most importantly, ministers agreed on a surveillance mechanism allowing the control and coordination of the preparations in the different member states. To this end, they agreed on the compilation of a so-called 'scoreboard'[3] as the basis for discussion. This mechanism was also intended to provide an incentive for individual countries to speed up their efforts with regard to the different technical issues. Most of the aspects of the preparatory process followed the principle of subsidiarity. The bulk of the technical preparation of the actual changeover process remained in the hands of the national authorities. The latter had to negotiate arrangements with the private banking sector for the changeover. For example, issues such as the financing of the changeover costs or the duration of the dual circulation period needed to be resolved. Finally, the activities of national governments and their agencies had to be coordinated with the ECB, which held key responsibilities in this area.

At the end of September the Eurogroup started its discussions on the state of the preparations. On 8 November the debate for the first time was conducted on the basis of the new scoreboard. The scoreboard consisted of a short working paper prepared by the Commission's DG ECFIN. This note was updated before each Eurogroup meeting and summarised the main developments in connection with the changeover preparations in a comparative fashion. The scoreboard highlighted the state of public awareness with reference to Eurobarometer surveys and reported on the different national information campaigns. It outlined the state of preparations with regard to enterprises and consumers, or particular parts of the population, such as pensioners. The regular briefing by the commissioner on the scoreboard was complemented by a presentation of the ECB president. In the following open debate ministers elaborated on country specific situations and expressed their concerns about deficiencies in the preparatory process. For example, a frequently raised problem was the lack of preparation of small and medium sized businesses.[4] In contrast to the debates on the key agenda items the discussions on the scoreboard tended to be relatively short and unspectacular. At the occasion of some meetings the regular briefings were complemented by more intensive debates focussing on particular concerns. The Eurogroup also sought to respond to concerns of the markets and the wider public through increased communication efforts. For example, at its meeting in June 2001 the group agreed on a press statement on the state of the preparations. Deviating from its usual preference for secretive behaviour the group was keen to send out a political message. The smoothness of the changeover process depended not least on the voluntary commitment of retailers and private banks. The Eurogroup wanted to remind them that the price neutrality of the exchange operations and the dual pricing of goods and services during the transition period were essential.

At the occasion of an informal ECOFIN Council meeting in Liège in September 2001 commissioner Solbes for the first time alerted the ministers to the risk of a general rise in prices in connection with the changeover.[5] The topic re-emerged within the Eurogroup discussions after the actual changeover on 1 January 2002. In general, ministers had been confident that the changeover would not lead to significant price hikes. At the beginning of January the new Eurogroup president Rodrigo Rato was keen to point out that there had been no indications of a general rise in prices during the second half of December. However, with the introduction of the new notes and coins, media reports on price increases emerged nearly every day. Obviously, many ministers sensed the political pressure, which could be triggered by the public concerns over price hikes. The topic became a regular item in the exchanges on the changeover process at the beginning of 2002. At its meeting on 11 February the Eurogroup decided to disperse concerns over price increases through a short press statement. However, this statement hardly found attention in the media because of the debate on the Commission recommendation to issue an early warning under the SGP to Germany and Portugal. This discussion had overshadowed the Eurogroup meeting and had attracted great attention by the media (see Chapter 5). In reaction to the continuing public debate ministers addressed the issue in a longer discussion at their meeting on 3 March. With this debate the Eurogroup's regular reviews of the changeover preparations ended.

Reflecting on economic governance in EMU

An important item on the Eurogroup's agenda is, finally, the reflection on the functioning of economic governance in EMU and the further development of the group's own work. Although these discussions represent only a relatively small share of the Eurogroup's overall workload they are an important element in structuring the fragile informal discussion process. The collective reflection exercises react to the fact that the Eurogroup has to invent and adjust its own working method (see Chapter 3). Moreover, orientation debates on the institutional aspects of economic governance in EMU are an important indicator of the underlying political preferences of the group members. Here, it emerges whether ministers are prepared to engage in closer coordination, or whether they would accept greater competences for the Commission in a specific area of the coordination process. Ever since its foundation the Eurogroup has scheduled such debates. On a few occasions ministers devoted a third or even half of the meeting to these issues but often debate on institutional issues simply takes place under the item 'miscellaneous'. This low profile of institutional issues is sometimes related to the fact that only a short *tour de table* is required for a first orientation on a particular subject, or that the group simply wants to conceal from the outside world that it devotes particular attention to an institutional problem. The following examples may illustrate the format and content of the Eurogroup's debates over economic governance. In addition, Table 4.2 (see page 110) provides an overview of the Eurogroup's major reflection exercises conducted so far.

One year after its foundation in June 1998 the Eurogroup took a first step in the refinement of its working method. At its first meeting under Finnish presidency on 12 July 1999 the Eurogroup held a discussion on the structure of the debates and the organisation of the work of the forum. Unlike at the occasion of discussions on the other main agenda items, the topic was introduced and discussed on the basis of an EFC paper. This pattern is characteristic for the more programmatic debates in the context of the Eurogroup. As regards the organisation of their own work ministers are reluctant to accept or even request policy guidance from the Commission.[6] Moreover, as demonstrated in Chapter 5 the central role of the EFC in the preparations of Eurogroup meetings implies that it is particularly suited to issue guidance on the organisation of Eurogroup debates. Eurogroup reflection exercises are usually preceded by similar exercises among EFC members. In addition, the EFC secretariat plays an important role in the drafting of new guidelines for the organisation of the Eurogroup's work.

At the occasion of the regular ECOFIN Council press conference the day after the Eurogroup's first discussion on its working method the group's president Sauli Niinistö briefly commented on the informal meeting. He characterised the agreed refinement of the working procedures as 'formalising the work informally'.[7] This statement reflected the wish to have more structured discussions within the group. During the first twelve months the discussion process within the group had simply evolved without any clear guidance. Many interventions had been fairly broad. However, the group had had its first experiences with regard to the main agenda items. Building on these experiences ministers agreed now on a range of measures proposed by the EFC and the Finnish presidency. They decided to circulate an annotated agenda among the group members before each meeting. In addition, the Commission was asked to prepare the debates on the economic and budgetary situation through written working papers, thus saving more time for the genuine debate over policies. The presidency was asked to invite lead speakers in preparation for Eurogroup meetings to introduce specific topics. Finally, the meeting led to the introduction of a regular letter by the president on the evolution of each meeting (see Chapter 3). As Chapter 5 will demonstrate in connection with the analysis of the development of the debates over budgetary policy, the impact of the measures agreed in the context of the Eurogroup's first reflection exercise was soon felt.

One year later a similar meeting under the incoming French Eurogroup presidency paved the way for a greater flexibility of the group's agenda. Participants had been unhappy with the tight time schedule of previous Eurogroup meetings, which used to take place in the early morning hours before ECOFIN meetings. This practice had often prevented a more thorough debate on individual topics. Now, it was decided that the group would convene on the eve before ECOFIN Council meetings in order to have more time for discussions.[8]

More recently, Eurogroup ministers saw themselves confronted with the question of the future of their informal deliberations. On 28 February 2002, the European Convention held its inaugural meeting in Brussels. The assembly of representatives from national parliaments and governments, the European Parliament (EP) and the Commission started its work on a draft constitution for an enlarged EU. As in the context of previous IGCs the Treaty provisions on EMU once more came under review. However, this time the debate was not only about the introduction of qualified majority voting and greater powers for the Commission but touched on the existence of the informal Eurogroup itself. In fact, ministers needed a certain period of time in order to realise the possible repercussions of the Convention process for their own informal discussions. At the occasion of the IGCs leading to the Amsterdam and Nice Treaties the EU finance ministers had been able to push through their own view on the constitutional framework of EMU without greater difficulties. Their conservative approach to the question of Treaty amendments in the area of EMU prevailed without much debate. This time, the public process of the Convention and the potential moral authority of a draft constitution made the outcome less predictable. Most importantly, the institutional dynamics of the enlargement process were likely to come into play sooner rather than later. The simple fact that euro area countries, which presented a powerful majority within the old EU, would soon be outnumbered by non-euro member states questioned the continued existence of the *status quo* of the euro area's economic governance set-up.

As the Convention process gathered momentum Eurogroup ministers were soon reminded that they had to form an opinion on the issues among themselves if they wanted to react to the debates on the future of the institutional framework. Commissioner Solbes increased the pace of the debate on economic governance on 2 May 2002, when he addressed the Brussels Economic Forum.[9] Solbes (2002) argued that the Eurogroup's

> informal and confidential nature has contributed to an improvement of the coordination through frank and open discussions. However, the question whether the current institutional set up remains appropriate for an EMU where a significant number of countries will not be members of the euro area for a period of time remains open. We should think about possibilities of different Council formats to respond to two objectives: to preserve the Community nature of the economic policy coordination and to respond to the different requirements of euro area/non euro area members. The need to have informal very restricted policy discussions should also be considered.

With this proposal the commissioner broke the taboo of questioning the unity of the Council. The respect of the unitary nature of the Council framework had so far been the main institutional constraint under which the Eurogroup had to operate. The commissioner also demanded a greater role for the Commission in the coordination process. In fact, Solbes and his advisers in DG ECFIN were convinced that the enlargement process posed a serious challenge to decision-making within the euro area. Nevertheless, the commissioner explicitly highlighted the possibility of continued informal discussions. For its part, the Commission had already recognised the important role of the Convention in the tackling of these institutional issues. Solbes's ideas were reiterated by an official Commission communication to the Convention on May 22, in which the supranational administration set out its own preferences in the debate on the future constitutional architecture of the EU (see Convention 2003a: 10). However, the conference speech of the commissioner provoked veritable debate among Eurogroup ministers when they met on 6 May. As a result of the debate, ministers were urged to further investigate the issues raised within the Convention and by Solbes within the context of the EFC. At its next meeting in June the Eurogroup held a first orientation debate. Ministers touched on the various aspects of institutional reform and also used the opportunity to remind each other of potential deficiencies in the organisation and conduct of the Eurogroup's work. In relation to the idea of a formal euro area forum, first concerns were raised that such a decision-making body besides the Eurogroup would be counterproductive.[10]

In the meantime the Convention had concluded its broader debates on the future of the EU and delegated parts of the drafting process to specific working groups. On 7 June the working group on economic governance held its first meeting. During the following meetings several members of the working group demanded a formalisation of the Eurogroup. At the same time, the informal debates among ministers were continued on the basis of EFC input in the context of the regular ECOFIN Council luncheons. This practice followed the rule that institutional issues, which touched on Treaty provisions, needed to be discussed among all fifteen EU finance ministers. Very soon it became clear that the ministers were determined to preserve the informal framework of Eurogroup meetings. Moreover, they sought to disentangle the question of formal euro area decision-making competences and that of the status of the Eurogroup. Instead of a separate euro area Council formation the ministers preferred to extend the list of suspended voting rights of non-euro countries in the ECOFIN Council (see Chapter 2). This solution allowed the keeping of the Eurogroup as it was and preserved the unity of the Council. As a participant in Eurogroup meetings explains:

> With regard to enlargement, however, decision-making in ECOFIN becomes more of a problem. That is why we need a euro area restricted decision-making process within ECOFIN. And in this context, it is important that the Eurogroup continues what it is. We need the informal group as we have it but we must change the decision-making. (Anonymous interview, participant C)

So far the Eurogroup's reflection exercises had occurred once or twice a year. The debate on the Convention's activities continued well into the year 2003. Moreover, the informal discussions on the future role of the Eurogroup brought the ministers back into business with the Convention – a process to which they had initially paid not much attention. The EFC president Jonny Åkerholm advocated the Eurogroup consensus in a

Table 4.2   Reflection exercises on the functioning of the Eurogroup and its role in the economic governance set-up of EMU (June 1998–October 2002)

Eurogroup meeting	*Scheduled discussion*	*Result**
12/07/1999	Organisation of the working procedures of the Eurogroup (initiative of the Finnish presidency)	Presidency letter, annotated agenda, lead speakers, regular Commission notes on economic and budgetary situation
16/07/2000	Functioning of the Eurogroup (initiative of the French presidency)	Evening sessions, press conference, structural matters
26/11/2000	Functioning of the Eurogroup	
18/01/2001	Follow-up on the Nice European Council meeting concluding the IGC	
12/02/2001	Commission communication 'strengthening economic policy coordination within the euro area'	
11/03/2001	The Eurogroup's working method and activities	Eurogroup working party within the EFC
14/12/2001	Functioning of the Eurogroup and its agenda	No regular press conferences
06/05/2002 03/06/2002 **	Functioning of the Eurogroup – European Convention	start of a reflection process on the future of the Eurogroup in an enlarged EU

* Empty spaces indicate that no significant changes occurred after the debate.
** Debate was continued within the context of ECOFIN luncheons.

Note: This information is based on data from *Agence Europe*, Bulletin (1999–2002), and anonymous interviews.

hearing of the Convention's working party on economic governance. On 7 September 2002, the chairman of the Convention's working party Klaus Hänsch was invited to the informal ECOFIN Council meeting in Copenhagen. He in turn reported on the results of the discussions within his group (European Convention 2002c). Most importantly, the frequent debates among ministers in connection with the Convention process showed that a strong working consensus on the role of the Eurogroup in the overall economic governance framework existed. However, the Eurogroup had so far found it difficult to communicate this position to the outside world. A participant in Eurogroup meetings summarises the result of debates as follows:

> Given that we will have a single monetary policy beside an independent fiscal policy also in the future, there is clearly a continuing demand for an informal body as the Eurogroup. I think this view is now pretty much shared between everyone. There is also a debate now on the formal decision-making competences of the euro area countries within ECOFIN. This is really a matter for the Convention to decide which formal decisions should be allocated to the euro area but the need for informal discussion will always remain. (Anonymous interview, participant B)

Notes

1 See, for example, *Financial Times* (25 August 2000); *Agence Europe*, Bulletin (30 September 2000).
2 See *Wirtschaftswoche* (1 March 2001); *Le Monde Economie* (19 March 2001).
3 See *Agence Europe*, Bulletin (9 September 2000 and 12 September 2000).
4 See *Agence Europe*, Bulletin (8 November 2000 and 28 February 2001).
5 See *Agence Europe*, Bulletin (4 September 2001).
6 An example was the Commission communication on the strengthening of economic policy coordination at the beginning of 2001 (see *Agence Europe*, Bulletin (8 February 2001)). Although the proposals were generally in line with considerations expressed by Eurogroup participants and coincided with the initiative of the Belgium Eurogroup presidency to strengthen the profile of the Eurogroup, ministers gave Commission president Prodi and commissioner Solbes the cold shoulder when the two wanted to discuss their initiative with the Eurogroup in February 2001 (anonymous interviews).
7 *Agence Europe*, Bulletin (14 July 1999).
8 See *Agence Europe*, Bulletin (18 July 2000).
9 The Brussels Economic Forum is a high profile conference for decision-makers and experts in the area of economic governance, which is sponsored by the Commission.
10 Anonymous interviews.

5

Informal governance and the operation of the SGP

This chapter analyses one specific policy discourse over time. It focuses on the Eurogroup's role in the operation of the SGP and demonstrates how the Eurogroup embraced the core themes of the SGP step by step and made them a key priority of its work. Reference to three instances of non-compliance with the SGP criteria during the years 2000 to 2002 illustrates how formal and informal governance structures interact in times of crisis.

The SGP constitutes the procedural framework for the enforcement of common rules and policy objectives with regard to economic policy coordination in Stage 3. As outlined in Chapter 2, the pact seeks to enhance compliance with the deficit rule and the BEPGs through strengthened multilateral surveillance and the further specification of the objective of budgetary consolidation. Consequently, the procedures and objectives of the SGP are at the heart of the operation of EMU's economic policy coordination set-up. The regulations of the pact have the status of secondary legislation. Together with the Treaty provisions on EMU they constitute the formal institutional framework for economic governance. Accordingly, the ECOFIN Council is the central decision-making body as regards the operation of the SGP.

Despite this formal assignment of competences the Eurogroup *de facto* intervenes at all stages of the decision-making process and has developed into the virtual political centre of the operation of the SGP. As regards SGP related issues, the activities of the Eurogroup have effectively emptied out the discussions within the ECOFIN Council. The previous chapter has demonstrated that the review of budgetary policy in the euro area ranks uppermost on the Eurogroup's agenda. The involvement of the group in the drafting processes leading to the formulation of common policy guidelines and objectives furthermore has shown how individual discussions in the run-up to formal decisions by the Commission or the Council become embedded in the wider discussion process within the Eurogroup. The illustration of the interaction of informal dialogue and aspects of formal decision-making is at the centre of the following discussion. Most decisively, the role of the Eurogroup in the operation of the SGP is not one that simply replicates the Council's agenda at the level of euro area ministers. It will be demonstrated how the key objectives of the pact became incorporated into the group's underlying working consensus. Finally, the in-depth analysis of four instances of non-compliance with the set of common rules and policy guidelines shows how this consensus is applied in times of crisis. As already outlined in Chapter 2 the revision of some provisions of the SGP in 2005 did not change the key governance patterns and instruments foreseen by the pact. Consequently, the account on Eurogroup involvement in the management of the SGP procedures given below also reflects the current practice of implementing the pact.

The medium term objective as a key reference point

From the time of the first Eurogroup meetings, debates on the budgetary situation in the euro area were a recurrent item on the agenda. However, no predefined pattern for the discussion of budgetary policy existed. Most importantly, it was not entirely clear what the particular role of the Eurogroup, in comparison with the ECOFIN Council, would be during Stage 3. Not surprisingly, initial debates under the chairmanship of the Eurogroup's first president, the Austrian finance minister Edlinger, were a mixture of more programmatic interventions and comments on specific developments. No unified vision existed among Eurogroup participants with regard to the role of budgetary policy coordination in Stage 3. A working paper of the Austrian presidency, which was circulated at the occasion of the third Eurogroup meeting in September 1998, reflected the different concepts circulating at the time. The paper is one of the rare Eurogroup working documents which was reproduced – partly – by the *Agence Europe* news bulletin one day after the meeting. The following summary of the paper's lead questions gives an impression of the diversity of the issues considered among ministers at the time:

> i) [the] effects of the single currency on macro- and microeconomic policies: – How long will it take for the cyclical positions of the States participating in EMU to become closely aligned? Will this synchronization occur automatically? Should economic policies contribute to this process? How will the single monetary policy react at the start of EMU, when cycles are not yet fully aligned? Will a specific reaction by monetary policy be necessary due to the Russian and Asian crises?
>
> ii) a stronger role for budgetary policies: – Are the Ministers agreed that budgetary policies should be modified to cope with unfavourable cyclical positions and with asymmetrical shocks? What sort of response do the Russian and Asian crises require? How can it be ensured that budgetary policies are capable of weathering national or regional economic shocks? Is closer coordination of budgetary policies necessary to make the budgetary position of the Euro zone more compatible with a single monetary policy?

[...]

v) better coordination of political decisions: – Is it recognised that effective coordination requires the 'broad guidelines' to become more binding? Are the Ministers agreed that economic policy decisions should be organised around these 'broad guidelines'? Is there agreement on the need for a consensus among the main institutions taking decisions on economic policy? Are the procedures projected by the European Central Bank and the Ecofin Council or Euro 11 adequate? In particular, is there agreement that the Monetary Committee (the future Economic and Financial Committee) should be asked to establish the necessary working relationships as quickly as possible?[1]

For example, some considered that the question of the role of budgetary policy coordination in response to asymmetric shocks would constitute an important part of the prospective Eurogroup activities. The reaction to asymmetric shocks within a currency union had been one of the key topics of the economics literature prior to Stage 3. However, at a practical level this question has been virtually irrelevant to the discussions on budgetary policy within the Eurogroup. In addition, the issue of 'unfavourable cyclical positions' of individual euro area countries, which is raised by the paper, has never played a significant role in the context of the common reviews of budgetary policy. Another question discussed in the early days of Eurogroup meetings was the one of the euro area's policy-mix. Many ministers stressed the role of the SGP for economic policy coordination in Stage 3. They demanded continued consolidation efforts in order to prepare for less favourable economic situations. In addition, the basic idea behind the pact that sound public finances are the basis for low interest rates in the euro area was reiterated in the discussions. This is the picture which emerges from interviews with participants in the relevant Eurogroup meetings and the statements of individual ministers reproduced in the *Agence Europe* news bulletins of the time. There was a general consensus among finance ministers that the SGP was needed for EMU. However, it is reasonable to assume that ministers diverged in their expectations with regard to the Eurogroup's role in the implementation of the objectives of the pact. Some obviously saw the need to highlight the role of budgetary consolidation as the key objective of coordination efforts in Stage 3. The Commission and the ECB also emphasised this position. In contrast, others did not prioritise the topic within the Eurogroup.

However, the more programmatic debates conducted during the time of the Austrian presidency did not result in a clear working plan for the group as regards the topic of budgetary policy. The debates can rather be seen as part of an orientation process. The group had to position itself within EMU's economic governance set-up. At the same time, the relatively favourable economic situation and the increased coordination efforts in the run-up to Stage 3 meant that the need for common action was not felt immediately. The pattern of discussions over budgetary policy only evolved by-and-by. It was following the Austrian presidency that the Eurogroup started to discuss the euro area's policy-mix in a more systematic way. In two successive meetings in February and March 1999 the Eurogroup focused on the topic of multilateral surveillance and the SGP. Based on the Commission's analysis ministers reviewed the budgetary situation in the euro area. These first surveillance exercises already pointed to the topics which would soon become regular items in Eurogroup discussions. Ministers reported and commented on the situation in their own countries. In addition, more general aspects of budgetary policy in the euro area were debated. Interventions pointed to the importance of the SGP and demanded sustained consolidation efforts. Moreover, some ministers emphasised the necessity to look increasingly on the potential for structural reform. Another aspect of the surveillance debates, which is still characteristic of Eurogroup discussions, concerned the evolutionary nature of EMU. In the course of their interventions on budgetary policy participants also expressed their wish that the Eurogroup study the relevance and role of different policy options in greater detail in subsequent meetings.

During the Finnish presidency in the second half of 1999 the common review of the budgetary situation clearly evolved into the Eurogroup's core business. Surveillance topics were scheduled for discussion at nearly every meeting. Moreover, in a round of subsequent meetings the Eurogroup discussed in greater detail country specific situations. Each meeting focused on a pre-defined group of euro area member states (see Table 5.1 on page 116). Moreover, the Finnish Eurogroup president Niinistö, who was an outspoken supporter of enhanced coordination efforts in the area of budgetary consolidation, sought to improve the preparations of the discussion process. He invited individual ministers to act as 'prosecutors'[2] in connection with country specific reviews. The intention behind this initiative was to add a structuring element to the discussions and to kick off debate amongst the group members. As indicated in the previous chapter, the role of the lead commentator is now exclusively left to the commissioner. Nevertheless, the experiment was part of the efforts to refine the functioning of the Eurogroup's informal working method in this policy area and to build an appropriate framework for peer review. Most importantly, the high frequency of budgetary debates soon led to a routinisation of the discussion pattern (see Figure 5.1 on page 118). The SGP's medium-term objective to bring budgets close to balance or in surplus became the key *criterion* for the review of budgetary policy in the euro area, as one participant in Eurogroup meetings points out:

Table 5.1   Establishing the agenda item 'budgetary situation' (policy-mix/ multilateral surveillance) June 1998–December 1999

Eurogroup meeting	*Scheduled topics for discussion*
04/06/1998	
06/07/1998	Budgetary situation in the euro area in 1998/1999
25/09/1998 (enlarged Eurogroup)	Austrian presidency paper on economic policy coordination
26/09/1998	
23/11/1998	
01/12/1998	
18/01/1999	
08/02/1999	Multilateral surveillance under the SGP
15/03/1999	Multilateral surveillance under the SGP
16/04/1999 (enlarged Eurogroup)	
10/05/1999	
12/07/1999	Budgetary situation in the euro area
10/09/1999	Budgetary situation in the euro area Country reviews (Belgium, France)
11/09/1999 (enlarged Eurogroup)	
08/10/1999	Budgetary situation in the euro area Country reviews (France, Ireland, Spain) (Lead commentator)
07/11/1999	Budgetary situation in the euro area Country reviews (Belgium, Finland) (Lead commentator)
29/11/1999	Budgetary situation in the euro area Country reviews (Austria, Portugal)

Note: This information is based on Agence Europe, Bulletin (1998–1999), and anonymous interviews. Blank fields indicate that no discussion on budgetary matters took place.

> The discussions between ministers have led to common standards and reference points with regard to the assessment of the quality of the national budget. Firstly, the interpretation of the 3 per cent objective through the Stability and Growth Pact as a reference point. Secondly, the central question of whether the actual consolidation of the national budget is in accordance with this reference point. Finally, is there sufficient preparation with regard to future problems, [i.e.] ageing populations, public health systems and the reduction of the public deficit? Politicians prefer to judge along these simple criteria and refrain from referring to more complex criteria raised by economists. (Anonymous interview, participant D)

The routinisation of the debate also implied that more programmatic considerations, such as the future evolution of the coordination framework or the composition of the euro area's policy-mix do not play a significant role in the context of the regular reviews of budgetary policy. The medium-term objective of the SGP has become part of an underlying working consensus which functions as the basis for policy assessment but is in itself not subject to contestation. As the interviews with participants in Eurogroup meetings unanimously suggest, individual ministers have never openly questioned the core objectives of the pact in the discussions. However, Eurogroup discussions see participants referring to the general economic ideas behind the pact (see Chapter 2) in specific situations. In particular, in times of crisis, or when individual member states are suspected of too lax an approach with regard to consolidation, ministers remind colleagues of the necessity of the existence of the SGP. Interventions refer to the need for a credible and stable economic policy framework for EMU. Individual participants stress the role of consolidation in securing low interest rates for the euro zone, thus creating a favourable environment for investment. Both the routinisation of the practical application of the pact's key criteria in the review of budgetary policy and the periodic reminders to consider the fundamental ideas behind the SGP have firmly anchored its political philosophy within the group. According to Eurogroup participants the regular informal discussions have stabilised and strengthened EMU's built-in focus on budgetary consolidation. As one of them explains:

> The Eurogroup has been a quantum leap with regard to the achievement of a common understanding of the fundamentals behind EMU. There is now an incredible convergence of views. As the example of us xxx [nationality deleted] shows our views have changed. When we started deliberations in the Eurogroup our position could be described as sceptical – if not hostile – as regards consolidation. These paradigm changes would have never been achieved within the context of ECOFIN which is a horse trading forum without proper discussions. (Anonymous interview, participant G)

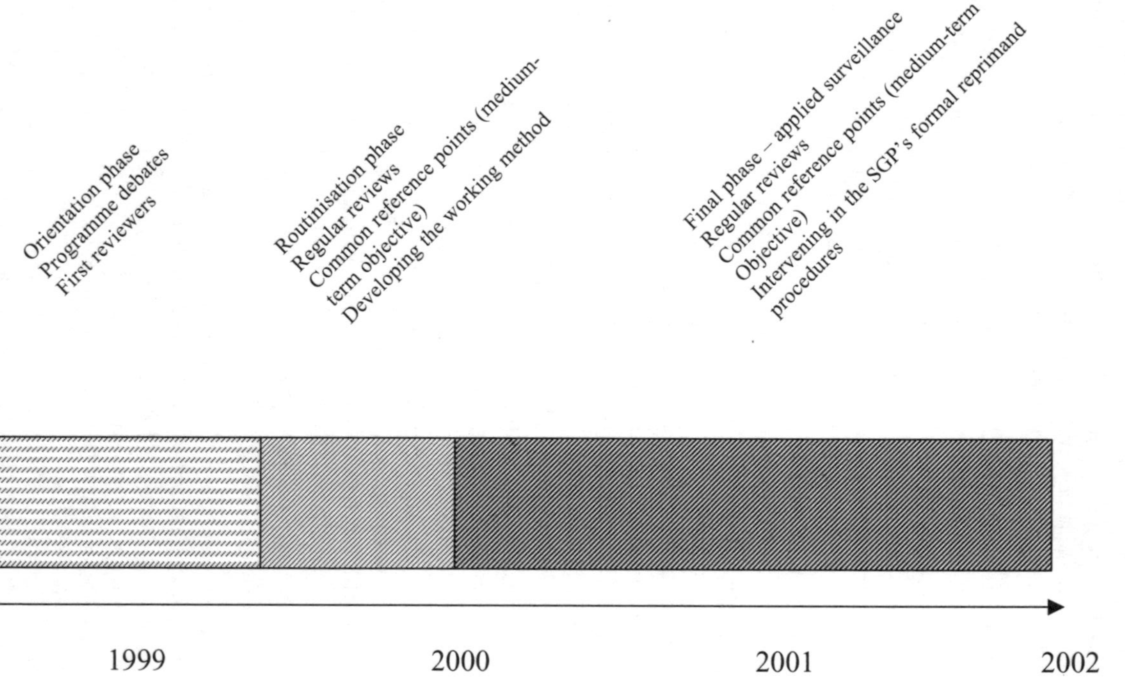

Figure 5.1   The common review of the budgetary situation in the euro area – evolution over time

The Eurogroup has developed into an important forum in operating the pact through firmly integrating the policy objectives of the SGP into its agenda, and by making them the central reference points of the analysis of the budgetary situations. Informal governance functions as a stabilising factor of the overall institutional set-up through fostering consensus formation among ministers. The Eurogroup has made discussion on the SGP criteria a priority by reserving considerable time for the topic, with each meeting addressing the budgetary situation and quite often devoting a third or even half of the time to the topic. Two features of the informal environment are of particular significance. Firstly, ministers have the time to engage in real discussions on individual cases. Those who are subject to criticism have the opportunity to respond. Secondly, the informal setting leaves room for reference to the economic ideas behind the pact, thus creating and keeping alive a consensus on the fundamentals. This consensus in turn acts as a key reference point to which ministers can refer when they remind individual colleagues of their obligations in relation to the euro area community.

In addition to mutual reassurance about the key objectives of the pact the common process of (re-)interpreting central aspects of its application and operation have played an important role. A prominent example is the convergence of views on the issue of how to assess budgetary situations which has been reached over time. The divergence of views on this issue goes back to the time when the SGP was first negotiated. The negotiations of the SGP unfolded over a period of two years. While general agreement on the basic idea of a stability pact for the EU was quickly achieved among all member states (Stark 2001) the individual aspects of the envisaged disciplining mechanism were more contested. As has been demonstrated in Chapter 2, the degree of political discretion reserved for the Council in the operation of the SGP was at the centre of the controversies. Similarly, different attitudes towards the objective of sustained consolidation existed. The differences mainly concerned the implementation of this objective over the economic cycle and the question of on which indicators the assessment of national budgetary situations should be based. To a large extent this economic question was linked to the political quarrel about the degree of discretion reserved for decision-makers in the operation of the pact. The definition of simple nominal criteria for the assessment of the appropriateness of national budgetary policy, such as the 3 per cent target of the medium-term rule, restricts the scope for political interpretation. Either a member state complies with this objective or not. The demand for procedural unambiguity with regard to the implementation of the SGP therefore goes hand in hand with the preference of simple nominal assessment criteria. However, from an economic point of view the nominal GDP deficit ratio does not necessarily reflect the actual budgetary situation of a country in an appropriate way because this figure explains nothing about the structural dimension of budgetary planning. For example, a continuously expanding annual deficit of 2.6 per cent of GDP in a country which is close to full employment, might ring the alarm bells of the guardians of the SGP. In contrast, the same nominal figure might be fully justified in a country which is in recession and witnesses a peak in its unemployment rate. However, due to the technical difficulties in calculating the accurate structural deficit of a country the latter assessment method can facilitate attempts to circumvent the rules.

If one looks back to the time when EMU was negotiated, but also later when the SGP was approved, it was possible to identify more or less clearly two camps within the EU. These camps differed in their attitude towards the assessment of budgetary situations. While one group of countries, led by Germany and the Netherlands, emphasised the role of nominal targets others, such as France and Italy, favoured a greater role for structural indicators. Due to the history of the SGP as a German project the assessment of the budgetary situation followed very much the idea that coordination should be based primarily on nominal targets. However, the practice of Eurogroup discussions shows that the actual working consensus, which has evolved over time, lies somewhere between the extremes. As one participant in Eurogroup meetings observes:

> Initially the discussion on budgetary policy within the Eurogroup was more based on the German view that nominal targets are the basis for policy coordination. Italy always emphasised together with France the need to take the structural situation into account as well. In total, the interpretation of budgetary policy has changed with less emphasis on nominal indicators today. (Anonymous interview, participant E)

And another participant in the discussions, who welcomes the greater focus on structural indicators, relates the evolution of the current practice to the improvement of the statistical methods for the analysis of the budgetary situation in the euro area. With regard to the initial experiences with the analysis of the budgetary situation in the Eurogroup the interviewee self-critically remarks that decision-makers paid

> excessive attention to targets as set in the stability programmes of individual member states. And then when the economy changes you don't fulfil the targets and so what? I mean that is to me not very surprising and I think one should not make too much of a fuss about it. To me it is in a way much more important that we should act in a way that keeps the 3 per cent limit without a risk, which is not necessarily the case now, for instance. There I would pay more attention. Otherwise I would indeed, and I think this has happened over time, we have increased the attention paid to cyclically adjusted balances. I think that will again improve the quality of the implementation because it makes for a more intelligent discussion, to have more weight laid on cyclically adjusted balances. The reason why we couldn't do it earlier might be perhaps that we didn't understand it very well, partly also

because we didn't have an agreed method of cyclical adjustment. Now, we have a better method developed by the Commission and the EPC – the production function method for making the adjustment assessments of output gaps. We are now on better grounds. (Anonymous interview, participant F)

This applied working consensus is the result of an intensive informal dialogue. The fact that the current working consensus has emerged from the actual experiences in reviewing budgetary situations has strengthened the perception that the pact is a genuinely common tool rather than a policy instrument imposed by one powerful player. Eurogroup discussions have reconciled two initially opposed positions. The overall orientation of the agenda towards the issue of budgetary consolidation has led to a strengthening of EMU's stability regime. This corresponds to the initial German wish to enhance compliance with the deficit rule in Stage 3 through supplementary measures. At the same time, the implementation of the pact is much more based on structural indicators than initially foreseen. The shared practice of the reviewing process has facilitated the surmounting of previously existing ideological cleavages. Most importantly, this practice has created an environment of mutual trust that allowed the discussion of alternative approaches to the assessment of budgetary situations which were previously rejected by those who suspected a loophole in the disciplining mechanism. Moreover, changes in the budgetary situation of the respective countries over time have demonstrated that the ideological preferences of individual governments and their finance ministries are subject to adjustment as well. Participants accept the Eurogroup as an environment for policy learning and are prepared to reconsider previously held beliefs. As a participant in the discussions explains:

It is a learning process. EMU has no historical precedent. What we are doing is completely new to all of us. That explains why the discussion we have is more a common understanding building process. Nobody is really right or wrong in the beginning. So, it is also explorative. We are learning by doing. One should be aware that this is also a fragile process. The people around the table have to be confident. There is no protection of the great and old EU institutions. You can't lean back because you know that somehow everything will go its way. The challenges are particularly high because there is so much subsidiarity in the economic pillar. And this is a matter of fact. We have to live with that reality. (Anonymous interview, participant C)

The revision of some provisions of the SGP in 2005 reflects the experiences made by policy-makers during the first five years of implementing the pact. To a large extent the revisions (see Chapter 2) formalise a practice of interpreting key aspects of the pact which had evolved informally within the Eurogroup up until then. Although political pressure from those member states having the greatest difficulties in implementing the policy recommendations derived from the pact played a decisive role in terms of the timing of the reform, the introduced changes did not emerge out of the blue. As the above review of the history of Eurogroup discussions on the core aspects of the pact reveals, the idea of putting greater emphasis on a more differentiated approach towards the determination of medium-term budgetary objectives for individual member states, or of better recognising efforts in the area of structural reform,[3] gradually evolved since the Eurogroup became involved in SGP procedures back in 1999. Moreover, the ECOFIN report on 'Improving the implementation of the Stability and Growth Pact' (European Council 2005: 25) explicitly acknowledges the pivotal role the Eurogroup has played in implementing the pact's objectives and governance mechanisms.

Apart from its ability to generate consensus among ministers through informal discussions, the Eurogroup has no means at its disposal to enforce the policies against the will of individual ministers. This fragility of the informal working method is all the more important with regard to actual cases of non-compliant behaviour of individual countries. Therefore, the following three episodes of Eurogroup involvement in formal reprimand procedures under the SGP illustrate in more detail how the informal setting responds to genuine stress tests of the coordination set-up.

Testing the pact: the early warning over the 2001 Irish budget

During the first two years of Stage 3 the Eurogroup's dialogue was not put to significant tests with regard to the application of the SGP criteria. However, as outlined above this period was important because it led to the routinisation of the pattern of budgetary discussions and allowed for minor tests when individual countries were singled out for slippage. More severe tests to the overall coordination set-up have only emerged in the more recent past. Although the real stress test for EMU's stability framework is far from over, important lessons can be learnt from the events during the period between the end of 2000 and the end of 2002 which is analysed in the following sections. This period allows the assessment of the interplay between the informal dialogue within the Eurogroup and the formal SGP reprimand procedures in different situations. Starting with the first so-called early warning ever issued under the SGP – a reprimand addressed to Ireland in connection with its 2001 budget – the following sections discuss four episodes of non-compliance with SGP criteria (see Figure 5.2 below). All four cases deal with the same situation. A member state comes close to breaching a formally defined rule or policy guideline, i.e. either the deficit rule or the BEPGs. In such a situation the procedural provisions of the SGP require the Commission to recommend that the Council address an early warning to the respective country. However, the cases differ in the way the actors who are subject to criticism have inter-acted with the informal governance set-up.

Each year during the course of December euro area member states submit their stability programmes to the Commission and the Council (see Chapter 2). This procedure, which is required under the SGP, responds to the Treaty's demand for the multilateral surveillance of economic policies. In a first step the Commission examines the stability programmes with regard to their consistence with the 3 per cent deficit criterion and the BEPGs. The disrespect of these criteria triggers a series of formal reprimand proceedings. In December 2000 the Commission was particularly concerned about Ireland. The Commission considered the outlined Irish budget for 2001 to be over-expansionary and pro-cyclical. At this time domestic inflation in Ireland was reported to be around 7 per cent. Moreover, the Commission was worried about the fact that the esti-mations of the Irish stability programme were in open contradiction to the current set of BEPGs which had been adopted in the summer 2000. The country-specific chapter on Ireland in the 2000 BEPGs stated:

> There are now firm signs of upward pressure on inflation in the economy and the emergence of supply constraints both physical, including infrastruc-ture, and in the labour market. In view of the above, budgetary policy should aim to:
> (i) be ready, already in 2000, to use budgetary policy to ensure economic stability given the extent of over-heating in the economy; gear the budget for 2001 to this objective;
> (ii) restrain growth in real public consumption from the 4.3% estimated in 1999 to 2.7.% in 2002 as shown in the updated stability programme [of the year 1999]; (Council of the European Union 2000: 57)

In fact, the specific situation of the fast-growing Irish economy had already been discussed before. Moreover, the two previous sets of BEPGs had urged the Irish government to contain inflationary pressures and the risk of overheating through further restrictions in public consumption. However, the Irish budgetary policy had thus far failed to comply with the set margins for a decrease in public consumption. Following the SGP procedures the Commission considered adopting a recommendation to the ECOFIN Council to issue an early warning on the matter to Ireland. However, before launching the formal procedure the economic and finan-cial affairs commissioner Pedro Solbes brought the case before the Eurogroup. At its meeting in January 2001 the group raised the issue with the Irish finance minister Charlie McCreevy. The views of ministers converged very quickly around the assessment presented by commissioner Solbes. Participants strongly urged their Irish colleague to correct the 2001 budget. At the same time McCreevy's critics around the table made clear that they were prepared to help him in case he wanted to act on the

Commission's guidelines. In such a situation the Eurogroup would have backed up his efforts through public statements and a delay of formal reprimand procedures for a certain period of time. However, a discussion about concrete adjustments to the Irish budget never took place. The Irish finance minister rejected outright the position advocated by the rest of the group. McCreevy defended his budget as appropriate and refrained from discussing the suggestions made by his colleagues.

The defiant stance of the Irish finance minister convinced the commissioner that a formal reprimand procedure was inevitable. Moreover, the commissioner had received the unqualified support of all other Eurogroup ministers for his position. This was particularly important because a Commission recommendation on an early warning to Ireland was seen as a decisive step in defending the credibility of the BEPGs as a coordination instrument. The renewed failure of the Irish government to comply with the guidelines demanded a response. In this context, possible difficulties in finding agreement on a Commission recommendation in the Council had further compromised the moral authority of the BEPGs. Only a week after the Eurogroup meeting the Commission for the first time ever adopted a recommendation to the ECOFIN Council to launch an early warning procedure on non-compliance with the BEPGs against Ireland. At the same time the dispute became public with all involved parties communicating their position through the media. While the Irish finance minister remained defiant and justified further budgetary expansion with the need to adjust the country's infrastructure to the booming economy, the Commission, the ECB and individual ministers urged a change in the Irish policy.

When the Eurogroup met again on 12 February 2001, ahead of the ECOFIN meeting, which had to decide upon the Commission recommendation, the positions had already hardened. McCreevy explained his negative reaction to the Commission recommendation. However, the critical stance of the other participants remained unambiguous. For the final time euro area ministers reassured each other that they supported the Commission recommendation. Only hours later the ECOFIN Council adopted the proposed early warning against Ireland. The pattern of the discussion clearly demonstrated the key role of informal discussions within the Eurogroup in relation to the management of the formal SGP procedures. For the Commission the discussions proved to be crucial because they ensured that the seriousness of the situation was conveyed to the Irish. The strong backing from ministers demonstrated that the commissioner was not alone in criticising the Irish policy. Moreover, the proceedings demonstrated that the Commission regards the Eurogroup as the pivotal forum for discussion of SGP related issues. The commissioner and ministers alike were also prepared to accept an informal commitment on the part of the Irish finance minister as a way of avoiding a formal reprimand. Such an offer demonstrated that the involved actors regarded the Eurogroup as the key forum for conflict resolution in EMU. However, the incident also demonstrated that the general atmosphere characterised by mutual trust and the readiness to offer support to countries which face difficulties in meeting common policy objectives is easily jeopardised when individual actors no longer engage in substantial discussion. The rest of the group very quickly united against McCreevy when it became clear that he fundamentally opposed a discussion on the Irish policy. The stance of the Irish minister did not resonate with the group consensus. The open rejection of previously agreed objectives in the Irish stability programme and the discussions only hardened the united front against him. As a participant in Eurogroup meetings observes:

> McCreevy was simply not prepared to give answers. That is why the whole thing went formal. Otherwise it could have been resolved without much noise. The consensus among the critics was there and emerged very quickly. All the major institutions such as the IMF, the World Bank and the Commission came to the same assessment. At the same time, people were really prepared to help Ireland but there was simply no way through. In the Austrian[4], German and Portuguese cases it was different. Ministers felt reassured by their colleagues. (Anonymous interview, participant E)

Avoiding a formal reprimand: the German-Portuguese early warning compromise

One year after the Commission had considered its first reprimand of a member state the next cases of non-compliance emerged. The budgets of Portugal and Germany gave reason for concern. While the Irish case had centred on the pro-cyclical effects of the country's budgetary policy this time the focus shifted to the core objective of the SGP – the control of public deficits. The rapid expansion of the public deficits in Germany and Portugal throughout the year 2001 conflicted with the SGP criteria. Against the background of sluggish growth prospects for the German economy a break of the 3 per cent ceiling for 2002 appeared to be a possibility. In the case of Portugal, the fact that the country had failed to restrain the expansion of its deficit at the beginning of the downturn despite a prolonged period of strong domestic growth over the last years gave reason for concern. In both cases the pattern of interaction between the critics and those who were singled out for slippage was very similar. Moreover, with regard to the time frame the Commission, the Council and the Eurogroup handled the German and Portuguese cases simultaneously. Therefore, the key developments in the two cases are discussed here in parallel. Despite the parallel time structure the two cases differ with regard to the size of the involved parties. As the biggest euro area economy Germany received by far the most attention in this scenario.

country size

Negotiation attitude		**big**	**small**	
	cooperative	*Dec 2001- Feb 2002* **Germany** Hans Eichel *(April 1999)*	*Dec 2001- Feb 2002* **Portugal** Guilherme Oliveira Martins *(July 2001)*	time period country minister (member of the group since)
	non-cooperative	*May - Oct 2002* **France** Francis Mer *(June 2002)*	*Dec 2000 – Feb 2001* **Ireland** Charlie McCreevy *(June 1998)*	

Figure 5.2 Discussing non-compliant behaviour under the SGP early warning scheme – the four cases

From the beginning the media and representatives from the smaller member states suspected that there would not be equal treatment for Germany. It was felt that the country would use its powerful political and economic position to fend off any substantial criticism raised within the context of the fragile reprimand procedures of the pact.

In contrast to the Irish case the consolidation course of the German social-democratic finance minister Hans Eichel had up to that point been very much in line with the common policy guidelines. Moreover, the minister, who had come into office in April 1999, enjoyed great respect among his colleagues within the Eurogroup. Eichel was known as an outspoken supporter of the informal discussions and a prominent advocate of the group consensus. Moreover, the minister felt strongly encouraged by the group in his efforts to gain domestic support for his consolidation course.[5] However, as regards the specific context of the year 2001 the problem of the German budget did not emerge out of the blue. It became visible to observers long before the German government submitted the annual stability programme before the Christmas break. At the beginning of October German deputy finance minister Karl Diller had acknowledged in a letter to the budgetary committee of the lower house of the German parliament, the Bundestag, that there were considerable cyclical risks which could lead to a deficit of more than 3 per cent in 2002 if the current budgetary plans were to be maintained. On 27 November German finance minister Hans Eichel told the Bundestag in Berlin that the room for manoeuvre included in his 2002 budget was indeed very narrow and that there were indications of a further deterioration of the cyclical situation during the course of the year 2002.

A week later the Eurogroup discussed the budgetary situation in the euro area ahead of the submission of the national stability programmes. Some participants were outspokenly critical with regard to the German budgetary plans and demanded adjustments.[6] Eichel argued along the line of his speech to the Bundestag saying that the drafted budget was tight but designed to meet the 3 per cent criterion. The concerns with the German situation were reflected in the statement commissioner Pedro Solbes made at the Eurogroup press briefing the next day. The commissioner said that he expected all member states to remain below the 3 per cent ceiling. However, without naming any particular country he warned that those countries which had not brought their budgets close to balance or into surplus before the current economic downturn, were now the subject of 'particular concern'.[7] This formula applied to France, Germany, Italy and Portugal which had only recorded a budget surplus for the year 2000.

In the case of Portugal, the figures suggested a rapid expansion of the government deficit in 2001. Moreover, the Portuguese government had announced that it was likely to miss by a few days the 15 December deadline for the submission of its national stability programme. In fact,

Portugal went through a domestic political crisis. On 17 December António Guterres resigned as Portuguese prime minister after six years in office. The socialist prime minister, who had presided over the Lisbon European Council meeting on economic reform, was seen by many as one of the ideational front runners of a new European approach to socialism. Guterres's resignation had been triggered by the humiliating defeat of his socialist party in a round of local elections. Observers linked the sharp decrease in the popularity of the prime minister and his party to the falling growth levels of the Portuguese economy. Moreover, Guetrres's cabinet had enforced unpopular spending cuts in an attempt to cope with falling tax revenues. Despite the government's record in the area of structural reform and consolidation, doubts emerged over the state of Portugal's public finances.[8] This speculation was further substantiated at the beginning of 2002 when the governor of the Portuguese central bank Vitor Constancio issued a statement warning about the state of the country's public finances. He criticised the Portuguese government for failing to use the unusually strong growth of its economy over the previous years to consolidate its budget. The central banker saw his country ill-prepared for the current economic downturn and considered the aim of a balanced budget as 'ambitious'.[9]

Although not mentioned on the draft agenda, which had been circulated to the media ahead of the meeting, the Eurogroup devoted some time to the German and Portuguese situation at its next meeting on 21 January 2002. Commissioner Solbes was by now convinced that the situation in the two countries was very serious and that action on the part of the Commission might be inevitable. In order to obtain the views of ministers on this position and to send a clear signal to the Germans and Portuguese he chose to inform the Eurogroup in advance that he seriously considered recommending an early warning for the two countries. This time the achievement of a consensus within the group was more difficult than in the Irish case. Whilst in general concern over the two budgets was shared, many did not consider that the situation was serious enough to justify a formal reprimand. In contrast to the Irish case the ministers in the spotlight did not question the common rules. Eichel argued that his budget already acknowledged the need to remain under the 3 per cent ceiling. His Portuguese colleague Guilherme Oliveira Martins stressed that his government had already reacted to the sharp fall in government revenues in 2001 through additional spending cuts. Given the deteriorating economic situation the question rather was about the credibility of the promises of the two ministers with regard to their plans for 2002.

The language used by Eurogroup president and Spanish finance minister Rodrigo Rato when he was speaking to the press after the meeting illustrated that the group was caught in a dilemma. On the one hand, the prevailing economic uncertainty made it difficult to give the German and

Portuguese budgets the green light. On the other hand, an immediate start of formal proceedings would have meant disregarding the promises given by the two ministers. Rato underlined that Eurogroup ministers thought that the overall budgetary policy of the countries was 'correct'[10] but warned that no further modifications should be made which could lead to increased risks. By emphasising that the Commission 'by now has not taken the initiative'[11] commissioner Solbes for his part made clear that the affair was far from over. In particular, the high degree of respect enjoyed by the German finance minister within the group made it difficult for many to reject his reiterated commitment to the SGP criteria as mere lip service. At the same time, the presentation of such a tight draft budget in a situation of great economic uncertainty appeared to be highly problematic, as a participant in Eurogroup meetings comments:

> Eichel appeared to be much more credible than others when he made his promises with regard to the German [2002] budget. However, to tell the group that Germany will not cross the 2.9 per cent exacerbated the smaller member states. This is quite something to say. In a situation where everything is unclear to claim to know that the budget will stay in such tight limits is absolutely incredible. (Anonymous interview, participant G)

Solbes was soon convinced that the German and Portuguese budgets in their then existing form were on the edge. For him it was clear that the deteriorating economic situation made further adjustments inevitable. Obviously, the commissioner had wanted to see some sort of commitment to additional measures on the part of the two ministers at the January Eurogroup meeting. This became clear when the Commission adopted a recommendation to the ECOFIN Council at the end of January to start an early warning procedure. For Solbes reassurance that the two countries were keen to remain within the set limits was not enough:

> For the Commission, such slides in the German and Portuguese public deficits are major, meaning that the conditions are there to launch an early warning procedure against these two countries.[12]

However, the commissioner also underlined that he was not critical of the overall orientation of German budgetary policy but that changes in the economic situation needed to be addressed more convincingly. He was particularly concerned that Germany could not achieve the common objective to balance its budget by 2004. Referring to the Portuguese situation Solbes highlighted that he was not concerned about the current level of the deficit but about its sharp rise in 2001. He spoke of a wrong budgetary policy for the year 2001. Portugal's deficit rose from 1.4 per cent in 2000 to 2.2 per cent in 2001. This stood in sharp contradiction with the 1.1 per cent deficit margin initially envisaged in the 2001 BEPGs and the recommendation to further restrain public expenditure (see European Economy

2001: 98). Solbes related the expansion of the deficit to cyclical and structural factors and demanded additional measures which would address the fall in government revenues. He stressed that the Portuguese government had to do everything in order to achieve its revised 1.8 per cent deficit objective for 2002 (see Portugal 2001: 7). The differentiated nature of the criticism was illustrated by Solbes's praise of the Portuguese government for having reacted to declining growth levels through extra spending cuts:

> It is true that the Portuguese government identified the risk of such a slide and thus adopted an extraordinary budget representing 0.6% of GDP. These measures contributed in reducing the growth in governmental spending, but were not enough to avoid a large slide.[13]

Commenting on the Commission's decision the Portuguese finance minister Oliveira Martins insisted that an early warning made no sense because Portugal was already in line with the common guidelines and had so far received the unqualified backing of the Commission for its budgetary policy approach. However, this defence stood in contrast to accusations raised during the ongoing parliamentary election campaign in Portugal. The centre-right Social Democratic Party (PSD) accused the ruling socialists of releasing false budgetary figures. The PSD leader José Manuel Durão Barroso even demanded an external audit of the public accounts after a potential election victory. He also pointed to a possible revision of Portugal's commitment to the budgetary objectives specified at the European level.[14]

The German government reacted even more forcefully to the Commission's decision. It increased the pressure on the Commission and other member states by openly questioning the appropriateness of the early warning recommendation. The German chancellor Gerhard Schröder rejected the initiative outright. As German newspapers reported, finance minister Eichel had hesitated to follow the more confrontational course of his chancellor. Initially, the minister had seen the Commission's decision as a boost for his own consolidation policy with regard to the political discussion within the domestic arena.[15] Finally, the French finance minister Laurent Fabius declared in a speech that he found it difficult to agree on an early warning to Germany because Germany's budgetary policy was solid.[16] Many observers judged this statement as an attempt to exploit the situation in order to change the rules of the game because the French knew that they could be the next country receiving an early warning. Only a few days after displaying his scepticism with regard to the Commission's initiative Fabius announced gloomy growth prospects for the French economy and admitted a rise in public debt.[17]

In this highly politicised atmosphere the Eurogroup met again on 11 February 2002 ahead of the decisive ECOFIN Council meeting which had to decide on whether to adopt or reject the Commission's recommendation. Participants were especially concerned about the announcement included in the German stability programme to delay the date for a balanced budget for two years. The Germans now were targeting the year 2006 instead of 2004 (see Bundesministerium 2001: 29). This intention contradicted the 2001 BEPGs. When the meeting started the participating ministers and their advisers were very well aware of the huge challenge to credibility which this situation posed. Many were irritated by the political pressure which was built up by the German chancellor. Nevertheless, the Eurogroup managed to form a consensus. During the discussion ministers pointed out that the Commission was not alone in considering the German and Portuguese situation to be very serious and that further reassurances had to be made. In addition, several ministers from smaller countries were concerned because a bigger member state was about to fend off an early warning while a smaller country like Ireland had received one without much discussion. This time the German finance minister Eichel went further than at the last meeting. Reacting to the criticism, he promised his colleagues that he would meet the 2004 objective for a balanced budget and not delay it until 2006, as foreseen in the German stability programme. Eichel reassured the group that he intended to do everything in order to avoid a breach of the 3 per cent objective. Moreover, the German finance minister promised to seek an agreement between the federal government and the federal states (Länder) on a national stability pact ensuring that Germany's budgetary position remained under control despite the autonomous budgetary competences of the federal states. Germany had to declare its intention to undertake increased stabilisation efforts in a public statement. The Portuguese government had to make similar reassurances. In turn, ministers agreed not to enact the Commission's recommendation in the ECOFIN Council.

As in the Irish case, the Eurogroup played a crucial role in the decision-making process (see Figure 5.3 below). In fact, the group proved to be the key handler of cases of non-compliance with the SGP procedures. Again the Commission used the Eurogroup to seek a consensual solution among euro area ministers prior to formal decisions. A Eurogroup participant underlines that the Commission

> had timed the whole thing deliberately in a way that the commissioner would first have the opportunity to announce the early warning in the Eurogroup and then in the Commission meeting afterwards the Commission enacted it. Thus the sequence was deliberately chosen in a way that one first could have a discussion informally within the Eurogroup and then the Commission would make its decisions. Consequently, the Eurogroup plays a decisive role in the preparation of these things ... and after the Commission's decision it was again in the Eurogroup. ECOFIN finally had to make the decision but it was pre-discussed in the Eurogroup the night before. (Anonymous interview, participant A)

In contrast to the Irish case the ministers who were subject to criticism reacted in a much more cooperative way. In particular, the behaviour of the German finance minister Eichel was carefully watched by the ministers from the smaller member states within the group. Instead of showing his outright opposition to the criticisms Eichel appealed to the existing group consensus on the SGP. The minister made it clear that he stood firmly behind the pact and that his budgetary policy was designed to fulfil the common criteria. Far from rejecting this as mere lip service the group was caught in a dilemma. The credibility enjoyed by Eichel so far stood in sharp contrast to the minister's initial reassurances in the January Eurogroup meeting that the German budget would under no circumstances breach the 3 per cent ceiling. Such a promise was not credible against the background of a deteriorating economic situation. Both for the Commission and the other ministers the Eurogroup discussions became the touchstone for the credibility of the two ministers under criticism. After the January meeting Solbes saw no alternative but to recommend early warnings to Germany and Portugal because he suspected inaction on the part of the two countries. However, the reassurances made during the February meeting responded to these concerns. Most decisively, Germany had promised to better coordinate budgetary developments within its federal system and pledged to comply with the objective of the 2001 BEPGs to strive for a balanced budget in 2004. Against this background it becomes clear how important the political role of the Eurogroup was in shaping the outcome. The group consensus emerged in a round of successive meetings. This process began with the December meeting and materialised only after long discussions at the final Eurogroup gathering before the ECOFIN decision on the recommendation by the Commission in February. When this final meeting had started a political consensus was still pending. Once this consensus had been found there was, as in the Irish case, no doubt which decision the ECOFIN Council would take.

France challenges the deficit rule

In March 2002, only a short time after the compromise over the early warning recommendations concerning Germany and Portugal, the European Council in Barcelona reaffirmed that EU governments stood behind the objective of national budgets being balanced or in surplus by 2004. Eurogroup ministers reportedly felt reassured that they had weathered the storm and that they had managed to organise strong support behind the SGP objectives. However, more trouble lay ahead. During the spring campaign for the re-election of French president Jacques Chirac he and his supporters declared several times that they did not feel bound by the commitment of EU leaders to achieve balanced budgets by 2004. Some

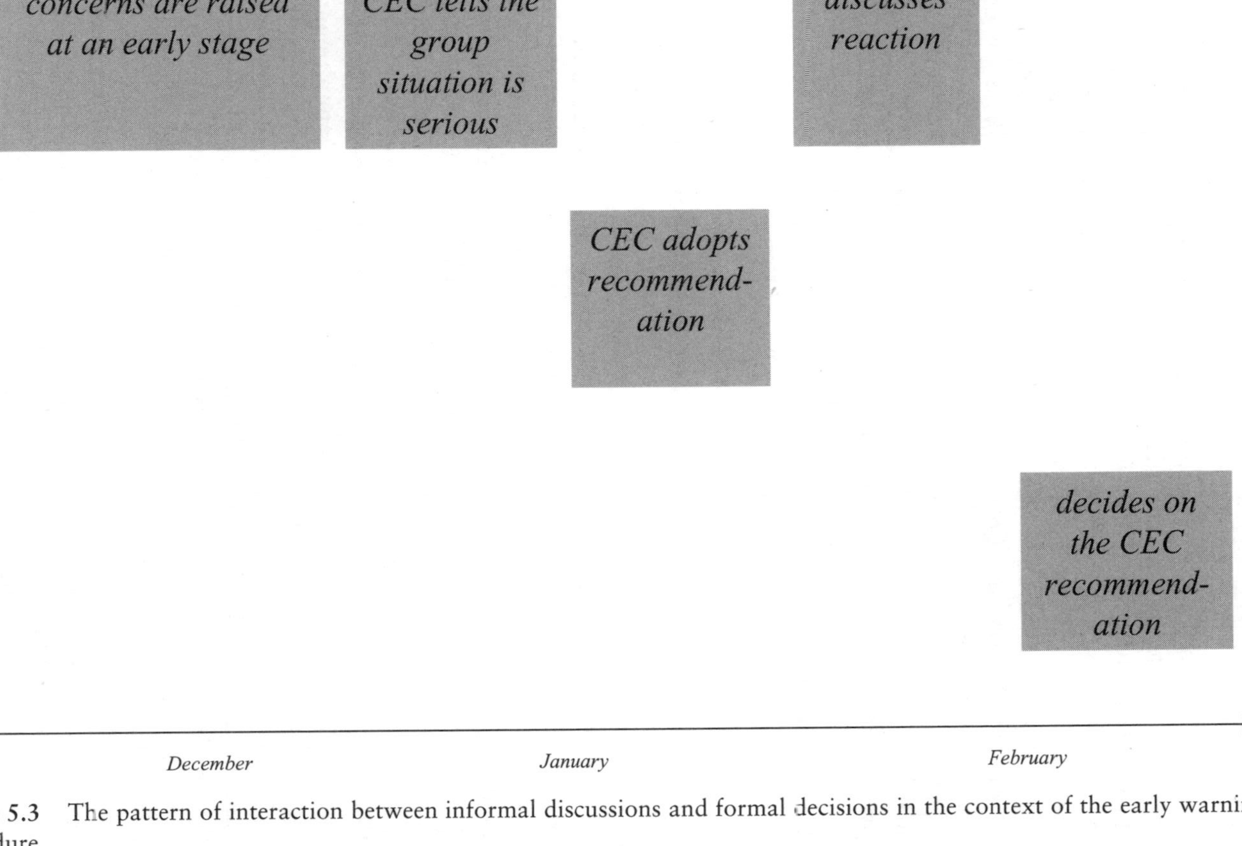

Figure 5.3   The pattern of interaction between informal discussions and formal decisions in the context of the early warning procedure

of the campaigners even spoke of a delay until 2007. On 6 May 2002 the
Eurogroup met in Brussels just one day after Chirac's election victory.
Shortly before the meeting French media reports had emerged that
Chirac's campaign statements were still valid. However, the French situation was not on the agenda and no clarification could be hoped for from
the French side. It was the night before the new centre-right interim
government under Jean-Pierre Raffarin was to be sworn in. However, the
public statements by members of Raffarin's new cabinet, which were
made over the next days, were unambiguous. The new French government
only intended to comply with the European criteria if growth would
permit it.[18] At this time, growth rates were already falling. With a view to
the upcoming elections to the national assembly politicians were keen to
emphasise that they were ready to enact the wide-ranging tax cuts which
had been promised during Chirac's campaign. These statements immediately provoked public reactions by several Eurogroup members. Amongst
the critics of the new French position was also German finance minister
Eichel who declared on 14 May 2002:

> I don't understand how Mr Chirac can vote in favour in Barcelona and say
> a few weeks later that this no longer applies.[19]

On the same day commissioner Solbes told the European Parliament in
Strasbourg that he did not think the French idea of postponement would
be helpful.[20] On 5 June 2002 the new French finance minister Francis Mer
participated in the Eurogroup for the first time. He admitted that there
were problems with the French budget and spoke of an uncertain situation ahead of the usual post-election assessment of the state of public
finances. In addition, Mer made the French commitment to the 2004
deadline depend on the completion of an internal audit of the state's
finances. This was particularly problematic because the ECOFIN Council
had to decide on the Commission's draft recommendation for the 2002
BEPGs before the final European Council meeting under the Spanish EU
presidency. The Commission's draft contained a renewed commitment to
the 2004 deadline. Mer's statement made an ECOFIN Council decision at
the beginning of June impossible. An additional meeting had to be scheduled for 20 June 2002 – the night before the summit of EU leaders in
Seville. After a six-hour debate France finally backed the 2004 deadline
although the original text was slightly revised allowing more room for
interpretation.

Meeting on 15 July the Eurogroup addressed the reluctant stance of the
new French finance minister with regard to the implementation of the
common consolidation objectives. During the discussion on the stance of
the French government participants intervened in favour of the principles
of the pact and sought to convince Mer that the consolidation objectives
needed to be respected. Interventions referred to the fundamental ideas

behind the pact and pointed to the beneficial aspects of the stability framework. The appropriateness and necessity of the objectives, which had been reaffirmed in Seville, was underlined. Following this discussion participants were confident that the Eurogroup was now firmly united behind the Madrid conclusions.[21] The impression prevailed that the row with the French minister was now less serious than before. As a participant in Eurogroup meetings explains, in times of crisis the informal discussions within the Eurogroup can provide crucial backing for the Commission in its role as a watchdog in the context of the SGP procedures:

> It is quite important that the ministers themselves engage in looking at such an issue and are also forced to listen to what the Commission, the ECB and other member states have to say. I think this is an experience which Germany and Portugal made at the beginning of this year and which is now made by France and Italy. Everybody knows approximately where the Commission stands but in the Eurogroup it emerges that the Commission is not at all isolated regarding these issues. Especially, the pressure built up by the smaller member states in relation to the bigger countries is very very high. ... And this creates a certain situation of group dynamic which very much helps the Commission. This is much more helpful than the Commission only talking with one finance minister or a big country. When in such a group situation six smaller countries – using partially very clear language – remind the bigger countries to what they have committed themselves then this has of course a very positive impact on these countries. That is why one must not underestimate the group dynamic situation in such a group. (Anonymous interview, participant A)

Over the summer break the economic situation and with it the tax revenues were further deteriorating. In background conversations with journalists senior Commission officials already indicated that France was close to a situation in which the launch of an early warning procedure would become inevitable. At the same time the public debate over the SGP intensified. The French position was defended as an attempt to counter the cyclical downturn. On 4 September 2002 the Finnish finance minister Niinistö speaking on behalf of a number of smaller member states used an interview with the *Financial Times* to defend the SGP and categorically rejected any slippage by bigger countries. Niinistö also referred to the promises of tax cuts made by the new French and Portuguese governments in the context of their respective election campaigns. He denounced such a strategy as free-riding in relation to other euro area countries. The finance minister highlighted the fact that it was easy for these countries to behave in such a way because the monetary union protected them from rising interest rates or a fall in the exchange rate of their national currency.[22]

On 6 September 2002 the finance ministers gathered in Copenhagen for the Eurogroup and the informal ECOFIN meetings. The Commission had already reduced its growth forecast for the euro area. After the meeting the French finance minister Mer declared that his country would not be able to meet the 2004 objective. Knowing very well that he was challenging the set of common rules once again Mer defended his stance by saying:

> It is not necessary to adhere too strictly to the letter. It is more important to act in the spirit of the SGP.[23]

Again a series of public criticisms mainly voiced by smaller member states was provoked. In this situation the Commission announced at the end of September the delay of the 2004 deadline for achieving budgets in balance or in surplus. With this decision the Commission had reinterpreted the medium-term rule. As has been outlined in Chapter 2, the SGP specifies the objective of bringing budgets close to balance or in surplus over the medium-term. The actual medium-term objective is specified in the national stability programmes. In addition, it is possible to define a concrete time frame within the BEPGs, as had happened in case of the 2004 deadline. Finally, the European Council may decide to increase commitment to this objective through a common declaration. The definition of the time period in which member states should achieve the target of a balanced or even positive budget can of course differ following the development of the economic cycle. Therefore, the Commission's adjustment of the medium-term rule was fully consistent with the SGP procedures. However, given the public debate over the validity of the SGP the adjustment further contributed to a general feeling of uncertainty over the implementation of the SGP criteria.

In this context, the members of the Eurogroup were determined to restore confidence in the common rules. At their meeting in October they sought to put an end to the public debate over the pact. The group's working consensus once more worked with all ministers firmly backing the pact and agreeing on a common understanding on the course of budgetary policy over the coming years. In a debate lasting for several hours they put considerable pressure on their French colleague and tried to convince him of the shared policy objectives. Finally, Mer agreed to back a common understanding on the condition that it noted his opposition concerning the objective of increased consolidation efforts by those member states not yet having budgets in balance or in surplus. The common understanding was published as a separate Eurogroup press statement – the second in the group's history. The decisive passage read as follows:

> Ministers re-affirmed their commitment to the Treaty obligation to avoid excessive deficits, and to the Stability and Growth Pact objective to achieve and maintain budgetary positions close to balance or in surplus over the

economic cycle. Ministers and the ECB concurred therefore with the Commission that those countries which have not yet reached that objective, need to pursue continuous adjustment of the underlying balance by at least 0.5% of GDP per year. All ministers but one accept this to start no later than in next year's budget. For any member state with an excessive deficit, this adjustment is clearly not enough. Ministers commit themselves to put forward in the 2002 updates of their stability programmes credible adjustment paths, based on realistic assumptions on the economic outlook, and well specified measures. (Eurogroup 2002)

With accepting this statement the French minister had agreed to being publicly singled out as the only participant with a deviating position. This was a clear indication that the group pressure had worked. One month later commissioner Solbes announced that he would propose a recommendation to the ECOFIN Council on an early warning to France because of the danger of the occurrence of an excessive deficit. This time Mer responded in a more conciliatory tone. The French minister underlined in public statements shortly after Solbes' announcement that he was committed to tackling the deficit problem and stood behind the pact. He also made clear that he did not intend to seek a veto of the Commission's recommendation in the ECOFIN Council by saying:

> It is the duty and the right of the Commission to address a warning to France over the approach of the 3% deficit criterion.[24]

Differing from the Irish and the German episodes the French case demonstrated the role the Eurogroup plays in defending the SGP in relation to one euro area member state over a longer period of time. As in the Irish case France openly challenged the rules and questioned the appropriateness of the common objectives. The ongoing dialogue within the group had essentially two functions. Firstly, the group sensed very quickly how serious the trouble with the French was. Therefore, participants referred frequently to the fundamental ideas behind the pact and sought to convince the newcomer Mer of the group consensus. Secondly, continued reassurance among the other ministers enabled them to take a determined stance over a longer period of time in their relation to Mer. This stance reflected the underlying working consensus within the group which had emerged since the review of the budgetary situation became a regular item on the Eurogroup's agenda. Asked about whether he believes that the continuing policy review has led to a convergence of views on the SGP a Eurogroup participant interprets the October statement as an expression of the group's underlying working consensus:

> Oh yes, I believe it! The discussion among ministers in the Eurogroup has led to a convergence of views on the SGP. Just to mention the October 2002 statement by the Eurogroup on budgetary objectives. This is the outcome of the long reflection process in the Eurogroup. And it is not only a conver-

gence of views among ministers but also with the ECB. It concerns the policy-mix and they [the decision-makers of the ECB] are obviously crucial for this and dialogue was important. (Anonymous interview, participant C)

Mer was constantly reminded of his duties towards the common interest of the euro area. Again, credibility played a decisive role. Opposition within the group to the French policies was decisively triggered by the outright rejection of the group's working consensus by the newcomer Mer. In addition, many participants were deeply frustrated with the French attitude towards the role of the Eurogroup as a key forum for coordination in Stage 3. Several interviewees expressed their frustration with the ambiguous stance of the French government towards closer policy coordination in EMU. In contrast to its role in the negotiations leading to the creation of the Eurogroup and its regular demands for closer coordination in Stage 3 the country had failed to comply with Eurogroup agreements several times. In the context of the Eurogroup's reaction to the oil price shock in September 2000 (see Chapter 4) the French finance minister had broken the group consensus only hours after the meeting. The row over the budget in 2002 had started with a broken promise and had ended in open resistance to the group's working consensus. As a consequence, confidence in the French commitment to common rules and policy objectives was severely damaged. A Eurogroup press statement from October 2002 literally placed the French minister outside the group. As one participant in Eurogroup meetings comments:

> On the one hand, the French always demand in a very abstract manner the creation of a European economic government; on the other hand, our experiences with the French ministers within the Eurogroup are one of the worst ones we made in the context of these meetings. The French ministers are the ones who show the fiercest resistance when it comes to concrete proposals for coordination. (Anonymous interview, participant G)

For another Eurogroup participant, who thinks in a similar way, the French case illustrates how difficult the issue of a further transfer of decision-making powers to the supranational level in the area of budgetary policy is:

> The French position towards the institutional set-up of the Eurogroup shows the self-contradiction of this set-up very nicely. They want more political power at the EU level but are not prepared to follow the rules set in Brussels. What would have happened in a situation as we have it at the moment [with France openly opposing the commonly agreed policy targets in 2002] if we had more decision-making powers within the Commission? (Anonymous interview, participant E)

Notes

1 *Agence Europe*, Bulletin (26 September 1998).
2 *Agence Europe*, Bulletin (9 September 1999).
3 For the introduced changes to the original Council regulations constituting the SGP see Council Regulations (EC) No. 1055/2005 and 1056/2005 of 27 June 2005, Official Journal (7 July 2005).
4 At the Eurogroup meeting in May 2000 the Austrian finance minister Karl-Heinz Grasser had to make comprehensive reassurances over its consolidation course following a Commission report that Austria's budgetary planning was not ambitious enough with regard to the achievement of common objectives. However, the incident was not related to a formal reprimand procedure. See *Frankfurter Rundschau* (6 May 2000).
5 Anonymous interviews.
6 See *Süddeutsche Zeitung* (18 January 2002).
7 *Financial Times* (5 December 2001).
8 See *Financial Times* (18 December 2001); *Le Monde* (18 December 2001).
9 *Le Monde* (30 January 2002).
10 *Agence Europe*, Bulletin (22 January 2002).
11 Ibid.
12 *Agence Europe*, Bulletin (31 January 2002).
13 *Agence Europe*, Bulletin (31 January 2002).
14 *Financial Times* (30 January 2002).
15 See *Süddeutsche Zeitung* (8 February 2002).
16 *Financial Times* (4 February 2002).
17 *Financial Times* (8 February 2002).
18 See interview with Philippe Marini, budgetary expert of Chirac's RPR, *Süddeutsche Zeitung* (11 May 2002).
19 *Financial Times* (15 May 2002).
20 *Frankfurter Allgemeine Zeitung* (15 May 2003).
21 Anonymous interviews.
22 *Financial Times* (4 September 2002).
23 *Süddeutsche Zeitung* (10 September 2002); my translation.
24 *Süddeutsche Zeitung*, 22 November 2002; my translation.

6

Assessing the Eurogroup's informal working method

The Eurogroup constitutes a unique framework for discussions among euro area finance ministers, the Commission and the ECB. As the preceding empirical analysis has shown, the Eurogroup is firmly anchored within EMU's economic governance framework. The following two chapters review the findings of the case studies in the light of the theoretical argument which was set out in Chapter 1. This chapter assesses the potential of the Eurogroup's informal working method to foster consensus-oriented policy deliberation among the euro area's top decision-makers. It reviews the features of the particular negotiation *setting* constituted by the Eurogroup. In a similar fashion it discusses whether the specific *content* of Eurogroup discussions is compatible with a deliberative style of discussion. Moreover, the discussion reflects on the outcome of the informal debates. Finally, these findings will be contrasted with the prevailing pattern of official Council negotiations, which represent the key framework for intergovernmental decision-making at the EU level.

The main argument brought forward by this study has been that the Eurogroup's influence over economic governance in the euro area depends on its ability to foster consensus on policy formation among ministers, the Commission and the ECB. In the absence of formal decision-making competences the Eurogroup relies on the voluntary commitment of its participants to advocate or enact informal agreements elsewhere. However, the generation of voluntary commitment among independent decision-makers with partially deviating preferences is not a foregone conclusion. Therefore, Chapter 1 paid particular attention to the question of what the conditions are of a successful informal policy dialogue. Here, in particular reference to legal approaches to EU comitology, the literature on policy learning and research on the role of arguing and deliberation in international negotiations has provided the basis of an analytical framework. Following major assumptions of this literature it has been possible to formulate a set of interrelated working hypotheses. It was expected that the occurrence of policy deliberation within the specific context of the Eurogroup is crucial for the potential impact informal governance structures can have on policy formation within EMU's overall governance framework. In order to enhance the applicability of the results of this study to other areas of EU decision-making a distinction has been made between the *setting* in which negotiations take place, i.e. the Eurogroup's informal working method, and the particular *content* of negotiations, i.e. issues related to economic policy coordination. This chapter argues that the empirical findings presented in the previous chapters suggest that the Eurogroup's informal working method is particularly suited to foster processes of policy deliberation. The features of the negotiation setting constituted by the Eurogroup are compatible with the criteria which have been defined in Chapter 1. The same applies to the content of the informal discussions among euro area ministers. The following sections review the empirical findings of this study in the light of these criteria. The discussion will first turn to the role of the negotiation setting and the content of discussions in fostering policy deliberation. It will then address the question of how processes of informal deliberation over policy translate into formal decision-making, both at the domestic and European level. Finally, the process of informal governance within the Eurogroup will briefly be compared with the pattern of formal negotiations within the Council of Ministers.

The negotiation setting

The Eurogroup's *restrictive participation regime* emphasises the role of face-to-face discussions among the euro area's key decision-makers. The review of Eurogroup agenda items has demonstrated that the small number of participants is of utmost importance in all areas of the group's work. Ministers can engage in real debates with arguments and counter-arguments. This form of communicative interaction is one of the most important preconditions of policy deliberation. Policy deliberation evolves on the basis of partially unconnected or even contradictory policy preferences and involves contestation as well as the affirmation of common positions. The interviews with Eurogroup participants unanimously suggest that the open exchange of views is regarded as the core value-added aspect of the informal negotiation setting. The common analysis of the economic situation and the review of budgetary policy particularly benefit from the interactive form of communication. The case studies have provided clear evidence that the frank exchange of views among ministers leads to the generation of political commitment as regards the implementation of common policy objectives. The same is true for the periodic reflection exercises and the discussions on the further development of EMU's institutional architecture. In the area of structural policy the interactive nature of the debate functions as a catalyst for processes of policy learning. The common discussion is highlighting best practices and alternative policy options. Even in the context of the discussions on the state of the preparations for the changeover to the euro the value-added aspect of interactive debates became visible. Although the focus was mainly on organisational and technical questions, the discussion of best practices on the basis of the Commission's scoreboard provided additional incentives for a timely and efficient conduct of the changeover process on the part of euro area member states.

The interactive and deliberative style of Eurogroup debates is further facilitated by the choice of the officials accompanying the ministers to Eurogroup discussions. The decision to pick only the most senior finance ministry officials rather than diplomats underlines the focus of the Eurogroup's agenda on policy deliberation instead of intergovernmental bargaining. Moreover, the advisers of Eurogroup ministers are the masterminds of the national finance ministries. These senior officials often exercise a considerable influence over the political agendas of their ministries. As members of the EFC and/or through their regular bilateral contacts these officials form a close community of senior European decision-makers and share common working experiences, policy ideas and a particular culture of collegiality. The *ideational affinities* prevailing within this circle of senior civil servants widens the 'middle ground for informed conflict' (Sabatier 1993: 140) within the Eurogroup. The existence of such a middle ground has been identified as a crucial basis for policy deliberation.

In general, the Eurogroup's informal working method allows combining political and technical aspects in the discussion process in a way which is hardly known in other EU negotiation contexts involving ministers (see last section of this chapter). The review of the literature on policy deliberation and learning in Chapter 1 has pointed to a dilemma arising in many negotiation settings. On the one hand, the ability of participants to refer to technical arguments in the discussion process has been considered as a crucial factor in adjusting the overall discussion process towards deliberative elements. Therefore, expert groups are generally considered to have fewer difficulties in reaching consensual solutions than circles of ministers. On the other hand, it has been argued that progress in expert negotiations is often hampered by the fact that experts lack the decision-making authority to put certain policy options on the table. Potential solutions, which appear to be reasonable from a technical point of view, might not be considered during the negotiations because of the narrow political mandate of the experts. The Eurogroup's working method partially overcomes this dilemma through assembling *participants with technical knowledge and the most senior decision-makers in the area of economic policy* in one small group. For similar reasons the decision to leave the preparations of Eurogroup discussions to the EFC as the competent expert committee in the area of EMU rather than to use the mixed model of diplomatic and technical preparations of the Council of Ministers has been crucial.

Moreover, the central role of the EFC in the preparations of Eurogroup meetings leads to the emphasis of a particular style of discussion. The *different topics for debate are introduced in the fashion of shared problems of euro area decision-making*. As has been outlined in Chapter 1, the organisation of the discussion around one or several clearly-defined shared problems triggers policy deliberation and learning processes. The Eurogroup has even been able to further improve this instrument through regular reflection exercises. The provision of background information through the Commission services and the lead presentations of the commissioner are vital elements of this preparation strategy. The oral or written summary exercises by the Eurogroup president follow the same logic. A further important improvement in this context has been the creation of the EFC's Eurogroup working party. The preparatory input of this group further emphasises the focus of Eurogroup discussions on shared problems for euro area decision-makers. In principle, the content of Eurogroup negotiations comprises issues of common interest (see below). However, this interest is quite often not as obvious as it might seem from a theoretical point of view. In other words, ministers agree in principle that the economic policies of their respective home countries are a matter of common concern and need to be discussed within the Eurogroup. The application of this underlying working consensus, however, proves to be more difficult. In the context of the debates over specific policies the focus is easily lost. In many situations ministers find it difficult to draw concrete conclusions for policy formation at the domestic level. Here, a more precise formulation of the specific challenges for decision-making and the existing policy options is decisive. The EFC's Eurogroup working party has pursued such a preparation strategy. The theoretical and empirical findings of this study clearly suggest that further improvements in this area are particularly promising with regard to a further strengthening of the Eurogroup's influence on domestic decision-making.

The empirical findings of this study also confirm the role of *confidentiality* as a trigger for policy deliberation in the context of informal discussions among finance ministers. In particular, the discussions on the economic situation and budgetary policy are characterised by a frank exchange of views. Such an atmosphere is crucial with regard to the critical review of national policies and alternative policy options, thus making the Eurogroup setting an important source of peer pressure in EMU's economic governance set-up. The relationship between ministers and the ECB is more complex. In general, the readiness on the part of the ECB to engage in a close policy dialogue with ministers is an indicator that the Eurogroup is regarded as a highly confidential negotiation setting. The central bank has always emphasised the role of confidentiality as a precondition for dialogue over its policy. However, the dialogue with the ECB is still characterised by a certain asymmetry. Whereas the ECB president is frank in his remarks on economic policy in the member states, ministers are less outspoken on the conduct of monetary policy. Further research is needed in order to establish the reason for this reluctance. However, as has been indicated by Chapter 4, this problem is likely to be related to historical sensitivities rather than to a deficiency of the informal working method. In general, the Eurogroup has demonstrated its ability to maintain a high degree of confidentiality over time. Moreover, participants are very well aware of the relationship between the respect of confidentiality and the quality of the discussion process. In particular, the repeated adjustments of the group's communication strategy have further optimised this feature of the informal working method.

The *flexibility of the agenda* is another characteristic feature of the Eurogroup's informal working method. Again, this feature has been identified at the beginning of this book as conducive towards policy deliberation. Both the empirical analysis of the preparation regime of Eurogroup discussions and the review of the different agenda items have demonstrated that the group frequently adjusts its agenda to the particular needs of the discussion process. This flexibility is not only important in the context of unforeseen events to which the group might want to react. Ministers also have the possibility of extending their discussions on specific issues in case it is not possible to find appropriate solutions within the envisaged time frame. Moreover, the Eurogroup has continuously extended the duration of its meetings. The most decisive step in this context has been the decision to reschedule Eurogroup meetings for the night ahead of ECOFIN Council meetings. This arrangement allows the extension of Eurogroup meetings into the night whenever a particular discussion so requires.

In addition, the Eurogroup setting has been found to grant *equal access to participation in the dialogue*. This is another precondition for consensus-oriented discussion behaviour. Equal access to the dialogue is facilitated by the fact that the nationality of individual participants is of less importance within the Eurogroup's informal negotiation setting than within the Council. Moreover, the small circle of participants emphasises psychological factors, such as the *evolution of a culture of mutual trust, assistance and consensus-orientation*. Here, the frequency and duration of face-to-face discussions among finance ministers is important. Eurogroup participants usually begin to know each other quite well after a certain period of shared discussion experience. The *ability to form an opinion on the trustworthiness of the respective counterparts in the discussions* is an important source of individual commitment to informally agreed policy objectives. Table 6.1 below summarises these findings.

Table 6.1 The informal negotiation setting as a catalyst for processes of policy deliberation

		Restricted number of participants	Organisation of the discussion around shared problems	Flexible agenda	Confidentiality	Participants with technical knowledge and decision-making authority	Psychological factors (mutual trust, ideational affinity)
Theoretical framework	**Catalysts for policy deliberation***						
Empirical findings	*Eurogroup's* **informal working method****	Minister plus one approach	EFC Eurogroup working party, lead presentations, presidency letter	Rescheduling of discussions, extension of the debates into the night	In camera meetings, communication is exclusively left to the president in office	Discussions among ministers are backed up by senior policy experts, EFC preparation of the meetings	Small group of only 30 members, high frequency of the meetings

*　*See chapter 1.*
**　*See empirical findings in chapters 3–5.*

The content of negotiations

Besides the negotiation setting the particular content of negotiations has been identified at the beginning of this study as a key factor influencing the orientation of the discussion process towards policy deliberation. In other words, depending on the specific nature of the Eurogroup's agenda items, processes of policy deliberation might be either hampered or triggered. In particular, four criteria for the assessment of the role of the content of negotiations have been specified. Policy deliberation will be triggered wherever the negotiation process involves: 1) reference to economic policy ideas; 2) reference to technical knowledge in the area of economics; 3) the prospect of a solution in the form of a cooperative positive sum game; 4) coordination through consultation and reinforcement. The empirical findings presented in Chapters 3–5 suggest that the topics of Eurogroup discussions essentially fulfil these criteria.

In general, all the key topics of Eurogroup discussions fulfil the *criterion of a cooperative positive sum game*. The Eurogroup understands itself as a community bound together by shared interests. These shared interests emerge from the creation of a monetary union among the Eurogroup countries. For example, the common reviews of the economic situation, which are a regular item on the Eurogroup's agenda, are conducted on that basis. Ministers are eager to provide information on the economic situation in their home countries in order to enable others to adapt to interdependencies, or to react to particular economic developments. As regards the discussion of the global economic situation and the euro exchange rate, the role of the euro area as a single economic and political entity is even more obvious. This particular content of the discussion process triggers processes of policy deliberation. Ministers perceive the economic development of euro area countries as a matter of common concern. As a result of these debates the views of ministers about key economic developments usually converge. This process is further helped by the fact that the discussion is largely based on thoroughly prepared *statistical and technical background information* which is provided by the Commission and the EFC.

Similarly the content of the discussions on budgetary policy has been found to trigger processes of policy deliberation. Budgetary policy coordination conducted within the framework of the Treaty's deficit rule and the SGP is in the interest of all involved actors. Given that the common efforts to maintain sound public finances across the euro area succeed, all countries within the monetary union will benefit in form of low interest rates and inflation levels. Moreover, this internal stability will secure confidence in the euro within international financial markets. Increased consolidation efforts during more favourable periods of economic development will enable euro area countries to maintain government spending during the downturn. This *economic policy idea* is widely shared among Eurogroup participants and can be described as being part of an underlying working consensus (see next section). They are prepared to engage in common discussions on the euro area's policy-mix and the consequences for national decision-making. This form of coordination is essentially based on *consultation and reinforcement*. The underlying collective interest in budgetary consolidation is conducive towards processes of deliberation as regards the analysis of the situation and the choice of appropriate policy options. The regular reviews have rallied consensus around the policy of consolidation among Eurogroup participants. However, this coordination scenario might be threatened by attempts of free-riding. Some euro area countries might decide to consolidate less then others, thus questioning the validity of their commitment to the common rules and objectives. In such situations the reference to key economic policy ideas behind EMU's consolidation regime has proved to be a crucial factor in maintaining and/or restoring the deliberative style of the discussions.

Similar to the discussions on the economic and budgetary situation, the debates about structural policy follow the idea that economic reform is a matter of common concern. The debates are based on the general concern that without more far reaching structural reforms economic policy will not be able to stimulate more pronounced economic growth within the euro area. Moreover, in the context of the discussions about budgetary policy Eurogroup participants regularly alert each other to the fact that monetary and budgetary policy alike might no longer be able to provide significant stimuli for increased economic activity. This common analysis substantiates a general interest among Eurogroup participants to engage in collective policy learning in the area of structural reform. The process of structural reform involves challenges to decision-making which are genuinely new to all Eurogroup participants. This further encourages a deliberative style of the discussion process.

The focus of the discussion on the state of the preparations for the euro changeover on technical and organisational questions limited the scope for policy deliberation. Nevertheless, the coordination of national activities was in the interest of all involved parties. Deliberation occurred in the form of the discussion of best practices as regards the national preparation activities. Finally, the content of the debates about the functioning of the Eurogroup has proved to be favourable to processes of policy deliberation. Eurogroup members strongly believe in the importance of informal discussions among themselves and share an interest in the further improvement of the Eurogroup's working method. In fact, the existence of regular Eurogroup reflection exercises most strikingly demonstrates how much the overall discussion process within the Eurogroup is geared towards policy deliberation. It is in the context of these reflection exer-

Table 6.2 The content of negotiations as a catalyst for processes of policy deliberation

Theoretical framework	Catalysts for policy deliberation*	Cooperative positive sum games	Coordination through consultation and reinforcement	Reference to economic policy ideas	Reference to academic and non-academic expert discourses
Empirical findings	**Content of Eurogroup debates****	Exchange of information and views on the economic situation, coordinated budgetary consolidation, creating stimuli for growth through structural reform, changeover to the common currency, improving the functioning of the Eurogroup	Critical reviews of the economic and budgetary situation, discussion of best practices	EMU's stability framework, limited capability of monetary and budgetary policies to stimulate economic growth highlights the role of structural reform	Discussions refer to economic analysis provided by the Commission and the EFC

*   *See chapter 1.*
** *See empirical findings in chapters 3–5.*

cises that Eurogroup participants seek to optimise the group's ability to generate commitment to the implementation of common policy objectives through continuing policy dialogue. These findings are summarised in Table 6.2.

Routinised informal dialogue and its impact on formal decision-making

The Eurogroup has proved to be a particularly favourable environment as regards the evolution of policy deliberation. Both the negotiation setting and the content of the discussions trigger a deliberative style of communication. This study has been based on the argument that policy deliberation among euro area ministers will translate into voluntary commitment with regard to the implementation of commonly agreed policy objectives. Therefore, the discussion now turns to the outcome of the informal deliberations among euro area ministers, the Commission and the ECB. In Chapter 2 informal governance has been defined as the process in which a certain group of decision-makers agrees *informally* to advocate or enact particular policies while acting in *formal* decision-making contexts. The activities of the Eurogroup follow this model of informal governance. Moreover, not all effects of informal governance are easy to identify – especially for an external observer. For example, the Eurogroup's spectacular crisis mediation exercises prior to ECOFIN Council decision-making in the context of the SGP receive the greatest attention by the media. In such situations the informal coordination of a common euro area position within the Eurogroup is no secret. Instead, the role of informal resources in the form of common policy guidelines or assessment criteria, which have emerged as a result of the informal discussions, is more difficult to identify.

The empirical findings presented in this book suggest that the most obvious manifestations of the group consensus are, in fact, highly intertwined with the more subtle effects of informal policy deliberation. In general, the discussions within the Eurogroup can be understood as a *routinised process of informal policy review* (see Figure 6.1 below). This process follows certain standards and procedures which have been established over time through repeated and successful application. The examination of the economic policies in the euro area is not a one-off event. National policies are permanently subject to scrutiny within the Eurogroup. The assessment of specific cases is influenced through previous experiences with regard to the applicability of certain policy instruments within a given economic situation. Moreover, this routinised process of informal policy review involves recurring reference to an underlying working consensus which has proved stable over time. This working consensus comprises core economic policy ideas, preferred policy options, and routinised procedures and practices with regard to the conduct of the Eurogroup's own work. Eurogroup participants refer to this working consensus when they discuss particular events or country specific situations. However, this working consensus has evolved ever since the Eurogroup started its informal discussions over economic policy. Often the experiences within the regular policy reviews have led to the reinforcement or further evolution of particular aspects of this working consensus. The continuing review of economic policy in the euro area has generated standards of appropriate policy formation. These informal resources guide the work of finance ministers at the domestic level. Individual Eurogroup participants function as advocates of particular policy options which are compatible with the results of Eurogroup discussions. Under certain circumstances the Eurogroup also explicitly coordinates the positions of its members with regard to formal decision-making within the ECOFIN Council or national cabinets.

In the following this general scheme of a routinised informal policy dialogue within the Eurogroup is discussed in greater detail with reference to the common reviews of budgetary policy. This activity figures uppermost in the Eurogroup's agenda and is, therefore, most suited for demonstrating the interplay of the different aspects of informal dialogue. Therefore, the empirical analysis of Eurogroup discussions in Chapters 4 and 5 has paid particular attention to the discourse over budgetary policy. In general, the discussions about budgetary policy have been found to follow a recurring pattern. The Eurogroup *regularly monitors the budgetary situation* in the euro area on the basis of Commission analysis and information on country specific developments by individual ministers. In addition, the group engages in a debate over appropriate policy responses. In a routinised procedure individual ministers face scrutiny as regards their own national policies. Depending on the circumstances a minister is criticised for pursing particular policies or encouraged to further follow an identified course.

This practice of peer review is widely accepted among ministers as an authoritative source of *policy guidance*. This form of policy guidance emerges as a result of the continuing process of peer review. However, this procedure does not imply that specific decisions of national cabinets are pre-agreed within the Eurogroup. In other words, in the context of the regular policy reviews ministers do not promise that their governments will enact a certain decision the day after the Eurogroup meeting. The outcome of these regular informal discussions are *informal resources* which impact on domestic decision-making in a more subtle way. These resources comprise shared beliefs on appropriate policy options, country specific policy guidelines or common understandings on economic and political developments. The impact of informal resources is felt when ministers act as advocates of the group consensus in their communications with the media, or defend certain policy options in debates with cabinet colleagues, parliament or interest groups. These informal resources have also been found informing the periodic formulation of policy guidelines and objectives in the context of EMU's formal coordination procedures. The Eurogroup discussions intervene in the drafting exercise of a new set of BEPGs and influence the formulation of the national stability programmes compiled under the SGP.

Nevertheless, the regular reviews of the economic and budgetary situation can also lead to more explicit forms of policy coordination. As the example of the Eurogroup debate about the oil price shock in September 2000 has demonstrated, ministers reassured each other to avoid national cabinet decisions which would have included the granting of subsidies in reaction to the price shock. Although this attempt failed, the incident became the template for a more direct form of informal policy coordination.

The existence of an *underlying working consensus* has been identified as a key factor in this routinised process of informal policy review. Seen from a historical perspective this working consensus emerged on the basis of core beliefs which were shared among EU policy-makers prior to Stage 3 (see Chapter 2). These beliefs concerned the overall orientation of economic governance in EMU. In this sense the process of informal discussions did not start from scratch. The prospective euro area decision-makers always agreed in principle that the conduct of economic policy within the monetary union remained a national responsibility. They also agreed on the necessity of a framework of common rules and coordination. In particular, the stability orientation of the system figured uppermost in the envisaged coordination agenda. Nevertheless, different interpretations with regard to specific policy objectives and coordination procedures remained. Finally, the ministers, the Commission and the ECB widely agreed that the group of euro area countries needed to advance policy coordination to a greater extent than the rest of the EU. Here, closer contacts among the euro area's top decision-makers were seen as the preferred option.

In the absence of any formal regulations of their work this set of shared beliefs enabled Eurogroup participants to navigate within the new environment. Step by step the increasing routinisation of the informal discussions led to a reinforcement of individual aspects of this working consensus. More and more, the sediments of the Eurogroup's own discussions supplemented the often very broad ideas which constituted the core beliefs of Eurogroup participants at the beginning. Here, the more detailed analysis of a specific discourse over time has been particularly insightful. The analysis of the evolution of the Eurogroup's discourse about budgetary policy has confirmed the above characterisation of the relationship between the continuing policy dialogue and the underlying fundamentals (see Chapter 5). The routinisation of the informal debates comprised both the introduction of assessment criteria and the establishment of working procedures. The SGP objective of bringing budgets close to balance or in surplus over the medium term became the key reference point in the common assessment exercises. In addition, the debates about the budgetary situation increasingly paid attention to structural indicators. This practice implied the reconciliation of previously existing differences with regard to the implementation of EMU's stability policies. As a result the underlying working consensus among Eurogroup participants was reinforced. These developments strengthened the moral authority of the guidance issued by the group in the context of its regular reviews.

These findings from the area of budgetary coordination also illustrate how the idea of a routinised informal policy dialogue helps in a better understanding of the nature of policy learning with EMU's system of economic governance. The notion of policy learning always implies policy choice. However, this choice can be quite restricted or rather open. Bringing in the historical dimension of the evolution of the Eurogroup's underlying working consensus allows a more precise definition of policy learning in the field of budgetary coordination. On the one hand, policy choice is constrained by a system of formal rules and procedures – notably the deficit criteria and the SGP. On the other hand, it has been demonstrated that these formal rules and procedures allow for a high degree of political discretion, a fact which has been explained by the uncertainty of policy-makers when EMU's system of economic governance was set up, and the general reluctance to transfer substantial political authority in the area of budgetary policy to the supranational level. Consequently, there is considerable room for policy choice, and, thus, learning. What is crucial here is to understand learning within the Eurogroup as an ongoing process rather than as a series of separate events. In fact, policy choice is essentially influenced by informal resources which have been generated at an earlier stage. In other words, policy choice is constrained by previous learning in the context of informal discussions. At some point these informal resources might materialise in the form of new supranational rules and procedures. The revision of some provisions of the SGP in 2005 provides an example for such a development.

In addition, the analysis of four cases of non-compliance with common rules and policy guidelines has demonstrated the Eurogroup's ability to act as a forum for crisis mediation. Such situations illustrate particularly well the interplay of the different aspects of the informal policy dialogue. The case of the Irish 2001 budget for the first time brought about a situation in which the Eurogroup intervened in formal decision-making procedures at the European level. The group coordinated the position of euro area countries prior to an official ECOFIN Council meeting which had to take the final decision on the matter. However, this most visible manifestation of the Eurogroup's ability to influence formal decisions through informal coordination marked only the end of a more complex process. When the Commission brought the case of a possible early warning decision over the Irish 2001 budget before the Eurogroup in January 2001 the group members very quickly united in their criticism of the Irish finance minister McCreevy. Two factors were crucial in connection with this unqualified display of support for the Commission's position. The criticism voiced by the Commission with regard to the conduct of Irish budgetary policy was not new to ministers. In fact, the regular reviews of the budgetary situation had frequently pointed to the particular situation of the fast growing Irish economy and the need for a more prudent approach with regard to the level of public consumption. At a more fundamental level the critical stance of Eurogroup participants was motivated by the fact that McCreevy had deliberately ignored, for a second time in a row, the policy guidance of the BEPGs – EMU's key coordination mechanism. The repeated ignorance of common policy guidelines stood in contradiction with the prevailing working consensus within the group that national policies should respect the framework of commonly agreed rules and policy objectives. These informal resources had been generated through numerous discussions in the context of the Eurogroup's continuing informal policy dialogue prior to the actual discussions on the start of formal proceedings against Ireland. Against this background the outright rejection of the criticism through Irish finance minister McCreevy only hardened the views of ministers, the Commission and the ECB. For the latter McCreevy's *non-cooperative* stance confirmed their suspicion that the Irish minister pursued too lax an approach with regard to the implementation of common policy guidelines.

The analysis of the German and Portuguese early warning compromise has confirmed the central role of the Eurogroup in the handling of crucial decisions within the context of the SGP procedures. Again, the Commission consulted the group prior to the launch of formal proceedings. In addition, the Eurogroup pre-agreed the position of euro area countries in preparation for the ECOFIN Council meeting which had to take the final decision on the Commission recommendation. Similar to the Irish case, the actual Eurogroup crisis mediation exercise during the months of January and February 2002 was guided by informal resources generated through the Eurogroup's continuing policy reviews which had taken place before this date. Once more, the Commission's criticism received the backing of ministers. The regular debates on the economic and budgetary situation in the euro area had created a general awareness of the risks inherent in the deteriorating economic situation. The problem of sluggish growth within the German economy was well known and the deterioration of the general economic situation further lowered expectations with regard to the prospects for the biggest euro area economy.

Moreover, the sharp rise in the Portuguese deficit had raised doubts about the sustainability of the envisaged consolidation course long before the beginning of 2002. Again, the empirical findings suggest that the Eurogroup's underlying working consensus informed the actual crisis mediation exercise. Whereas the Irish case had centred on pro-cyclical effects of the national budget, this time the process of budgetary consolidation was at stake – a key element of the working consensus.

How far the crisis talks were embedded in the wider informal discourse over budgetary policy was further highlighted by the form of interaction between the two ministers, who were subject to criticism, and the rest of the group. In contrast to the Irish case the attitude of the criticised ministers was *cooperative*. The German and Portuguese ministers had not questioned the validity of common policy guidelines. Moreover, the two underlined their commitment to achieve the commonly agreed consolidation targets. This position was in accordance with the Eurogroup's underlying working consensus. On the basis of this position it was possible to reach a compromise over the procedural handling of the two cases. Another important informal resource guiding the discussions in this situation concerned the personal profile earned by German finance minister Eichel within previous Eurogroup discussions. The main reason for the credibility enjoyed by Eichel was his personal record as an advocate of the group consensus. As in the Irish case the crisis talks within the Eurogroup were concluded by an informal agreement on a common euro area position for the following ECOFIN Council meeting. This time the talks within the Eurogroup had led to the termination of the formal early warning procedure. Nevertheless, in contrast to the Irish case the Eurogroup discussions had brought about a formally stated commitment on part of the German and Portuguese governments to enact a set of additional measures ensuring the viability of the consolidation targets.

In addition, the central role of the Eurogroup in connection with the operation of the SGP procedures has been confirmed by the analysis of the conflict over the French budget in 2002. In contrast to the three other cases the actual decision to issue an early warning against France came at the end of a series of crisis talks within the Eurogroup. Whereas the actual period of crisis meditation within the Eurogroup had been relatively short in the Irish, German and Portuguese cases, the French finance minister Mer engaged the group in a struggle which lasted for several months. Again, the informal resources generated within the context of the regular policy reviews and the Eurogroup's underlying working consensus played a pivotal role in the discussions. As in the Irish case the minister who was subject to criticism reacted in a *non-cooperative* way. As a newcomer within the group Mer did not feel bound by the fundamental beliefs held by the rest of the group. Moreover, against the background of a further deteriorating economic situation the French display of opposition to common policy guidelines threatened the unity of the Eurogroup. In this difficult situation several participants sought to unite the group and to convince the newcomer Mer by making reference to the fundamental economic policy ideas behind the SGP. Again, the deliberative style of the discussion was crucial in the formation of a consensus among ministers. As a result, the Eurogroup was able to rally vital support for the Commission in its role as a watchdog within EMU's surveillance framework. Moreover, the group resisted the attempt by the French government to revise the framework of common rules. At the same time, individual ministers, the commissioner and the ECB president acted as advocates of the group consensus in their communications with the media.

Finally, the analysis of the four episodes has pointed to the relationship between country size and the informal dialogue. In principle, a country which becomes subject to a formal reprimand decision by the Council, can always choose to retreat to the classical means of Council bargaining if it is not prepared to accept the Eurogroup as the central forum for the solution of such problems. In particular, the German and French cases have illustrated that this option always remains open to national governments and that bigger member states especially might be tempted to retreat to this option. However, in none of the analysed cases did strategic action on the part of the countries which were subject to criticism prevent the characteristic features of the Eurogroup's working method coming into play. As a result the Eurogroup was still able to function as a moral authority and could exercise peer pressure on the non-compliant countries. The French case has illustrated that the group can resist external pressures over a longer period of time and that it provides a crucial forum for smaller member states in rallying support against free-riding tactics of bigger member states in the context of the SGP. This is not to say that the discussions within the Eurogroup can prevent incidences such as those in the second half of 2003 and the following years when the three biggest euro area countries chose to cooperate against the Commission. The *simultaneous occurrence of multiple cases of non-cooperative behaviour*, in particular on the part of the bigger member states, constitutes the greatest obstacle to crisis mediation in the context of the SGP procedures within the informal forum. However, even in such situations the group continues to remain a relevant player in the economic governance set-up and is still able to put pressure on non-complying countries, although the latter find it much easier to fend off formal reprimand procedures once they form a bigger coalition: a problem which can hardly be avoided in a predominantly intergovernmental setting. Figure 6.1 below illustrates how the Eurogroup functions as a generator of informal resources in EMU.

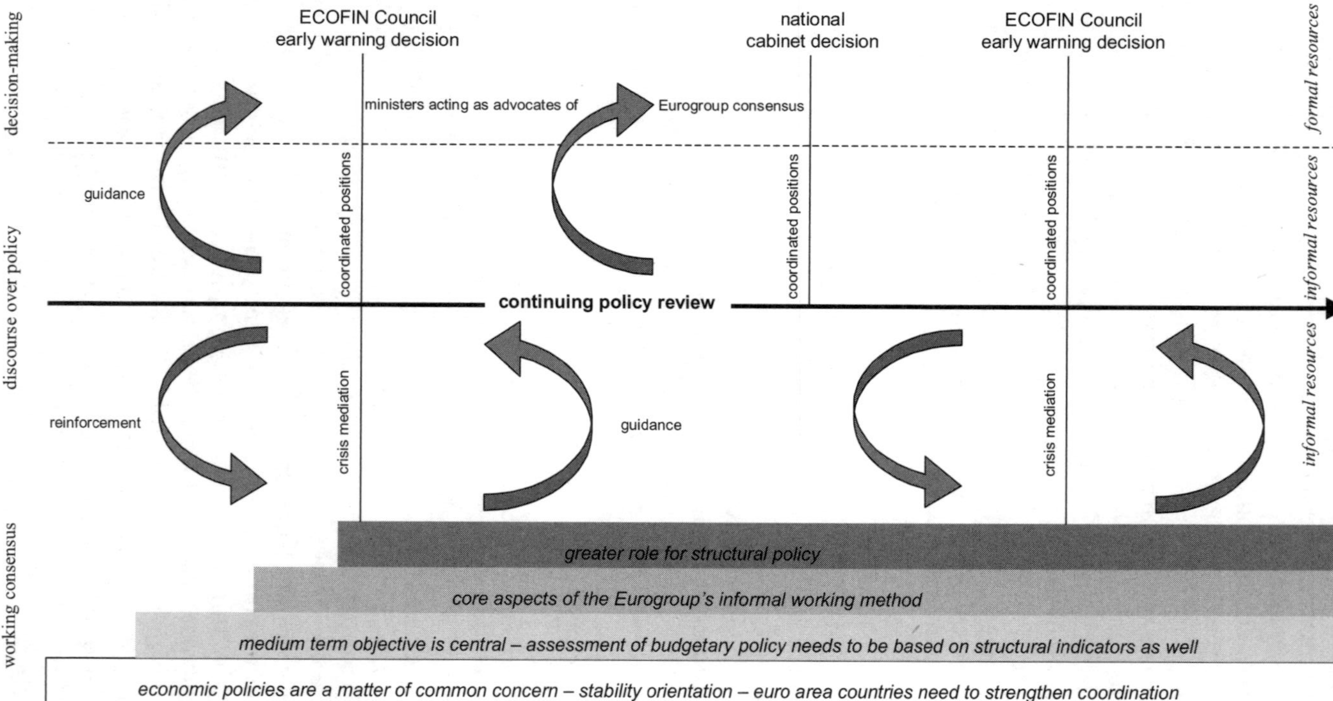

Figure 6.1 The generation of informal resources through continuing policy review within the Eurogroup

Comparing the informal dialogue with the pattern of Council negotiations

A central argument brought forward by this book is that the Eurogroup opens up new possibilities for policy dialogue which do not exist within the framework of formal Council meetings. Before discussing the institutional implications of this study for EU governance it is, therefore, helpful to briefly contrast the above findings on the functioning of the Eurogroup's informal working method with the prevailing pattern of negotiations among ministers within the Council. Fiona Hayes-Renshaw and Helen Wallace (1997: 7) have characterised the Council as a negotiation forum where

> ministers hammer out often difficult and tense agreements. Most of their time is spent poring over the details of texts, as separately and together they strive to put them into a form that they can live with.
>
> In such negotiations the participants often want to speak in unvarnished terms and to deploy arguments that they would not so easily repeat in more explicit and public form. Ministers and their officials build coalitions, exercise leverage and do deals, benefiting from the veil of secrecy that mostly cloaks their actions, as do ministers within cabinets in national governments.

It follows that Council negotiations are about the conclusion of *formal agreements*. The Council is the central decision-making body with regard to the approval of EU legislation. In addition, the Council exercises core executive functions within the system of EU governance. This is, for example, of particular importance in the area of foreign policy (Lewis 2003: 149). As an institution of the member states the Council is characterised through the manifestation of national interests as far as the definition of EU legislation and activities is concerned. Philippa Sherrington has concluded that 'member states are the Council' (Sherrington 2000: 164). She sees the initial attitude of member states towards a given proposal which is to be discussed within the Council as the main factor influencing the operation of the decision-making forum.

The Council's preoccupation with formal decision-making is reflected in the *regularisation* of its work.[1] It has even been noted that the process of the regularisation of Council negotiations further continues in response to negative negotiation experiences (Hayes-Renshaw and Wallace 1997: 264). Council negotiations usually mark the end of a long process of preparatory work involving the Commission, the EP and the various expert committees of the Council. Related to the complexity of the preparations of Council negotiations is the phenomenon that national delegations at Council meetings consist of a number of diplomats and experts who assist their ministers within the meeting room (Westlake 1999: 57–75). A technical detail or a pre-agreement reached during the preparatory phase of negotiations can be crucial when concluding a formal outcome.

Moreover, the Council negotiates common legislation and Community activities across many different policy areas involving different cost and benefit calculations on the part of individual member states. The finalisation of European decision-making, therefore, also constitutes the final opportunity for individual member states to correct the cost and benefit balance according to their own preferences. Consequently, negotiation behaviour is guided by a number of different strategic considerations. For example, the question of voting power and the formation of winning and losing coalitions is considered to be an important factor in influencing outcomes (Hayes-Renshaw and Wallace 1997: 245–253; 267–270). As a result of the high degree of institutionalisation of Council decision-making and the continuity of the Council's work in different policy areas, individual Council negotiations are highly intertwined. Adopting a neo-functionalist perspective Hayes-Renshaw and Wallace understand Council negotiations as a series of package deals, both within and across issue areas, and argue that this nature of the negotiation process socialises the negotiators in a particular way:

> The quality and value of the compromise could vary from those based on rather minimalist definitions of shared interests to expansive definitions of shared interests, some of which might be about anticipated future gains as well as immediate interest satisfaction. ... In this way participants came to acquire an interest in the maintenance of the forum itself; they became 'locked in', and socialised by the intensity and rewards of their interaction. This is not to say that nationally based participants would always prefer European-level solutions, but that they would in principle be amenable to them. (Hayes-Renshaw and Wallace 1997: 254–255)

In principle, this process of socialisation is self-reinforcing, thus strengthening the role of the Council as a forum for common decision-making in comparison with national governments over time. However, as Hayes-Renshaw and Wallace admit with reference to Scharpf's (1985) seminal contribution on the 'Politikverflechtungsfalle' (joint-decision trap) of federalist systems, an institutionalised negotiation system based on issue linkages and package deals permanently risks producing sub-optimal outcomes. A deal might pay off in the sense that it compensates individual actors for previously accepted disadvantages. However, this form of deal-making is not concerned with the provision of optimal solutions to shared problems of decision-making. Based on his analysis of negotiations between the federal government and the federal states in West Germany Scharpf has attributed these adverse effects to the prevalence of *bargaining* as the main negotiation mode instead of problem-solving (see Scharpf 1985: 338–346). The latter mode, however, is only applicable in the context of cooperative positive sum games and, thus, not compatible with a negotiation system focused on issue linkages and package deals. In this context, Sherrington's (2000: 165) observation that the Council generally takes its decisions by consensus is noteworthy. Although qualified majority voting is foreseen in many areas of Council decision-making this mechanism is only used in exceptional circumstances. This practice further underlines that Council negotiations are highly interlinked. Negotiators do not want to jeopardise the carefully negotiated balance of interests.

Despite the strong role of strategic considerations in Council negotiations the Council is generally seen as a negotiation forum in which a common culture of decision-making and shared normative ideas play an important role as well. Hayes-Renshaw and Wallace (1997: 265) have highlighted that negotiators also see the negotiation setting as 'an end in its own right and not just instrumental'. In a similar way the impact of policy ideas on the negotiation process is considered to be relatively high. However, these ideas are mainly attributed to 'influential epistemic communit[ies]' (Hayes-Renshaw and Wallace (1997: 266). Policy ideas emerge from, or are debated within, the expert committees of the Council's sub-structure. They might inform negotiations among ministers through these channels but are rarely the subject of debate in the actual meetings of the most senior decision-makers.

As has been noted above, Council negotiations among ministers mark only the end of a long preparatory process. Consequently, the Council's sub-structure plays a crucial role in the preparation and conduct of the negotiations. This applies in particular to COREPER as the central pre-negotiation forum. COREPER is widely seen as a key stabilising factor in the Council system. In this context, Martin Westlake (1999: 289) has highlighted that COREPER has an important effect on the Council's work in terms of 'socialisation'. He has pointed to the fact that the 'permanent representatives frequently outlast their political bosses' (ibid.). Moreover, the fact that COREPER meets on a weekly basis triggers the evolution of an atmosphere of friendship, familiarity and mutual trust among its members (see also Hayes-Renshaw et al. 1992; Lewis 1998a and b). Consequently, the key role of the diplomats in Council negotiations lends continuity and stability to the process. The greater confidentiality of COREPER meetings compared to Council sessions is seen as crucial for the committee's ability to overcome situations of deadlock and to hammer out compromises.

Notes

1   See for an encompassing overview of the different procedures and rules Westlake 1999.

7

Conclusion

> Oh yes, in the absence of the Eurogroup the evolution of EMU would probably have been a lot more disruptive. It is really a question of governance. We can say that the Eurogroup is the core of EU economic governance. (Anonymous interview, participant C)

The Eurogroup generates informal resources which guide policy-makers in the absence of formal provisions or form the basis of formal resources such as Treaty provisions, Council decisions at the EU level or cabinet decisions at the national level. The Eurogroup represents a framework for routinised informal policy dialogue among the euro area's key decision-makers. In this context the deliberative style of the informal discussions plays a pivotal role. Policy deliberation fosters consensus among decision-makers on appropriate policy options. Moreover, routinised informal policy dialogue within the Eurogroup is based on an underlying working consensus implying that actors share a common understanding on the fundamentals of the coordination process within the area of EMU – be it called a 'culture of coordination' (Fabius 2000) or a 'single economic philosophy' (Jacquet and Pisani-Ferry 2001). In the absence of legally binding coordination instruments this is the only way to ensure that policy-makers stick to their commitments made within the informal context of Eurogroup discussions, or in the form of formal but non-binding policy guidelines adopted by the Council. Building on this assessment of the Eurogroup's informal working method this book concludes with interpreting the routinised informal policy dialogue among ministers as a form of *deliberative intergovernmentalism* and assesses the value-added dimension of this alternative mode of governance within the context of the EU. More specifically, the following sections highlight which lessons can be learnt in the area of EMU from the experiences gained within the Eurogroup so far. In this context, the discussion pays particular attention to the consequences for economic governance within the euro area of the enlargement of the EU by ten new member states in 2004. Moreover, the future use of deliberative intergovernmentalism will be considered in the light of concerns that the creation of informal negotiation settings at the intergovernmental level contradicts basic democratic principles. Finally, the discussion points to the possible use of this governance mode in other policy areas than EMU.

Deliberative intergovernmentalism: an alternative mode of governance

The question of the contribution of informality as a working method for negotiations among euro area finance ministers is closely related to the more general question of the role of intergovernmental decision-making as the central source of political authority within the EU polity. Here, the Council plays a twofold role. On the one hand, the Council guarantees the representation of the member states. Each member state uses the forum as a safeguard against the violation of its national interest. Seen from this perspective, the role of the Council appears to be one of restricting the development of common policy objectives and their implementation. On the other hand, it is important to have in mind that negotiations within the Council are actually the way the common interest of the member states is formally defined. From this point of view the Council plays a creative role within the system of EU governance. The approval of common legislation or activities through the Council lends both legitimacy and impetus to the integration process. In fact, 'the Council has a central consensus-building function in the EU policy process' (Bulmer 1996: 38). In the absence of a strong supranational authority, which allocates resources autocratically, this role as a consensus-building forum is vital for both the definition and the implementation of common policies. This consensus-building process is essentially based on two elements. The first element concerns the general nature of the integration process as an instrument advancing the interests of all member states. In other words, the basis for agreement is that all involved actors are convinced that they achieve better solutions to common problems when acting together rather than on their own. The second element of the consensus-building process within the Council reflects the fact that member states also act as competing political and economic entities. Depending on the specific subject of the negotiations some countries might benefit more than others from integration. Some of them might even be entirely opposed to integration in a given policy area while others are strongly in favour of common action. The complexity and scope of the integration process, however, makes it necessary to find solutions to these diverging positions. As a result, the finalisation of EU legislation or decisions over common action within the Council becomes highly biased towards redistributive bargaining. However, this focus on issue linkages and compensation is not always possible or desirable as it leads to suboptimal outcomes with regard to the choice of policy options (Scharpf

1985). The inevitable tendency of Council negotiations to follow the logic of bargaining implies that the ability of decision-makers to explore innovative solutions to shared problems of decision-making is reduced. In other words, the ability of the Council to trigger processes of policy deliberation among ministers is limited.

Redistributive bargaining implies that the voluntary commitment to commonly agreed activities is relatively low (see Chapter 1). This explains why Council negotiations are highly regularised. However, once the negotiations are concluded the outcome has the status of EU law, and, in principle, the struggle ends. Moreover, within the framework of the Community method the role of policy initiation and innovation falls to the Commission. The bias of Council negotiations towards bargaining rather than deliberation is part of this division of labour. However, as the literature on comitology in the regulatory field has shown, this framework might not lend the necessary legitimacy to EU law. Policy deliberation among member state representatives is, therefore, an important additional element in the drafting of EU law and an important source of legitimacy (Joerges 2002; Joerges and Neyer 1997a, 1997b; Neyer 2000).[1] In other words, redistributive bargaining alone cannot provide the necessary legitimacy of EU law. The first element of consensus-building within the Council is important as well. Member states need to be convinced that they achieve better solutions to common problems when acting together rather than on their own. In this context it is essential to overcome diverging preferences within the negotiations through persuasion on the basis of normative, or technical, arguments rather than through redistributive bargaining.

The deliberative element, which is added to the Community method by comitology, has been called 'deliberative supranationalism' (Joerges and Neyer 1997b: 299). Alternatively, it is argued here that the work of the Eurogroup constitutes a form of *deliberative intergovernmentalism* (see also Puetter 2003). Policy deliberation within the committee system lends legitimacy to *supranational* law. Instead, the informal discussions within the Eurogroup focus on the generation of voluntary commitment to non-binding policy objectives among the most senior representatives of *national* governments. Moreover, informal discussions among ministers are explicitly political and are not regularised by law. Formal procedures protect the committee system as a space for deliberation and help to overcome the stubborn focus on the national interest. The informal process among ministers, however, has to create its own rules and procedures concerning the preparation of the sessions, the role of the presidency, the communication with the press or even the place where the group meets. Since these rules and procedures are fragile the conduct of the informal dialogue depends exclusively on the 'self-discipline'[2] of the involved actors.

This study has shown that the concept of deliberative intergovernmentalism is of particular importance in areas which are less regulated by EU law but in which the conduct of national policies becomes increasingly a matter of common concern. EMU's economic pillar is characterised by a decentralised system of governance (see Chapter 2). Economic policy remains a national responsibility and the Commission has no executive powers in this area. With the exception of the excessive deficit rule, formal procedures for policy coordination are based on non-binding Council recommendations. Moreover, even the enforcement of the excessive deficit rule is not a foregone conclusion since the Council enjoys far-reaching discretionary competences. In this context, the creation of a small group for informal discussions among the ministers, the Commission and the ECB has been the adequate institutional choice. The evolution of a routinised informal policy dialogue among the euro area's key decision-makers has overcome a central weakness of the Council system with regard to the governance of a decentralised policy area such as EMU's economic pillar. By engaging ministers in processes of policy deliberation the Eurogroup's informal working method has opened up new possibilities for the political stabilisation of the fragile formal coordination framework. Eurogroup discussions increase the commitment to common policies and create new incentives for addressing collectively so far unknown challenges to decision-making. In many ways the Eurogroup integrates what falls apart within the Council structure. The Council structure encourages the separation of policy deliberation and bargaining whereas Eurogroup discussions focus on both the development of policy options and the political question of their implementation. This feature of the Eurogroup setting also makes it particularly suited to dealing with crisis situations in the context of pending Council decisions on SGP matters. The bargaining about the conditions of a potential formal reprimand for non-compliant behaviour becomes embedded in a normative and ideational framework generated through the regular policy reviews.

For the first time, a group of ministers systematically applies this working method of informal policy deliberation in the context of EU decision-making. Deliberative intergovernmentalism represents an alternative mode of governance which can complement the process of formal decision-making within the Council of Ministers in an ideal way. In fact, the comparison of informal discussions within the Eurogroup with Council negotiations suggests that neither the system of official Council negotiations, nor the routinised informal policy dialogue, could replace the other. The occurrence of redistributive bargaining as a key feature of Council negotiations belongs to the unavoidable side effects of confederalist and federalist systems. In this respect, the highly regulated system of Council negotiations represents the appropriate institutional choice because it limits the risk that conflicts over specific policies jeopardise the whole system of EU governance. The fragile informal framework of Eurogroup discussions could never provide this stability in the way the Council system does. In turn, the Council structure is less suited to dealing with challenges to EU decision-making emerging in less regulated areas which do, however, require close policy coordination. Deliberative intergovernmentalism is a mode of governance needed in policy areas where interdependencies are particularly high but a more centralised system of governance is not feasible or desirable because member states do not want to transfer sovereignty to the supranational level indefinitely.

Enhanced policy coordination in areas which are not regulated by Community legislation is also the rationale behind the so-called open method of coordination (OMC). The Lisbon European Council in March 2000 introduced the OMC as an umbrella method for policy coordination in the area of economic and social policy. The OMC is based on a strong agenda-setting role for the European Council in these policy areas. The heads of state and government commit themselves to fix non-binding common policy guidelines and define specific timetables for the achievement of these policy objectives. The implementation of these objectives is then monitored on the basis of commonly defined indicators and benchmarks, thus forming a system of peer review (see European Council 2000, paragraph 37). As Scharpf (2001, chapter 6.2) has argued, the OMC could prove to be an effective mechanism for policy coordination in areas where no supranational competences exist:

> Instead, responsibility for those policy choices that cannot or should not be made directly by the 'political' institutions of the Union (Council and Parliament) would be left to Member States, where they would become the responsibility of politically accountable national and subnational governments. These policy choices, however, would not be those of sovereign, 'Westphalian' nation states. They would be taken in an institutional setting in which 'common concerns' are integrated into the preference function of national and subnational actors, and in which the effectiveness of nationally divergent solutions needs to be demonstrated in comparative analyses under conditions of peer review. The Council, moreover, would remain as a fleet in being that could intervene, by decisions taken by qualified majority, against specific deficiencies and the 'beggar-my-neighbor' practices of individual Member States.

However, the intersection between the OMC and the Eurogroup both in terms of the applied working method and the agenda is less significant than it might appear in the first place. Above all, the routinised informal policy dialogue within the Eurogroup implies a much closer form of coordination than the OMC mechanism, which is essentially an umbrella method applicable to various aspects of economic and social policy within the EU. Instead, the Eurogroup's continuing policy dialogue represents a much more sophisticated environment for policy deliberation and learning. Most importantly, as regards the Eurogroup's two main agenda items, the discussions about the economic situation and the review of budgetary policies move far beyond a formalised procedure of benchmarking. Ministers directly scrutinise the policies of their counterparts and remind each other of their commitments with regard to the common interest of the euro area. The other difference between the work of the Eurogroup and the OMC concerns the coordination agenda. The introduction of the OMC had little effect on the practice of budgetary coordination within EMU which is the central topic of Eurogroup discussions. Coordination in this policy area is based on the BEPGs and the SGP mechanisms as before. Whereas the European Council is the main agenda setter in the context of the OMC, the Eurogroup discussions play an important role in the development of the group's working priorities. Finally, the OMC is a working method for the Community institutions emphasising many aspects of the traditional division of labour between and within these institutions. Most importantly, policy learning in the form of interactive discussions among representatives of the Commission and the national governments mainly takes place within expert committees notably the EPC and the Employment Committee. At this level the OMC has promoted policy dialogue on questions such as structural reform, research and development and social inclusion.[3] Here, the debates on structural reform within the Eurogroup might provide a context for the discussion of the committee's work at a more political level. In fact, the president of the EPC has already participated in Eurogroup discussions on structural matters. This link between the informal dialogue among the ministers and the expert committee could be further strengthened.

Lessons for EMU

> Summing-up, the Eurogroup is a logical and reasonable institution within the context of EMU. However, Europe has come to a deadlock. The institutions are there but the implementation is missing. The Commission is very weak in this policy area. I have no solution for the dilemma that national egoism blocks progress regarding the European interest. Nobody wants a new transfer of sovereignty. In principle, the Eurogroup is an intelligent solution but if ministers do not stick to their commitments, then it does not work. ... How does an election campaign in which everybody promises everything fit into the Maastricht framework? Perhaps this is all a temporal problem. There is no doubt that we have to get used to the new situation – and this is a task for the Eurogroup. (Anonymous interview, official C)

It would be misleading to judge the work of the Eurogroup against the template of an imaginative European economic government with supranational decision-making powers. Instead, it is important to assess the group's value-added aspect in the context of the current decentralised policy framework of EMU. This framework reflects both economic conviction and political reality. Decision-makers widely believe in the sustainability and advantages of national discretion within the boundaries of a limited set of supranational rules. In addition, the political coordinates of the European integration process did not and still do not allow a more centralised form of economic policy-making. Member states are reluctant to agree on formally transferring sovereignty in this sensitive policy area to the EU level. Instead of being an embryonic European economic government the Eurogroup supplements and further develops the formal coordination instruments foreseen by the Treaty. The informal format of the group has facilitated decision-makers to navigate within the constitutional framework of economic governance which was drafted at a time when policy-makers were not fully aware of the precise challenges to economic policy coordination under the conditions of a single currency. It was mainly through its internal discussions that the Eurogroup defined its working priorities. Consequently, the debate inside the Eurogroup is in itself a crucial factor in determining the shared interest of euro area ministers in enhanced policy coordination.

The Eurogroup's informal working method is both a result of political compromise and an innovative attempt to create a more suitable environment for discussion over economic policies in Stage 3. On the one hand, the group's informal format responds to particular institutional constraints associated with the multi-speed nature of European monetary integration. The creation of a formal euro area forum would compromise the unity of the Council. Equal access to the decision-making process is one of the fundamental principles of EU governance. Already the Treaty provisions on EMU's flexible entry mechanism challenge this principle (Tuytschaever 2000). Given these institutional sensitivities there are hardly any alternatives to a low official profile of the Eurogroup. In addition, the dialogue between economic and monetary policy authorities requires an informal environment because of the independent status of the ECB. On the other hand, Eurogroup participants praise the group's informal working method as a major achievement. The fact that ministers can engage in real debates and a frank exchange of views is perceived as the key advantage of the Eurogroup in comparison with the ECOFIN Council. Seen from a historical perspective, the choice of an informal format for the Eurogroup was, in fact, not simply an unintended side effect of political compromise but also constituted the attempt to find a new working method for policy coordination in Stage 3. The above reflections on the role of a routinised informal policy dialogue as an alternative mode of governance have explained why this attempt has largely been successful.

However, room for a further improvement of the Eurogroup's working method and the wider coordination set-up remains. The Eurogroup has strengthened the instrument of peer pressure and has lent support to EMU's extremely fragile set of formal coordination instruments. This does not, however, imply that the Eurogroup can counter principal opposition by national governments to policy coordination at the European level by other means than those described in this book. It remains to be seen which conclusions euro area decision-makers draw from the most recent cases of persistent non-compliance with the common rules. However, the discussion of a potential adjustment in the allocation of political authority between the national and supranational level is beyond the scope of this study. Apart from these wider institutional considerations, room remains for a further strengthening of informal dialogue inside the Eurogroup with regard to individual agenda items. For example, the review of budgetary policy in the euro area is still focused on the identification of both policy failure and best practices with regard to past experiences. A more detailed discussion of national budget drafts prior to their approval at the domestic level remains the exception.[4] The debates within the Eurogroup have demonstrated that the commitment towards greater coordination in the area of budgetary policy often implies painful learning processes. Decisions in this area have enormous effect on the position of individual finance ministers and their governments within the domestic arena. The fact that the discussions within the Eurogroup have done a great deal to socialise the long-term members of the group in their commitment to the objective of budgetary consolidation is noteworthy in this regard.

Nevertheless, a lot still remains to be done in order to anchor a 'European thinking'[5] within national debates about budgetary policy. Here, it is important to further strengthen the role of individual ministers as advocates of the group's consensus in domestic debates. Eurogroup discussions have also demonstrated that the group finds it particularly difficult to influence developments which are beyond the immediate decision-making authority of finance ministers. For example, depending on the political system of an individual member state a finance minister might not enjoy the full decision-making authority required for informal ad hoc coordination in the area of budgetary policy.[6] In fact, informal policy coordination within the Eurogroup requires a high degree of self-commitment not only on the part of individual ministers but also on the part of their governments. The debates over structural policy have demonstrated how much the success of informal dialogue depends on the structure of the discussions. The organisation of the debates around clearly identified shared problems of decision-making is a crucial pre-condition for policy learning. Finally, the informal dialogue between EMU's monetary and economic pillar still lacks an important element. Although individual ministers have repeatedly raised different expectations in public statements Eurogroup meetings rarely see a critical review of the ECB's policy.

Governing the euro area in an enlarged EU

The 2004 EU enlargement poses a twofold challenge to informal governance within the Eurogroup. Firstly, the group of euro area countries no longer represents the overwhelming majority of EU member states. This situation is likely to lead to an increasing demand for exclusive euro area decision-making competences during the intermediate period. Secondly, the doubling of the number of Eurogroup participants becomes a real possibility in the not so distant future. Following the results of this study of Eurogroup negotiations this development is likely to bring key features of the informal working method into question. The problem of formal euro area decision-making in an enlarged EU is relatively well known. In fact, the Convention and the Constitutional Treaty have presented a potential solution to the problem. As a result, the principle of euro area restricted decision-making within the Council is likely to be extended to a number of other Treaty articles (see Chapter 4). However, the potential effects on the functioning of the Eurogroup's informal working method through the increase in the number of participants have received less attention by policy-makers. There is little doubt that the doubling of the number of participants will have considerable repercussions for the discussion process within such a small group as the Eurogroup. Building on the findings of this study the rest of this section considers potential solutions to the problems posed by the enlargement of the informal group.

An increase in the number of participants could impact on the discussion process in the following ways. Technically, the greater number of participants will reduce the duration of interventions by individual participants and/or reduce the frequency of these interventions. Given the current time frame of Eurogroup meetings this would limit the potential for real debates with arguments and counter-arguments. An alternative scenario would imply that the discussion process becomes more hierarchical. The discussions would be conducted among a group of leading participants. Such a development could be further triggered by the fact that long-term Eurogroup members set the informal rules of the discussion process while incoming members are expected to accept the existing practices. However, another risk is that in analogy to the Council setting the nationality of participants becomes increasingly important. In other words, those who really matter in terms of formal decision-making will also speak within the informal meetings. This would question the informal principle of equal access to participation in the informal dialogue. Moreover, a larger number of participants are also likely to lead to a lower degree of confidentiality. Finally, much will depend on whether the Eurogroup enlarges slowly over time or whether a large number of EU member states join at the same point in time. As the case studies have demonstrated, the informal dialogue is easily jeopardised by incoming group members who have not internalised the group consensus. In such a situation much depends on the ability of the other members of the group to unite on the basis of the currently existing working consensus. A large number of new participants joining the discussions at the same point in time is likely to make this procedure even more difficult. Under such circumstances a split of the group into those who still stick to the working consensus and those who oppose it becomes a real risk.

The EFC, for example, reacts to the increase in the number of its participants through the exclusion of those EFC members from the national central banks. The reduction of the number of participants is, however, not an option in the context of the Eurogroup. It is already common practice that the ministers are those who speak most. The role of the advisers does not pose a significant obstacle to the discussion process in terms of the duration and frequency of individual interventions. Alternatively, a potential exclusion of particular countries from the discussions, or a system of rotating membership would contradict the purpose of a close policy dialogue as conducted within the Eurogroup. Instead, one possible response to the increase in the number of participants could be the extension of the time frame of Eurogroup meetings. In addition, the frequency of Eurogroup meetings could be increased. It is, however, possible that the simultaneous process of the extension of the Eurogroup's agenda would counterbalance the positive effects of such measures. The encounter of new common challenges has provoked the constant expansion of the time frame of the informal discussions over the last years.

This leads to another factor influencing the consensus-oriented nature of the discussion process. Much depends on how far individual group members feel committed to an underlying working consensus. Currently, newcomers in Eurogroup discussions subscribe to (or resist) this group consensus in the course of the discussion process. The duration of this process depends on the understanding and persuasion of individual participants. In order to be able to deal with a large number of ministers joining the informal discussions at the same time, the process of socialisation could be anticipated at an early stage. In particular, two options are conceivable. Firstly, meetings in the format of the so-called enlarged Eurogroup could soon start to address the challenges of the convergence process more thoroughly. In particular, common reviews of the budgetary situation in the fashion of current Eurogroup meetings are conceivable. Alternatively, prospective euro area countries could meet informally in a separate group together with the Commission, the ECB and a troika of Eurogroup ministers. Such a grouping could apply the Eurogroup's informal working method in the particular context of the convergence process. In comparison with the format of enlarged Eurogroup meetings the more restricted format would allow the devotion of more time to the particular needs of accession countries. Besides budgetary policy, discussions could also focus on the particularities of the economies of the accession coun-tries. Most of these countries share the same problems as regards, for example, the need to sustain economic growth above the EU average over a longer period of time in order to close the gap with the old EU economies.

In general, the 2004 EU enlargement readjusts the relationship between euro area countries and the out-group towards EMU's original flexibility regime (see Chapter 2). This regime was built on the assumption that the exclusion of some member states from the single currency would only be temporary. In comparison with the euro-sceptic movement within the old EU-15, the new member states are eager to join the single currency. It is, therefore, necessary to emphasise the 'centripetal forces' (Tuytschaever 2000: 186) of the economic governance set-up. The impression of being only second-class members of the enlarged EU may well lead to the read-justment of political attention away from the process of convergence with EMU's entry criteria. The above suggested increasing use of the instru-ment of a close policy dialogue in an enlarged EU could be an important step in the right direction. At the level of formal decision-making the extended use of exclusive euro area voting rights in the ECOFIN Council rather than the creation of independent euro area decision-making struc-tures should be the preferred option.

A model for the future?

> Fiscal and foreign policy are very similar because both are test cases with regard to the question of how far the EU goes. In both cases ex ante coor-dination was considered to be only possible if the EU would become fundamentally more federal. Considering that the latter has not happened yet we got relatively far. (Anonymous interview, participant G)

This study has argued that routinised informal dialogue among the most senior decision-makers of the euro area is an effective instrument to improve economic governance within EMU. Finally, the question remains whether the concept of deliberative intergovernmentalism could be a model for the future which is also applied in other policy areas than EMU. Since the Eurogroup widely escapes accountability and judicial control at the EU level the main question is whether the continued use of this alter-native mode of governance is desirable on the basis of democratic considerations. Moreover, a possible use of the Eurogroup's informal working method in other policy areas raises the question of whether the results of this study are transferable to other fields than the one of EMU.

The idea of an informal circle of decision-makers has always been asso-ciated with a lack of democratic control. Indeed, the fact that the Eurogroup operates outside the regular Community institutions while exercising at the same time considerable influence over decision-making procedures gives reason for concern. Michael Zürn (2000: 193) has summarised the dilemma inherent to informal intergovernmental arrangements:

> On the one hand, consensus-oriented deliberations and negotiations are, as a rule, more successful with a small number of actors and (at least sometimes) *in camera*. Yet both closed sessions and a biased selection of participants contradict democratic principles. Most importantly, the accountability of decision-makers decreases significantly. Negotiation systems as a whole are not directly subject to any form of democratic scrutiny.

In a similar way Tuytschaever (2000: 194) has pointed to the fact that

> intergovernmental co-operation outside the Treaty framework has been heavily criticised because of its lack of transparency, its democratic deficit and the absence of an independent judicial review mechanism.

Confidentiality, which was identified as an integral part of the informal working method, is a major obstacle to democratic scrutiny. Informal circles of ministers, which can have a considerable impact on decision-making and directly affect the lives of citizens across Europe, are difficult to control. While one should expect that the principle of domestic scrutiny matches the intergovernmental nature of the body (Weiler 1999: 276), it is nearly impossible for the public to assess the role that is played by individual ministers in the group. Even senior officials in the finance ministries or the Commission, who are briefed by their ministers and deputy ministers, do not get the full picture. While ministers insist that the issues discussed during the sessions require confidentiality because they can lead to disruptions in financial markets or undermine the effectiveness of decisions, the most critical observers deny that there is any justification for secrecy with regard to the content of discussions.[7] There is, by definition, no easy way out of this dilemma of informality. The opening of the doors of the meeting room would only lead to a situation in which ministers read out prepared statements. There is little doubt that they would find other channels for their informal discussions. However, in this case the framework provided by the Eurogroup, which allows for more exhaustive discussions on the basis of Commission analysis and background information, would be lost.[8] Another aspect for consideration is that informal gatherings of ministers in the context of the EU – as in the case of the Eurogroup – are essentially a reflection of the fact that more and more aspects of the day-to-day business of the executive branch have a European dimension and have to be therefore coordinated at the EU level. Many of the issues on the Eurogroup's agenda indeed attract little public attention when they are discussed behind closed doors within national cabinets. However, this does not solve the fundamental problem of accountability. Here, new solutions have to be found which reflect the peculiarities of the informal working method. National finance ministers could, for example, regularly appear before national parliaments in other member states than their own. This idea was introduced by the then French finance minister Laurent Fabius during his presidency of the Eurogroup in the second half of 2000 and has been practised by France and Germany. It reflects the interdependencies between national budgetary decisions. In addition, the president of the Eurogroup could regularly report to the Economic and Monetary Committee of the European Parliament. This would of course require that the participants in the sessions trust their presidency and feel that their position is represented in an appropriate way.

At a procedural level the Constitutional Treaty produced by the Convention and the following IGC has offered a possible solution to the problems associated with the Eurogroup's status as an institution operating outside the Community structure. The draft constitution foresees a so-called Eurogroup protocol which is annexed to the constitution (European Convention 2003, Article III, 85b and Annex II, Protocol on the Euro Group). This protocol defines the Eurogroup as a forum for informal gatherings of euro area ministers, the Commission and the ECB. Moreover, the protocol regulates the preparations of the meetings and asks the ministers of the euro area to elect a president for two years. The protocol formalises the current practice of Eurogroup meetings without affecting the informal working method applied by the group. This procedure not only preserves the positive aspects of the informal working method but also opens up new possibilities for a greater transparency of the Eurogroup's work. An important improvement would be that the Eurogroup president and/or other Eurogroup members explain in parliament, both at the national and the EU level, the main results of Eurogroup discussions and point to their political implications. On the basis of the current legal situation such reporting exercises are problematic because they would lend an official status to a group which formally does not exist.

So, is the concept of deliberative intergovernmentalism applicable to other policy areas? Seen from a historical perspective the field of economic and monetary cooperation seems to be a unique example with regard to the occurrence of regular informal discussions among finance ministers. Westlake (1999) has pointed to the fact that prior to the creation of the ECOFIN Council in 1974 the Community's finance ministers had already established the practice of regular informal meetings. Since the 1960s the ministers had discussed questions of economic policy coordination and the coordination of positions in international financial institutions. This study has demonstrated why the topic of economic policy coordination is particularly suited to informal policy deliberation at the level of ministers. However, this is not to say that informal policy dialogue among ministers cannot be practised in other areas as well. An obvious case would be the field of the EU's foreign and security policy. In this area the coordination agenda constantly expands. At the same time, member states are reluctant to formally transfer sovereignty to the supra-national level. Routinised informal dialogue among the top decision-makers in this area could help to back up the existing coordination procedures. Moreover, the content of the debates over foreign policy seems to be compatible with the criteria specified by this study. Shared normative ideas and principles, but also technical knowledge, are of particular importance in this policy area. Ben Tonra (2001) has high-lighted that in the area of EU foreign policy negotiators generally do not arrive with pre-defined positions at the negotiation table. This is a further indication that the conditions for the evolution of a routinised informal policy dialogue are in place. Finally, the occurrence of closer cooperation among a limited number of member states still remains a possible scenario in this policy area.

Notes

1   Charles Sabel and Jonathan Zeitlin (2003: 21) have pointed to the fact that the current practice of deliberation within the committee system deviates from the initial objective pursued with the creation of the committee system. Historically, the system of comitology has been created in order to ensure that the Commission does not exceed its competences. However, as the empirical studies on the committee system have demonstrated, the *de facto* role of the system is to provide a framework for policy deliberation at an intergovernmental level during the drafting of EU legislation.

2   Anonymous interview.

3   It is important to note that the explicit definition of the OMC through the Lisbon European Council conclusions only marks the end of a series of European Council meetings introducing aspects of this working method for the above policy areas (see Chapter 4 on the discussions about structural policies within the Eurogroup).

4   As a participant critically remarks, budgetary coordination has not yet worked 'in the sense that ministers discuss plans rather than only what they have already done. You can have good debates on what you have done but it is essential to focus on your plans. The Eurogroup is the forum where they can have this discussion for which confidentiality is needed, where you can think aloud and try different things in order to get feedback from your colleagues.' (Anonymous interview, participant B)

5   German finance minister Hans Eichel, interview in *Die Zeit* (No. 23, 2002).

6   See example of the oil price shock in 2000 in Chapter 4.

7   See German deputy finance minister Kaio Koch-Weser, *Der Euro – wie geht es weiter mit der europäischen Integration*, presentation and discussion, Forum Constitutionis Europae, Humboldt Universität, Berlin, 15 January

2002 and Christa Randzio-Plath, president of the Economic and Monetary Committee of the European Parliament, round table discussion, CEUS, University of Bremen, 28 January 2002.
8   As one interviewee put it: 'If you close down the Eurogroup ministers would meet over coffee or tea or would extend their lunches in order to discuss confidential issues. There is always a way around.' (Anonymous interview, official E).

References

Interviews

I would like to thank the following persons for their cooperation in the series of expert interviews substantiating this research:

Åkerholm, Jonny: President of the EFC until April 2003, Ministry of Finance, Helsinki (now European Bank for Reconstruction and Development, London).
Bini-Smaghi, Lorenzo: Director General, Treasury Department, Ministry of Finance, Rome.
Brouhns, Grégoire: Secretary General, High Representative for macroeconomic and financial stability issues, Ministry of Finance, Brussels.
Buti, Marco: Head of Unit, Economic and Financial Affairs Directorate General, European Commission, Brussels.
Carré, Hervé: Director, Economic and Financial Affairs Directorate General, European Commission, Brussels.
Grosche, Günter: Secretary of the EFC and the EPC, Director, Economic and Financial Affairs Directorate General, European Commission, Brussels.
Hay, Charles: Economic policy section, Permanent Representation of the United Kingdom, Brussels.
Jansen, Anita: European currency policy section, Federal Ministry of Finance, Berlin.
Julien, Catherine: Deputy Head of Bureau, Foreign Exchange and Economic Policy, Treasury Department, Ministry of Economics, Finance and Industry, Paris.
Korkman, Sixtén: Director General, Social and Economic Affairs Directorate General, Council Secretariat, Brussels.
McNally, Donal: Second General Secretary of the Department of Finance, Dublin.
Regling, Klaus: Director General, Economic and Financial Affairs Directorate General, European Commission, Brussels (previously Federal Ministry of Finance, secretary of state, Bonn).
Schönfelder, Wilhelm: Ambassador, Permanent Representation of the Federal Republic of Germany, Brussels.
Stark, Jürgen: Vice-President, Deutsche Bundesbank, Frankfurt (previously Federal Ministry of Finance, secretary of state, Bonn).

Wieser, Thomas: Director, Economic Policy and Financial Markets, Federal Ministry of Finance, Vienna.

Media sources

The following media sources have been used in connection with this thesis. In order to improve readability only direct quotes are fully referenced in footnotes containing issue numbers and/or the respective date of publication. The date of publication can deviate by plus or minus one day from printed versions of the respective publications as far as online sources are concerned.

Agence Europe, Bulletin Quotidien, daily news bulletin, Brussels 1998–2003.
Europe-by-satellite, online video on demand archive, Brussels 2000–2002, www.europa.eu.int/comm/ebs/index_en.html.
Financial Times, newspaper, London 1998–2003.
Financial Times Deutschland, newspaper, Hamburg 2001–2003.
Frankfurter Allgemeine Zeitung, newspaper, Frankfurt am Main 1998–2003.
Guardian, newspaper, London 1998–2003.
Handelsblatt, newspaper, Frankfurt am Main 2000–2003.
Irish Times, newspaper, Dublin 2000–2002.
La Libre Belgique, newspaper, Brussels 2000–2002.
Le Monde, newspaper, Paris 1998–2003.
Les Echos, newspaper, Paris 1998–2003.
Libération, newspaper, Paris 1998–2003.
Süddeutsche Zeitung, newspaper, München 1998–2003.
Wirtschaftswoche, Frankfurt am Main 2001–2002.

Books and articles

As the location of individual online documents on the servers of the publishers might be subject to change, the references specify the domain name of the publishing institution rather than the direct link to the respective document.

Adler, Emanuel and Haas, Peter M. (1992): 'Conclusion: epistemic communities, world order, and the creation of a reflective research program', *International Organization*, Vol. 46, No. 1, pp. 368–390.
Artis, Michael J. and Buti, Marco (2000): '"Close-to-balance or in surplus": A policy-maker's guide to the implementation of the Stability and Growth Pact', *Journal of Common Market Studies*, Vol. 38, No. 4, pp. 563–591.
Bennett, Colin J. and Howlett, Michael (1992): 'The lessons of learning: Reconciling theories of policy learning and policy change', *Policy Sciences*, Vol. 25, No. 3, pp. 275–294.
Benz, A. (1990): 'Verhandlungen, Verträge und Absprachen in der öffentlichen Verwaltung', *Die Verwaltung*, No. 23, 1990, pp. 83–98.
Berger, Suzanne and Dore, Ronald (eds) (1996): *National diversity and global capitalism*, Cornell University Press, Ithaca.
Bini Smaghi, Lorenzo and Casini, Claudio (2000): 'Monetary and fiscal policy co-

operation, institutions and procedures in EMU', *Journal of Common Market Studies*, Vol. 38, No. 3, pp. 375–391.

Boulhol, Hervé (2002): 'Le pacte de stabilité et de croissance à l'épreuve du ralentissement économique', *Problèmes Économiques*, No. 2755, pp. 18–23.

Boyer, Robert and Dehove, Mario (2002): 'Un « gouvernement économique » pour l'Europe', *Problèmes Économiques*, No. 2744, pp. 22–25.

Bryant, Ralph C. and Hodgkinson, Edith (1989): 'Problems of international cooperation', in: Cooper, Richard N., Eichengreen, Barry, Henning, C. Randall, Holtham, Gerald and Putnam, Robert D. (eds), *Can nations agree?*, The Brookings Institution, Washington DC.

Brouhns, Grégoire (1999): *La coordination des politiques dans l'UEM et le role de l'Euro 11*, Ministère des Finances Belgique, Service d'Etudes et de Documentation, Vol. 59, No. 2.

Bulmer, Simon J. (1998): 'New institutionalism and the governance of the Single European Market', *Journal of European Public Policy*, Vol. 5, No. 3, pp. 365–386.

Bulmer, Simon J. (1996): 'The European Council and the Council of the European Union: shapers of a European confederation', *The Journal of Federalism*, Vol. 26, No. 4, pp. 17–42.

Bulmer, Simon J. and Wessels, Wolfgang (1987): *The European Council – decision-making in European politics*, Macmillan Press, Basingstoke.

Bundesministerium (2001) der Finanzen: *German stability programme*, December 2001 update, Berlin, www.bundesfinanzministerium.de.

Busch, Klaus (1996): 'Spill-over-Dynamik und Spill-back-Potential in der europäischen Währungsintegration – ein Beitrag zur Integrationstheorie', in: Kohler-Koch, Beate and Jachtenfuchs, Markus (eds), *Europäische Integration*, Leske+Budrich, pp. 281–311.

Cabral, António J. (2001): 'Main aspects of the working of the SGP', in: Brunila, Anne, Buti, Marco and Franco, Daniele (eds), *The Stability and Growth Pact – The architecture of fiscal policy in EMU*, Palgrave, Houndmills, Basingstoke, pp. 139–157.

Cabral, António J. (1999): 'The Stability and Growth Pact: Main aspects and some considerations on its implementation', in: Bernard, Luc D., Cabral, António J. and Lamfalussy, Alexandre: *The euro-zone: A new economic entity?*, Bruylant, Bruxelles.

Cameron, David R. (1998): 'Creating supranational authority in monetary and exchange-rate policy: The sources and effects of EMU', in: Sandholtz, Wayne and Stone Sweet, Alec (eds), *European integration and supranational governance*, Oxford University Press, pp. 188–216.

Campanella, Miriam L. (2000): 'The battle between ECOFIN-11 and the European Central Bank: A strategic interaction perspective', in: Green Cowles, Maria and Smith, Michael (eds), *The state of the European Union – risks, reform, resistance, and revival*, Oxford University Press, Oxford, pp. 110–126.

Campanella, Miriam L. (1995): 'Getting the core: neo-institutionalism and the EMU', *Government and Opposition*, Vol. 30, No. 3, pp. 347–369.

Chayes, Abram and Handler Chayes, Antonia (1993): 'On compliance', *International Organization*, Vol. 47, No. 2, pp. 175–205.

Checkel, Jeffrey T. (2001a): 'Why comply? Social learning and European identity change', *International Organization*, Vol. 55, No. 3, pp. 553–588.

Checkel, Jeffrey T. (2001b): 'Social construction and European integration', in: Christiansen, Thomas, Jørgensen, Knud Erik and Wiener, Antje (eds), *The social construction of Europe*, Sage, London, pp. 50–65.

Christiansen, Thomas, Jørgensen, Knud Erik and Wiener, Antje (eds) (2001): *The social construction of Europe*, Sage, London.

Coeuré, Benoît (2002): 'L'Eurogroup: Bilan et perspectives', *Revue d'Economie Financiere*, Vol. 65, pp. 69–80.

Collignon, Stefan (2002): 'Two years into the euro: The next step for Europe', in: Caesar, Rolf and Scharrer, Hans-Eckart (eds), *European Economic and Monetary Union: An intial assessment*, Nomos Verlagsgesellschaft, Baden-Baden, pp. 39–52.

Collignon, Stefan (2001): *Economic policy coordination in EMU: Institutional and political requirements*, paper presented at the Center for European Studies (CES) Harvard University and L'Institut d'Etudes Européennes de l'Université de Montréal et de l'Université McGill, revised version, May.

Commissariat Général du Plan (1999): *Le gouvernement économique de la zone euro*, Rapport du groupe "Coordination des politiques macro-économiques en Europe", La Documentation française, Paris.

Council of the European Union (2000): *Broad guidelines of the economic policies 2000*, Office for Official Publications of the European Communities, Luxembourg.

Council of the European Union (1999): *The euro and economic policy – legal and political texts adopted by the Council of the European Union and the European Council*, Office for Official Publications of the European Communities, Luxembourg.

Crouch, Colin and Streeck, Wolfgang (eds) (1997): *Political economy of modern capitalism: Mapping convergence and diversity*, Sage, London.

Culpepper, Pepper D. (2002): 'Powering, puzzling, and "pacting": the informational logic of negotiated reforms', *Journal of European Public Policy*, Vol. 9, No. 5, pp. 774–790.

De Búrca, Gráinne and Scott, Joanne (eds) (2000): *Constitutional change in the EU – From uniformity to flexibility?*, Hart Publishing, Oxford, pp. 173–195.

De Búrca, Gráinne and Zeitlin, Jonathan (2003): *Constitutionalising the Open Method of Coordination – What should the Convention propose?*, CEPS Policy Brief, No. 31, March.

Druckman, Daniel (2002): 'Case-based research on international negotiation: Aproaches and data sets', *International Negotiation*, Vol. 7, pp. 17–37.

Druckman, Daniel (2001): 'Turning points in international negotiation: A comparative analysis', *Journal of Conflict Resolution*, Vol. 45, pp. 519–544.

Dyson, Kenneth (ed.) (2002): *European states and the euro – Europeanization, variation, and convergence*, Oxford University Press, Oxford.

Dyson, Kenneth (2000): *The politics of the euro-zone – stability or breakdown?*, Oxford University Press, Oxford.

Dyson, Kenneth (1994): *Elusive union: The process of Economic and Monetary Union in Europe*, Longman, London.

Dyson, Kenneth and Featherstone, Kevin (1999): *The road to Maastricht:*

Negotiating economic and monetary union, Oxford University Press, Oxford.
ECOFIN Council (1997a): Brussels, November 17, press release, No. 12242/97, http://ue.eu.int/newsroom/.
ECOFIN Council (1997b): Brussels, December 1, press release, No. 12671/97, http://ue.eu.int/newsroom/.
Edwards, Geoffrey and Philippart, Eric (1999): 'The provisions on closer cooperation in the Treaty on European Union: Politics of a multi-faceted system', *Journal of Common Market Studies*, Vol. 37, No. 1, pp. 87–108.
Egeberg, Morten (1999): 'Transcending intergovernmentalism? Identity and role perceptions of national officials in EU decision-making', *Journal of European Public Policy*, Vol. 6, No. 3, pp. 456–474.
Ehlermann, Claus Dieter (1998): 'Differentiation, flexibility, closer co-operation: The new provisions of the Amsterdam Treaty', *European Law Journal*, Vol. 4, No. 3, pp. 246–270.
Elgström, Ole and Jönsson, Christer (2000): 'Negotiation in the European Union: bargaining or problem-solving?', *Journal of European Public Policy*, Special Issue: *Negotiation and Policy-Making in the European Union – Processes, System and Order*, Vol. 7, No. 5, pp. 684–704.
Elgström, Ole and Smith, Michael (2000): 'Introduction: negotiation and policy-making in the European Union – processes, system and order', *Journal of European Public Policy*, special issue: *Negotiation and Policy-Making in the European Union – Processes, System and Order*, Vol. 7, No. 5, pp. 673–683.
Elster, Jon (ed.) (1998): *Deliberative democracy*, Cambridge University Press, Cambridge.
European Convention (2003): *Draft Constitution*, Volume II, Draft revised text of Parts Two, Three and Four, CONV 805/03, Brussels, 12 June 2003, http://european-convention.eu.int.
European Convention (2002a): Communication from the Commission to the Convention, 22 May 2002: *A project for the European Union*, CONV 229/02, Brussels, 3 September 2002, http://european-convention.eu.int.
European Convention (2002b): *Final report of Working Group VI on Economic Governance*, CONV 357/02, Brussels, 21 October 2002, http://european-convention.eu.int.
European Council (2005): *Brussels, presidency conclusions*, March 22–23, press release, No. 7619/1/05, REV1, http://ue.eu.int/newsroom/.
European Council (2000): *Lisbon, presidency conclusions*, March 23–24, press release, No. 100/1/00, http://ue.eu.int/newsroom/.
European Council (1999): *Cologne, presidency conclusions*, June 3–4, press release, No. 150/99, http://ue.eu.int/newsroom/.
European Council (1998a): *Cardiff, presidency conclusions*, June 15–16, press release, No. 00150/1/98 REV1, http://ue.eu.int/newsroom/.
European Council (1998b): *Vienna, presidency conclusions*, December 11–12, press release, No. 00300/1/98 REV, http://ue.eu.int/newsroom/.
European Council (1997a): *Amsterdam, presidency conclusions*, June 16, press release, No. SN00150/97, http://ue.eu.int/newsroom/.
European Council (1997b): *Extraordinary meeting on employment, Luxembourg, presidency conclusions*, November 20–21, press release, No. SN300/97, http://ue.eu.int/newsroom/.

European Council (1997c): *Luxembourg, presidency conclusions*, December 12–13, press release, No. SN400/97, http://ue.eu.int/newsroom/.

European Council (1996): *Dublin, presidency conclusions*, December 16, press release, No. 00401–x/96, http://ue.eu.int/newsroom/.

European Economy (2001): *2001 Broad economic policy guidelines*, No. 72, Office for Official Publications of the European Communities, Luxembourg.

Fabius, Laurent (2000): 'France's mission in Europe', *Financial Times*, 24 July.

Fligstein, Neil, Sandholtz, Wayne and Stone Sweet, Alex (2001): 'The institutionalization of European space', in: Fligstein, Neil, Sandholtz, Wayne and Stone Sweet, Alex (eds), *The institutionalization of Europe*, Oxford University Press, Oxford.

Finnemore, Martha and Sikkink, Kathryn (1998): 'International norm dynamics and political change', *International Organization*, Vol. 52, No. 4, pp. 887–918.

Fischer, Jonas and Giudice, Gabriele (2001): 'The stability and convergence programmes', in: Brunila, Anne, Buti, Marco and Franco, Daniele (eds), *The Stability and Growth Pact – The architecture of fiscal policy in EMU*, Palgrave, Houndmills, Basingstoke, pp. 158–184.

Garrett, Geoffrey and Tsebelis, George (1996): 'An institutional critique of intergovernmentalism', *International Organization*, Vol. 50, No. 2, pp. 269–299.

Garret, Geoffrey and Weigast, Barry (1993): 'Ideas, interests and institutions: Constructing the European Community's internal market', in: Goldstein, Judith and Keohane, Robert (eds), *Ideas and foreign policy*, Cornell University Press, Ithaca NY.

Gehring, Thomas (1994): 'Der Beitrag von Institutionen zur Förderung der internationalen Zusammenarbeit – Lehren aus der institutionellen Struktur der Europäischen Gemeinschaft', *Zeitschrift für Internationale Beziehungen*, Vol. 1, No. 2, pp. 211–242.

Glomb, Wolfgang (1998): 'Bedarf die WWU einer gemeinsamen "Wirtschaftsregierung"?', in: Caesar, Rolf and Scharrer, Hans-Eckart (eds), *Die Europäische Wirtschafts- und Währungsunion – Regionale und globale Herausforderungen*, Europa Union Verlag.

Haas, Peter M. (1992): 'Introduction: Epistemic communities and international policy coordination', *International Organization*, Vol. 46, No. 1, pp. 1–35.

Haas, Peter M. (1989): 'Do regimes matter? Epistemic communitites and Mediterranean pollution control', *International Organization*, Vol. 43, No. 3, pp. 377–403.

Habermas, Jürgen (1998): *Faktizität und Geltung – Beiträge zur Diskurstheorie des Rechts und des demokratischen Rechtsstaats*, Suhrkamp Verlag, Frankfurt am Main.

Habermas, Jürgen (1995): *Theorie des kommunikativen Handelns*, Vol. 1–2, Suhrkamp Verlag, Frankfurt am Main.

Hall, Peter (1993): 'Policy paradigms, social learning and the state: The case of economic policymaking in Britain', *Comparative Politics*, Vol. 25, pp. 275–296.

Hall, Peter (ed.) (1989): *The political power of economic ideas: Keynesianism across nations*, Princeton University Press, Princeton, NJ.

Hall, Peter and Soskice, D. (eds) (2001): *Varieties of capitalism*, Oxford

University Press, Oxford.

Hancké, Bob (2003): 'The political economy of fiscal policy in EMU', *European Political Economy Review*, Vol. 1, No. 1, pp. 5–14, www.eper.org .

Hayes-Renshaw, Fiona, Lequense, Christian and Mayor Lopez, Pedro (1992): 'The permanent representations of the member states to the European Communities', *Journal of Common Market Studies*, Vol. 28, No. 2, pp. 119–137.

Hayes-Renshaw, Fiona and Wallace, Helen (1997): *The Council of Ministers*, Macmillan Press, Basingstoke.

Heipertz, Martin and Verdun, Amy (2004): 'The dog that would never bite? What we can learn from the origins of the Stability and Growth Pact', *Journal of European Public Policy*, Vol. 11, No. 5, pp. 765–780.

Heisenberg, Dorothee (2003): 'Cutting the bank down to size: Efficient and legitimate decision-making in the European Central Bank after enlargement', *Journal of Common Market Studies*, Vol. 41, No. 3, pp. 397–420.

Henning, C. Randall and Putnam, Robert D. (1989): 'The Bonn Summit in 1978: A case study in coordination', in: Cooper, Richard N., Eichengreen, Barry, Henning, C. Randall, Holtham, Gerald and Putnam, Robert D. (eds), *Can nations agree?*, The Brookings Institution, Washington DC.

Héritier, Adrienne (1993): 'Policy-Analyse. Elemente der kritik und perspektiven der neuorientierung', in: Héritier, Adrienne (ed.), *Policy-Analyse – Kritik und Neuorientierung, Politische Vierteljahresschrift*, special issue (Sonderheft), No. 24, pp. 9–38.

Hodson, Dermot and Maher, Imelda (2002): 'Economic and Monetary Union: Balancing credibility and legitimacy in an asymmetric policy-mix', *Journal of European Public Policy*, Vol. 9, No. 3, pp. 391–407.

Hodson, Dermot and Maher, Imelda (2001): 'The open method as a new mode of governance: The case of soft economic policy co-ordination', *Journal of Common Market Studies*, Vol. 39, No. 4, pp. 719–746.

Hoffmann, Stanley (1995): *The European sisyphus. Essays on Europe 1964–1994*, Westview Press, Oxford.

Hollingswood, J. and Boyer, R. (1997): *Contemporary capitalism: The embeddedness of institutions*, Cambridge University Press, Cambridge.

Hollis, Martin and Smith, Steve (1990): *Explaining and understanding international relations*, Clarendon, Oxford.

Hosli, Madeleine O. (2002): 'Preferences and power in the European Union', *Power Measures*, No. 2, pp. 311–326.

Hosli, Madeleine O. (2000): 'The creation of the European Economic and Monetary Union (EMU): Intergovernmental negotiations and two-level games', *Journal of European Public Policy*, special issue: *Negotiation and policy-making in the European Union – processes, system and order*, Vol. 7, No. 5, pp. 744–766.

Hosli, Madeleine O. (1996): 'Coalitions and power: effects of qualified majority voting in the Council of the European Union', *Journal of Common Market Studies*, Vol. 34, No. 2, pp. 255–273.

Howarth, David J. (2001): 'The French road to European Monetary Union', Palgrave, Basingstoke.

Howarth, David J. (1999): *French aversion to central bank independence and the*

EMU project, paper presented at ECSA, Biannual Conference, Pittsburgh, June.

Howarth, David J. and Loedel, Peter (2003): *The ECB: the new European leviathan*, Palgrave, Basingstoke.

Institute of European Affairs (IEA) (1997): *EMU update*, No. 4, Dublin.

Jachtenfuchs, Markus (1995): 'Ideen und internationale Beziehungen', *Zeitschrift für International Beziehungen*, Vol. 2, No. 2, pp. 417–442.

Jacquet, Pierre and Pisani-Ferry, Jean (2001): *Economic policy co-ordination in the euro-zone: What has been achieved? What should be done?*, Centre for European Reform, London.

Jenkins-Smith, Hank C. and Sabatier, Paul A. (1993): 'The dynamics of policy-oriented learning', in: Jenkins-Smith, Hank C. and Sabatier, Paul A. (eds), *Policy change and learning: An advocacy coalition approach*, Westview Press, Boulder, CO.

Joerges, Christian (2002): '"Deliberative supranationalism" – two defences', *European Law Journal*, Vol. 8, pp. 133–151.

Joerges, Christian and Neyer, Jürgen (1997a): 'Transforming strategic interaction into deliberative problem-solving: European comitology in the foodstuffs sector', *Journal of European Public Policy*, Vol. 4, No. 4, pp. 609–625.

Joerges, Christian and Neyer, Jürgen (1997b): 'From intergovernmental bargaining to deliberative political processes: The constitutionalisation of Comitology', *European Law Journal*, Vol. 3, No. 3, pp. 273–299.

Kaelberer, Matthias (2003): 'Knowledge, power and monetary bargaining: Central bankers and the creation of monetary union in Europe', *Journal of European Public Policy*, Vol. 10, No. 3, pp. 365–379.

Kant, Immanuel (1990): *Kritik der reinen Vernunft*, Felix Meiner Verlag, Hamburg.

Kant, Immanuel (1983): *Kritik der praktischen Vernunft*, in: Werke in sechs Bänden, Vol. IV, Wissenschaftliche Buchgesellschaft, Darmstadt.

Katzenstein, Peter J. (ed.) (1996): *The culture of national security – norms and identity in world politics*, Columbia University Press, New York.

Keck, Otto (1997): 'Zur sozialen Konstruktion des Rational-Choice-Ansatzes', *Zeitschrift für Internationale Beziehungen*, Vol. 4, No. 1, pp. 139–151.

Keck, Otto (1995): 'Rationales kommunikatives Handeln in den internationalen Beziehungen – Ist eine Verbindung von Rational-Choice-Theorie und Habermas' Theorie des kommunikativen Handelns möglich?', *Zeitschrift für Internationale Beziehungen*, Vol. 2, No. 1, pp. 5–48.

Keck, Otto (1993): *Information, Macht und gesellschaftliche Rationalität – Das Dilemma rationalen kommunikativen Handelns, dargestellt am Beispiel eines internationalen Vergleichs der Kernenergiepolitik*, Nomos, Baden-Baden.

King, Gary, Keohane, Robert O. and Verba, Sidney (1994): *Designing Social Inquiry*, Princeton University Press, Princeton.

Kissling-Näf, Ingrid and Knoepfel, Peter (1998): 'Social learning in policy networks', *Policy & Politics*, Vol. 26, No. 3, pp. 343–367.

Kitschelt, H. et al. (1999): *Continuity and change in contemporary capitalism*, Cambridge University Press, Cambridge.

Korkman, Sixtén (2001): 'Fiscal policy coordination in EMU: Should it go beyond the SGP?', in: Brunila, Anne, Buti, Marco and Franco, Daniele (eds), *The*

Stability and Growth Pact – The architecture of fiscal policy in EMU, Palgrave, Houndmills, Basingstoke, pp. 287–312.

Kröger, Jürgen (2002): 'Problems of incentives within EMU: Experience with the Stability and Growth Pact', in: Caesar, Rolf and Scharrer, Hans-Eckart (eds), *European Economic and Monetary Union: An initial assessment*, Nomos Verlagsgesellschaft, Baden-Baden, pp. 197–208.

Lewis, Jeffrey (2003): 'The Council of the European Union', in: Cini, Michelle (ed.), *European Union politics*, Oxford University Press, Oxford.

Lewis, Jeffrey (2000): 'The methods of Community in EU decision-making and administrative rivalry in the Council's infrastructure', *Journal of European Public Policy*, Vol. 7, No. 2, pp. 261–289.

Lewis, Jeffrey (1998a): 'Is the "hard bargaining" image of the Council misleading? The Committee of Permanent Representatives and the local elections directive', *Journal of Common Market Studies*, Vol. 36, No. 4, pp. 479–504.

Lewis, Jeffrey (1998b): *The institutional problem-solving capacities of the Council: The Committee of Permanent Representatives and the methods of Community*, Max-Planck-Institut für Gesellschaftsforschung Discussion Paper 98/1.

Liebert, Ulrike (2001): 'Constructing monetary union: euro-scepticism and the emerging European public space', in: Magnusson, Lars and Stråth, Bo (eds), *From the Werner Plan to the EMU. In search of a political economy for Europe*, PIE-Peter Lang, Brussels.

Lodge, Juliet E. and Pfetsch, Frank R. (1998): 'Negotiating in the European Union: Introduction', *International Negotiation, A Journal of Theory and Practice*, special issue: *Negotiating in the European Union*, Vol. 3, No. 3, pp. 289–292.

Louis, Jean-Victor (2000): *The institutional framework of economic policy co-ordination*, paper for the Jean Monnet Group on the IGC 2000 Conference, Brussels 6–7 July.

Majone, Giandomenico (1993): 'Wann ist Policy-Deliberation wichtig?', in: Héritier, Adrienne (ed.), *Policy-Analyse – Kritik und Neuorientierung*, *Politische Vierteljahresschrift*, special issue (Sonderheft), No. 24.

Mancini, G.F. (2000): *Democracy and constitutionalism in the European Union – collected essays*, Hart Publishing, Oxford/Portland Oregon.

March, James G. and Olsen, Johan P. (1998): 'The institutional dynamics of international political orders', *International Organization*, Vol. 52, No. 4, pp. 943–969.

March, James G. and Olsen, Johan P. (1989): *Rediscovering institutions. The organizational basis of politics*, The Free Press, New York.

Marcussen, Martin (2000): *Ideas and elites: The social construction of economic and monetary union*, Aalborg University Press, Aalborg.

Martin, Lisa L. and Simmons, Beth A. (1998): 'Theories and empirical studies of international institutions', *International Organization*, Vol. 52, No. 4, pp. 729–757.

Maystadt, Philippe (1997): 'Le role du Conseil ECOFIN en tant que gouvernement économique européen, exposé', in: Notre Europe, Groupement d'études et de recherches: *L'Europe en quête de politique économique, Colloque sur la convergence économique et l'emploi en Europe*, Brussels, 29 May, www.notre-europe.asso.fr/.

McNamara, Kathleen R. (1998): *The currency of ideas – monetary politics in the European Union*, Cornell University Press, Ithaca, NY.

Milner, Helen (1992): 'International theories of cooperation among nations – strengths and weaknesses', *World Politics*, Vol. 44, pp. 467–468.

Milward, Alan S. (1992): *The European rescue of the nation-state*, Routledge, London.

Minkkinen, Petri and Patomäki, Heikki (eds) (1997): *The politics of Economic and Monetary Union*, Kluwer Academic Publishers, Dordrecht.

Mooslechner, Peter and Schuerz, Martin (2001): 'International macroeconomic policy coordination: Any lessons for EMU? – A selective survey of the literature', in: Hallett, Andrew Hughes, Mooslechner, Peter and Schuerz, Martin (eds), *Challenges for economic policy coordination within European Monetary Union*, Kluwer Academic Publishers, Dordrecht, pp. 65–90.

Moravcsik, Andrew (1998): *The choice for Europe. Social purpose and state power from Messina to Maastricht*, Cornell University Press, London.

Müller, Harald (2001): *Arguing, bargaining and all that – reflections on the relationship of communicative action and rationalist theory in analysing international negotiations*, paper prepared for the 4th Pan-European International Relations Conference, Universtiy of Kent, 8–10 September.

Müller, Harald (1995): 'Spielen hilft nicht immer – Die Grenzen des Rational-Choice-Ansatzes und der Platz der Theorie kommunikativen Handelns in der Analyse internationaler Beziehungen', *Zeitschrift für Internationale Beziehungen*, Vol. 2, No. 2, pp. 371–391.

Müller, Harald (1994): 'Internationale Beziehungen als kommunikatives Handeln – zur Kritik der utilitaristischen Handlungstheorien', *Zeitschrift für Internationale Beziehungen*, Vol. 1, No. 1, pp. 15–44.

Müller, Harald and Risse, Thomas (1999): *Arguing and bargaining in multilateral negotiations*, grant proposal to the Volkswagen Foundation, December.

Neyer, Jürgen (2000): 'Justifying comitology: The promise of deliberation', in: Neunreither, Karlheinz and Wiener, Antje (eds), *European integration after Amsterdam: Institutional dynamics and prospects for democracy*, Oxford University Press, Oxford, pp. 112–128.

Notre Europe (1997): Groupement d'études et de recherches: *L'Europe en quête de politique économique, Colloque sur la convergence économique et l'emploi en Europe, Brussels*, 29 May 1997, www.notre-europe.asso.fr/.

Official Journal of the European Communities/ European Union, Brussels (individual issues as specified in the text).

Office for Official Publications of the European Communities: *Consolidated Treaties. Treaty on European Union. Treaty establishing the European Community*, Luxembourg 1997 (quoted as TEU and TEC as specified in the text).

Pierson, Paul (1998): 'The path to european integration: A historical-institutionalist analysis', in: Sandholtz, Wayne and Stone Sweet, Alec (eds), *European integration and supranational governance*, Oxford University Press, Oxford, pp. 27–58.

Pollack, Mark A. (2001): 'International relations theory and European integration', *Journal of Common Market Studies*, Vol. 39, No. 2, pp. 221–244.

Polster, Werner (2002): *Europäische Währungsintegration – Von der Zahlungsunion zur Währungsunion*, Metropolis-Verlag, Marburg.

Portugal (2001): *Stability and growth programme, update for the period 2002–2005*, Lisbon, December, as published on the website of the European Commission, Directorate General for Economic and Financial Affairs, Brussels, http://europa.eu.int/comm/economy_finance/index_en.htm.

Puetter, Uwe (2003): 'Informal circles of ministers – A way out of the EU's institutional dilemmas?', *European Law Journal*, Vol. 9, No. 1, pp. 109–124.

Puetter, Uwe (2001): *An institutional framework for arguing and deliberation: The Eurogroup as a generator of informal resources*, paper prepared for the 4th Pan-European International Relations Conference of the ECPR Standing Group on International Relations, University of Kent, 6–10 September.

Reichenbach, Horst, Emmerling, Thea, Staudenmayer, Dirk and Schmidt, Sönke (1999): *Integration: Wanderung über europäische Gipfel*, Nomos Verlagsgesellschaft, Baden-Baden.

Reynders, Didier (2001): 'La présidence belge de l'Eurogroupe: vers un renforcement de la coordination économique', *Reflets, Perspectives de la Vie Économique*, Vol. 40, No. 3, pp. 139–142.

Risse, Thomas (2000): '"Let's argue!": communicative action in world politics', *International Organization*, Vol. 54, No. 1, p. 1–39.

Risse, Thomas, Engelmann, Daniela, Knopf, Hans-Joachim and Roscher, Klaus (1998): *To Euro or not to Euro? The EMU and identity politics in the European Union*, European University Institute, Working Paper RSC No 98/9.

Risse, Thomas and Ulbert, Cornelia (2001): *Arguing and persuasion in multilateral negotiations: theoretical approach and research design*, paper presented at the 4th Pan-European International Relations Conference, University of Kent, 7–10 September.

Risse, Thomas and Wiener, Antje (1999): '"Something rotten" and the social construction of social constructivism: a comment on comments', *Journal of European Public Policy*, Vol. 6, No. 5, pp. 775–782.

Rosamond, Ben (2003): 'New theories of European integration', in: Cini, Michelle (ed.), *European Union politics*, Oxford University Press, Oxford.

Sabatier, Paul A. (1998): 'The advocacy coalition framework: revisions and relevance for Europe', *Journal of European Public Policy*, Vol. 5, No. 1.

Sabatier, Paul A. (1993): 'Advocacy-Koalitionen, Policy-Wandel und Policy-Lernen: Eine Alternative zur Phasenheuristik', in: Héritier, Adrienne (ed.), *Policy-Analyse – Kritik und Neuorientierung, Politische Vierteljahresschrift*, special issue (Sonderheft), No. 24, pp. 116–148.

Sabatier, Paul A. (1988): 'An advocacy coalition framework of policy change and the role of policy-oriented learning therein', *Policy Sciences*, Vol. 21, pp. 129–168.

Sabel, Charles F. and Zeitlin, Jonathan (2003): *Active welfare, experimental governance, pragmatic constitutionalism: The new transformation of Europe*, paper prepared for the conference 'Debating the democratic legitimacy of the European Union', Mannheim Centre for European Social Research (MZES), 27–29 November.

Sandholtz, Wayne (1993): 'Monetary bargains: The Treaty on EMU', in: Cafruny,

Alan W. and Rosenthal, Glenda G. (eds), *The state of the European Community. Vol. 2. The Maastricht Debates and Beyond*, Longman, London, pp. 125–144.

Scharpf, Fritz W. (2001): *European governance: common concerns vs. the challenge of diversity*, Max-Planck-Institut für Gesellschaftsforschung Working Paper 01/6.

Scharpf, Fritz W. (1985): 'Die Politikverflechtungs-Falle: Europäische Integration und deutscher Föderalismus im Vergleich', *Politische Vierteljahreszeitschrift*, No. 4, pp. 323–356.

Schelkle, Waltraud (2002): 'Disciplining device or insurance arrangement? Two approaches to the political economy of EMU policy coordination', *Working Paper Series European Institute*, LSE WP1-02.

Schimmelfennig, Frank (2001): 'The Community trap: liberal norms, rhetorical action, and the Eastern enlargement of the European Union', *International Organization*, Vol. 55, No. 1, pp. 47–80.

Schimmelfennig, Frank (1997): 'Rhetorisches Handeln in der internationalen Politik', *Zeitschrift für Internationale Beziehungen*, Vol. 4, No. 2, pp. 219–254.

Schimmelfennig, Frank (1995): *Debatten zwischen Staaten – Eine argumentationstheorie internationaler systemkonflikte*, Leske+Budrich, Opladen.

Schmidt, Vivien A. (2001): 'The politics of economic adjustment in France and Britain: When does discourse matter?', *Journal of European Public Policy*, Vol. 8, No. 2, pp. 247–264.

Schönfelder, Wilhelm and Thiel, Elke (1996): *Ein Markt – eine Währung – Die Verhandlungen zur Europäischen Wirtschafts- und Währungsunion*, Nomos, Baden-Baden.

Sherrington, Philippa (2000): *The Council of ministers – political authority in the European Union*, Pinter, London.

Simmel, Georg (1992): *Soziologie – Untersuchungen über die Formen der Vergesellschaftung*, Gesamtausgabe, Band 11, edited by Otthein Rammstedt, Suhrkamp Verlag, Frankfurt am Main.

Singer, Otto (1993): 'Policy communities und diskurs-koalitionen: experten und expertise in der wirtschaftspolitik', in: Héritier, Adrienne (ed.), *Policy-Analyse – Kritik und Neuorientierung, Politische Vierteljahresschrift*, special issue (Sonderheft), No. 24, pp. 149–174.

Solbes, Pedro (2002): *Economic policy coordination: the way forward*, speech delivered to the Brussels Economic Forum, SPEECH/02/192, Brussels 2 May 2002, http://europa.eu.int/.

Somers, Frans (ed.) (1998): *European Union economies – A comparative study*, 3rd edition, Longman, London.

Stark, Jürgen (2001): 'Genesis of a pact', in: Brunila, Anne, Buti, Marco and Franco, Daniele (eds), *The Stability and Growth Pact – The architecture of fiscal policy in EMU*, Palgrave, Houndmills, Basingstoke, pp. 139–157.

Stubb, Alexander (2000): 'Negotiating flexible integration in the Amsterdam Treaty', in: Neunreither, Karlheinz and Wiener, Antje (eds), *European integration after Amsterdam: Institutional dynamics and prospects for democracy*, Oxford University Press, Oxford, pp. 153–174.

Stubb, Alexander (1997): 'The 1996 Intergovernmental Conference and the management of flexible integration', *Journal of European Public Policy*, Vol. 4, No. 1, pp. 37–55.

Susskind, Lawrence E., Chayes, Abram and Martinez, Janet (1996): 'Parallel informal negotiation: A new kind of international dialogue', *Negotiation Journal*, Vol. 12, No. 1, pp. 19–29.

Sutter, Matthias (2000): *Der stabilitäts- und wachstumspakt in der Europäischen währungsunion. Grundlagen, abstimmmungsmacht und glaubwürdigkeit der sanktionierung übermäßiger defizite*, Nomos Verlagsgesellschaft, Baden-Baden.

Taylor, Paul (1983): *The limits of European integration*, Croom Helm, Beckenham.

Tonra, Ben (2001): 'The Europeanisation of national foreign policy: Dutch, Danish and Irish foreign policy in the European Union', Ashgate, Aldershot.

Traxler, Franz (2003): 'Bargaining institutions and the monetary regime: a cross-national comparison and its implications for European monetary union', *Journal of European Public Policy*, Vol. 10, No. 4, pp. 596–615.

Tuytschaever, Filip (2000): 'EMU and the catch-22 of EU constitution-making', in: De Búrca, Gráinne and Scott, Joanne (eds), *Constitutional change in the EU – from uniformity to flexibility?*, Hart Publishing, Oxford, pp. 173–195.

Tuytschaever, Filip (1999): *Differentiation in European Union law*, Hart, Oxford.

Ungerer, Horst (1997): *A concise history of European monetary integration*, Quorum Books, Westport.

Van Dijk, Teun A. (ed.) (1985): *Handbook of discourse analysis, Vol. 1, Disciplines of discourse*, Academic Press, London.

Verdun, Amy (2000a): *European responses to globalization and financial market integration – perceptions of Economic and Monetary Union in Britain, France and Germany*, St. Martin's Press, New York.

Verdun, Amy (2000b): 'Governing by committee: the case of monetary policy', in: Christiansen, Thomas and Kirchner, Emil, *Committee governance in the European Union*, Manchester University Press, Manchester, pp. 132–144.

Verdun, Amy (1999): 'The role of the Delors Committee in the creation of EMU: an epistemic community?', *Journal of European Public Policy*, Vol. 6, No. 2, pp. 308–328.

Wallace, Helen (2000): 'Flexibility: A tool of integration or a restraint on disintegration?', in: Neunreither, Karlheinz and Wiener, Antje (eds), *European integration after Amsterdam: Institutional dynamics and prospects for democracy*, Oxford University Press, Oxford, pp. 175–192.

Wallace, Helen (1985): *Europe: The challenge of diversity*, Royal Institute of International Affairs, Chatham House Papers, No. 29, Routledge & Kegan Paul, London.

Wallace, Helen and Wallace, William (eds) (2000): *Policy-making in the European Union*, 4th edition, Oxford University Press, Oxford.

Warleigh, Alex (2002): *Flexible integration: Which model for the European Union?*, Sheffield Academic Press, Sheffield.

Webb, Michael C. (1995): *The political economy of policy coordination*, Cornell University Press, Ithaca.

Weiler, Joseph H.H. (1999): *The constitution of Europe: 'Do the new clothes have an emperor?'*, Cambridge University Press, Cambridge.

Wendt, Alexander (1998): 'On constitution and causation in international relations', *Review of International Studies*, Vol. 24, No. 5, pp. 101–117.

Wessels, Wolfgang (1980): *Der Europäische Rat. Stabilisierung statt Integration? Geschichte, Entwicklung und Zukunft der EG-Gipfelkonferenzen*, Europa Union Verlag, Bonn.

Westlake, Martin (1999): *The Council of the European Union*, 2nd edition, John Harper Publishers, London.

Wicks, Nigel (1999): 'A decentralised model of economic governance', in, Centre for European Reform: *Will EMU lead to European economic government?*, London.

Wiener, Antje (2003): *The evolution of EU constitutional norms – British and German elites in Berlin*, Brussels and London, book manuscript.

Wiener, Antje (2001): *Social facts in world politics – The value-added of constructivism*, paper prepared for presentation to the 42nd annual convention of the International Studies Association, Chicago, 20–25 February.

Wiener, Antje (1998): *The embedded acquis communautaire – transmission belt and prism of new governance*, EUI Working Paper RSC No. 98/35.

Wolf, Dieter (1999): *Integrationstheorien im vergleich – neo-funktionalismus versus intergouvernementalismus am beispiel der WWU*, Nomos, Baden-Baden.

Zürn, Michael (2000): 'Democratic governance beyond the nation-state: The EU and other international institutions', *European Journal of International Relations*, Vol. 6, No. 2, pp. 183–221.

Zürn, Michael (1998): *Regieren jenseits des Nationalstaates*, Suhrkamp Verlag, Frankfurt am Main.

Index